REFUGEES AND REBELS

Indonesian Exiles in Wartime Australia

Jan Lingard

Australia Indonesia Association of NSW

© Jan Lingard 2008

First published 2008
Australian Scholarly Publishing Pty Ltd

Second edition 2022
Australia Indonesia Association of NSW
GPO Box 802, Sydney NSW 2001, Australia
www.australia-indonesia-association.com
Email: info@ australia-indonesia-association.com

ISBN 978 0 646 85941 5

All rights reserved

Cover photograph: Tribune 19.10.1945
Cover design: Tarny Burton & Robert Shepherd (32phillip)
Design and typesetting: Laurin McKinnon

For Sally

14.6.1959 – 19.9.2007

Contents

	Acknowledgements	ii
	A note on spelling and place names	iv
	Map: Main sites for Indonesian presence in Australia 1942-1948	v
	Introduction	1
1	Refuge in White Australia	9
2	Bad Boys and Good Boys	35
3	The Coming of the Nationalists	61
4	Cowra and Beyond	77
5	Battle Lines are Drawn	103
6	The Indonesian Revolution Comes to an Australian Country Town	123
7	Mates and Merdeka	143
8	The First Repatriation	161
9	Turbulent Times	183
10	New Year, New Challenges	201
11	People to People	225
12	Now is the Hour	249
	Conclusion	277
	Endnotes	283
	References	301
	Index	309

Acknowledgements

There are many people I must thank for helping to make Refugees and Rebels possible, the first being the actors in this story whom I was fortunate enough to interview both in Australia and in Indonesia. They shared their memories with generosity of time and spirit. In Jakarta I am grateful to Kam Nasution and Enid Achmad; in Bandung to George Worang and family, particularly Selfia; in Yogyakarta to R.M. Roeslan, and in Madura to the late Moh Hodrie and his family. In Australia I thank Lionel Boorman, Des Darragh, Colin Duce, Bonita Ellen, Ted Fryer, James Gibson, John Guthrie, Gordon Hooton, Lew Hughes, Phyllis and Johnno Johnson, Matina King, Nancy Loan, Bob and Margaret McLean, Miriam Nicholls, Lilian Perston, Jan Ritchie, Sheila Tattersall, John Treloar and Jean Wachyo. For their equally generous contributions by letter my thanks to James Baillie, Ruth Barrett, Elva Beck, Allan Brownlee, Lola Burke, Laureen Collins, Eva Cusack, Wendy James, Leo Lane, F.X. Lasman, H. Abdul Rachman, G. Wallace Campbell and Margaret Wright. For good-natured helpfulness and patience I am grateful to the research staffs at the National Archives of Australia in Sydney, Canberra and Melbourne offices, the Australian War Memorial, the State Archives of Queensland, the Noel Butlin Archives at the Australian National University, the Mitchell Wing of the State Library of NSW, State Library of Victoria, State Library of Queensland and the National Library of Australia, for all of whom no request was too much trouble. In Cowra, special thanks are due to Graham Apthorpe who enthusiastically supported and assisted my research there and organized access to the records kept in the Cowra Court House. In Jakarta, Robert Paath kindly allowed me access to the library of the newspaper Suara Pembaruan. I am particularly grateful to Iskandar P. Nugraha who generously used some of his precious and limited research time in Leiden to find useful material for me in the Dutch Archives, and also to him, and Rudy De Jong for translating some of this material into English, my Dutch having long ago been forgotten.

I have been blessed by having friends who encouraged me with their continued interest in the project and helped in practical ways. During research trips, Carol and Graham Vaughan were wonderfully supportive travelling companions in Java and Madura and Doug Ramage and Richard Howard gave me friendship and home comforts in Jakarta. In particular I acknowledge with gratitude and love the personal support and assistance given by my dear friend the late Wayne Levy, who drove me around Melbourne to interviews and lent his skills to help reproduce some of the photographic material from old glass slides. Special thanks are also due to John Turner, who meticulously and patiently worked his way through the first draft and whose perceptive comments set me on the road to producing a coherent manuscript and to Ruth Turner, English teacher extraordinaire, who spotted my spelling and grammatical lapses. Keith Foulcher gave me the benefit of his wisdom, experience and analytical skills to suggest further improvements. Any deficiencies in the text are entirely my own doing.

I was able to seriously start the research for this book during a period of study leave from the University of Sydney in 1997, for which I am grateful, as I am for the small seeding grant from the then School of Asian Studies. I am also grateful to the School of Languages and Cultures for its generous contribution towards the publication costs of this book.

Finally I must thank Michael Kramer and the Australia Indonesia Association NSW for their support in publishing this edition of my work, and my good friends Laurin McKinnon, Tarny Burton and Robert Shepherd who contributed hours of their time and their artistic and technical expertise to make the publication of this book possible.

A note on spelling and place names

The Indonesian spelling system has undergone several changes from its original Dutch orthography. Similarly there have been changes of place names since the Dutch colonial era ended. Throughout this book I have used modern spelling and modern place names unless quoting from original documents. For example I refer to Boven Digul rather than Boven Digoel, and Jakarta rather than Batavia, unless directly quoting from primary sources.

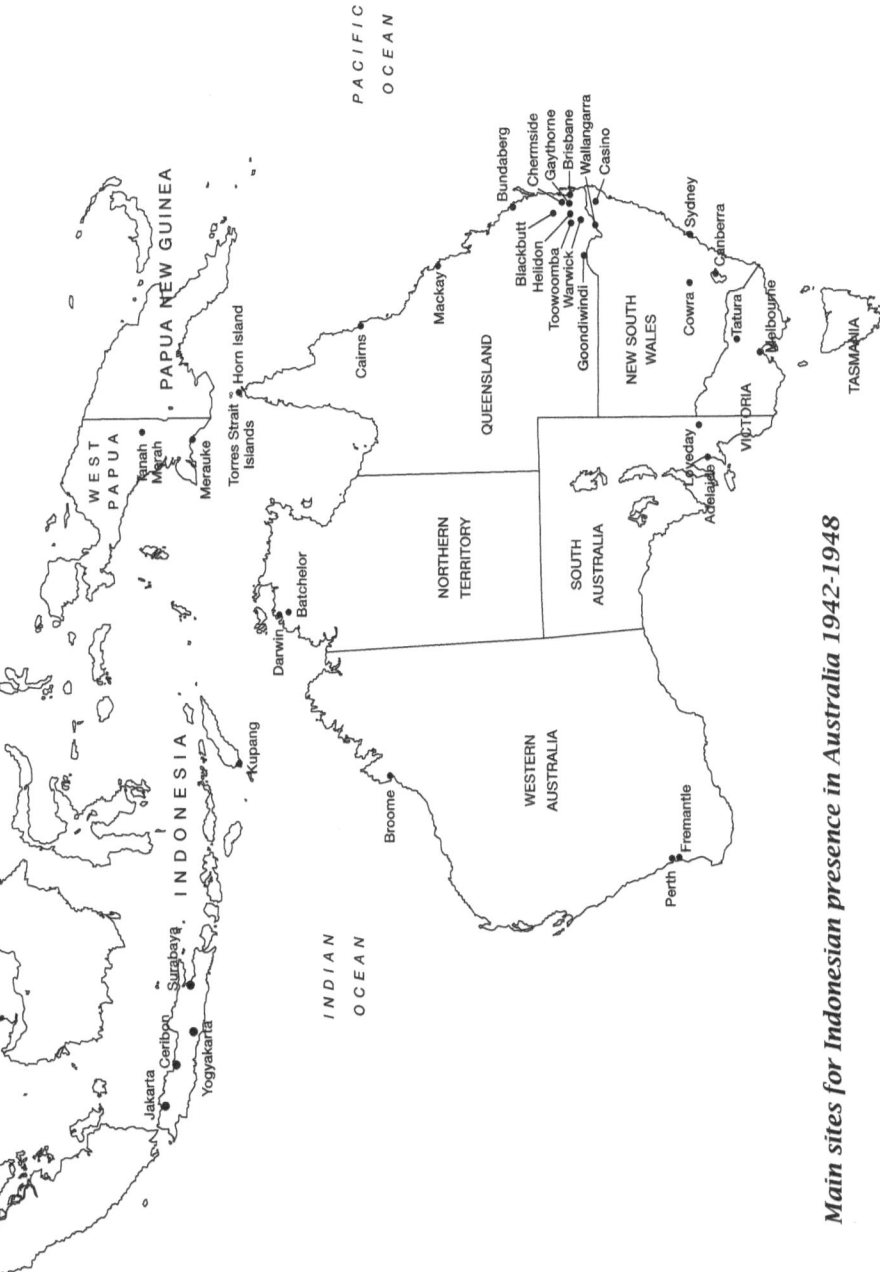

Main sites for Indonesian presence in Australia 1942-1948

Introduction

This book relates a unique chapter of Australia's social and political wartime history – the sojourn in Australia of some five and a half thousand Indonesians, for varying lengths of time between 1942 and 1947, and its aftermath. Their experiences living among local communities, urban and rural, and their engagement with Australians, provided the social context for the significant political effects of their stay.

Before this period, Australians and Indonesians had little contact with or knowledge of each other, despite their geographic proximity. Australia was a country whose racism was enshrined in the Immigration Restriction Act, commonly known as the White Australia Policy, put in place from the beginning of federation in 1901 to ensure that the entry of 'coloureds' was kept to a minimum. Australian thought about Asia was generally focused on fears of an invasion of some kind, based on the assumption that the vast empty spaces down south were an irresistible attraction to the 'teeming millions' in Australia's near north, that floods of cheap labour would threaten local jobs and that the white gene pool could be polluted by lascivious, morally corrupt Asian men who lusted after white women. These fears were particularly directed to China from 19th century onwards when the goldfields attracted many Chinese to Australia to seek their fortunes, and to a lesser extent, to Japan. The British, French, Portuguese and Dutch colonies in the region were hardly regarded as being 'Asian' at all but rather, like Australia itself, as outposts of European civilization, whose 'native' populations attracted little interest.

Notwithstanding this, there were some limited contacts between Australians and Indonesians over the years before 1942.

Indonesians in Australia

As part of the Darwin festival of September 1999 a cast comprising Indonesian Makassarese from South Sulawesi and Australian Yolngu people from Northeast Arnhem Land performed an operetta called *Trepang*, which was about the earliest known visits of Indonesians to Australian shores: these were the trepang collecting voyages of sailors from Makassar (now Ujung Pandang), thought to have begun around 1700 before European settlement, and which continued for about 200 years.[1]

They sailed their proas south in search of the trepang (also known as sea cucumber or beche-de-mer) that abounded in the waters near the Arnhem Land coast and the north-west coast of the Kimberley, Western Australia. Well-established trading contacts between eastern ports of the Indonesian archipelago and South China ensured a ready market for this product from Australia, which when processed was a prized aphrodisiac delicacy for the Chinese.[2] When from 1893 the Makassarese were required to buy licences and pay customs duties to the colonial authorities these imposts gradually led to declining profits, with the result that by 1910 their voyages came to an end. They were only ever in Australia on a temporary basis, purely for a profitable commercial industry. Their visits impacted on the Aborigines with whom they traded goods for labour, but would have been largely unknown to white Australians after settlement.

At the same time as the Makassarese were fishing for trepang in the north of Australia in the nineteenth century, hundreds of Javanese were being recruited as indentured labourers to work in the sugar cane industry in northern Queensland, as part of the drive to obtain cheap labour. The Javanese constituted a small part of a work force dominated by Pacific Islanders, but records do indicate that in 1886 nearly 900 were employed on Colonial Sugar Refinery's estates.[3] By 1911, nine years after the Immigration Act had come into effect, the number of Javanese in the north Queensland sugar districts had dwindled to just over a hundred[4] and soon they had all left, having played their part in a coercive indentured labour system which had itself declined.

In the town of Port Hedland, on the northern coast of Western Australia, grow several large trees, identified by a plaque as 'Midi Bin Brahim's Trees.' The plaque tells us that Midi Bin Brahim was

Introduction

born in East Java in 1880, and came to Broome in 1900 as an indentured crewman in the pearling fleet. He later moved to Port Hedland and married an Aboriginal woman by whom he had nine children. He planted the trees – a species native to Southeast Asia – in the early 1930s, was a practising Muslim and had a *musolah,* a prayer house, built in his back yard. Midi bin Brahim was one of a wave of Indonesians who came as indentured workers employed in the pearling industry, beginning in the latter part of the nineteenth century, particularly in Broome. Once the Immigration Restriction Act became effective, the pearlshelling industry was the only one exempt from the ban imposed on importing cheap Asian labour. The government agreed that Asian labour was necessary for the survival of the industry and Asian labourers were issued with Certificates of Exemption from the conditions of the Act.[5] Government records known as the Annual Returns, show that between 1902 and 1941, over 2,000 Indonesians from such places as Kupang, Java and Ambon came as pearlers.[6]

When World War II expanded to the Pacific region the pearling industry was forced to suspend its operations, and the 100 or so Indonesian workers still in Australia were evacuated from Broome and scattered to other states to become part of the Indonesian population in Australia for the duration of the war. Like the cane workers, the pearling workers were brought to Australia as cheap labour to increase the wealth of white entrepreneurs. When their contracts ended, they were sent home and Australia remained 'Australia for the White Man,' as the masthead slogan of the *Bulletin* magazine proudly proclaimed.

Trepang fishermen, sugar cane labourers and pearling workers: this was likely the full extent of an Indonesian presence in Australia at different times prior to 1942. The nature of their labour and the conditions under which they were in the country would have ensured their contacts with white people were minimal, and confined to specific geographic and hierarchical boundaries.

Australians in Indonesia

There are no records available to show how many Australians ventured to Indonesia before duty during World War II sent Australian soldiers to some parts of the archipelago, but the way was open

3

for Australian travellers to venture to the Indies when the Dutch-owned Royal Packet Navigation Company, KPM, inaugurated its Java-Australia Line in 1908. In March 1919, Miss Dorothy Fry from Lindfield in Sydney sailed to Java to take up a position as a stenographer with a British company. Her letters to her family during the years she worked in Jakarta provide a fascinating glimpse of the experiences and attitudes of a young expatriate woman from White Australia, living in an Asian country. They reveal that she was little interested in the local population, except in their capacity as servants about whom she often complained. Excerpts from her letters published in the Sydney Morning Herald in 1921 revealed another of her concerns. 'Certainly the colour question hits you at every turn: you cannot get away from it,' she wrote.[7] Her feelings were graphically revealed in her description of the recent arrival in town of a Dutch woman, married to a 'nigger'. 'It is a horrid sight to see them together,' she wrote, 'even the Dutch people were shocked and they are not particular about a tinge or two'.[8] Dorothy Fry was indeed a product of her time and homeland.

Beginning in the 1920s, advertisements began appearing in Australia offering travellers the chance of luxury cruises to the East. These tours found a market and 'Java was a fashionable holiday destination for adventurous Australians in the late 1920s and early 1930s'.[9] One of these was Mr S. Elliott Napier, a Sydneysider who journeyed to Java and Bali in 1934, and on his return wrote at great length about his travels in *The Sydney Morning Herald* (6.10.1934). Apart from his account of the sights he saw, on the relationship between the Javanese and their colonial masters Napier observed, '... so far as we can see, the Javanese instead of worrying overmuch about Dutch rule, are eminently satisfied with it', a rather naive observation given that the Indonesian nationalist movement was slowly gathering momentum at the time. Besides tourists some Australians travelled to Indonesia for creative inspiration. These included photographer Frank Hurley, painter Margaret Preston, author Frank Clune and documentary film makers Mel Nicholls and Fred Daniell.

One impetus which often motivates people to explore new horizons is commercial gain, and in this regard Australia and the NEI were no exception, with trading enterprises beginning between the two countries in 1908.[10] In an effort to introduce new products and

Introduction

to even up the balance of trade which favoured the Dutch, in 1933 the Manufacturers Association of Australia sponsored The Australian Trade and Goodwill Delegation, whose members travelled to a number of destinations in the NEI aboard the Dutch ship *Nieuw Holland*, taking with them a floating trade fair. At each port of call swarms of visitors came on board to view the goods. But as proof of the Australians' ignorance about the non-European population of the region, the delegates suddenly realized that none of the printed promotional literature they had prepared, such as pamphlets, catalogues and posters was in Malayan, the language of the seventy million 'prospects' they had come so far to court. Like Napier before them the delegates' perceptions of the relationship between the Dutch colonisers and the indigenous population reflected the prevalent attitudes of the day —

> Their world has been made for them by generous nature, assisted ably by the methodical and omniscient Dutch Administration. For these obedient, tractable little brown men have been assembled bright skies, blue seas ... all the complexities and burdens of government they allow to rest on the broad and willing shoulders of their Dutch overlords ... the brown man is aware that always the Superior Power is his refuge and guide.[11]

In common with the vast majority of their compatriots, these Australian travellers to the NEI would have had little or no knowledge of the burgeoning nationalist movement in the vast archipelago from the 1920s onwards. Their comments demonstrate the success of the Dutch propagated idea that the Indonesians were childlike, happy, inferior people who needed and were content with the guidance, protection and overlordship of their benign colonisers – colonisers who had in reality oppressed them, particularly the Javanese, politically, and in cahoots with their own ruling class, exploited them economically for over three hundred years. But as war clouds gathered, all that was about to change. When, in May 1940, Germany invaded the Netherlands and the Dutch declared war, the NEI and Australia found themselves Allies and as the Japanese threat loomed both governments were well aware of their mutual strategic concerns. In January 1941 the Australian Prime Minister, Robert Menzies, visited

The Netherlands Empire Prepares For Its Hour.
Netherlands Information Bureau 1942.

Jakarta promising arms, supplies, and an AIF division to bolster the defences of the NEI.[12] The Dutch invited an Australian Press Delegation, including the managing director of the *Argus* newspaper, Mr E.G. Knox, to visit the Indies to inspect Dutch defences. Mr Knox was eloquent in his comments to NEI military leaders about the impending threat of invasion from Japan, promising that 'the Australian people would shed their last drop of blood to prevent the ravages of war coming to the East Indies …'[13] Mr Knox's rhetoric was matched by that of Dr C.O. van der Plas, the Governor of East Java, and leader of a NEI press delegation which made a reciprocal visit to Australia in October 1941, when he declared, 'We of the Dutch East Indies shall help to defend Australia's strategic Barrier Reef foot by foot and inch by inch, and we will never surrender.'[14]

When war in the Pacific broke out after the Japanese attack on Pearl Harbour, suddenly from January 1942 Australian newspaper

Introduction

reports provided a lesson in the geography of the Indonesian archipelago as the previously little known islands, cities and towns of the NEI fell to the Japanese, one by one. The inadequately reinforced and equipped NEI armed forces were able to offer little resistance. In the end the Australian people did not 'shed their last drop of blood to prevent the ravages of war,' as Mr Knox had promised, and contrary to Dr van der Plas's vow, the Dutch did surrender, with one result being that several thousand Indonesians ended up as exiles in Australia.

They came as refugees and for the most part loyal 'native' subjects of the Dutch colonial empire, to a xenophobic country where keeping aliens far away and preserving a white Australia was part of the established national identity. When they were repatriated to their homeland several years later, the majority of them returned as rebels fighting for their freedom from colonial domination. In the interim they had commenced or in some cases continued their struggle against the Dutch whilst on Australian soil and been politically supported by their Australian friends, particularly waterside workers and other unionists. This is their story.

1

Refuge in White Australia

The Japanese invasion of the Netherlands East Indies in World War II brought about one of the most unusual episodes in Australia's wartime history. This was the arrival of several thousand Indonesian evacuees – men, women and children – who spent some of the war and immediate post war years in Australia, between 1942-1947. During this period they were dispersed to various parts of the country, to capital cities and rural towns. Consequently many Australian and Indonesian people, largely unaware of each other until then, came into contact and formed personal relationships for which there were no precedents.

Invasion and exodus

On 10 February 1942 the *Sydney Morning Herald* carried the dramatic headlines, 'Java Stands Ready to Meet Invaders. Protecting the Natives. Every Man to Stay at Post.' But despite these brave words defeat was inevitable. Lacking adequate resources, and with the non-arrival of anticipated reinforcements, the Royal Netherlands Indies Army (KNIL) forces and their Allies could offer little resistance. With heavy losses of Allied shipping in the Battle of the Java Sea on 27 and 28 February, the way was clear for the Japanese invasion force to land on the north coast of Java west of Surabaya, and sweep towards the capital, Jakarta (then called Batavia). The Netherlands East Indies (NEI) government was forced to flee from Jakarta to Bandung where it made one last broadcast on 7 March, before, as the ominous headline of the Sydney Morning Herald announced, silence fell over Java.[1] On 8 March the Governor of the NEI surrendered unconditionally to the Japanese. In the final frantic days before the surrender, evacuations of some of the NEI and Allied personnel commenced by air and sea from the port of Cilicap on the south coast of Java. Their destinations were Broome and other Australian ports, with the result that Australia became host to an influx of refugees from the Indies – Dutch, Eurasian and Indonesian.

Thus the exigencies of war brought about a situation that would have been impossible to imagine previously in White Australia – the entry of some thousands of 'native' Asian evacuees. The precise numbers are difficult to determine because many Indonesians engaged in wartime tasks, particularly the crews of Dutch merchant ships, were entering, leaving and re-entering. The journalist Rupert Lockwood estimated the number of Indonesians entering Australia between 1942 and 1945 at 10,000,[2] whereas official sources recorded that between 1942 and 1946, 5,416 Indonesians were admitted temporarily.[3] The majority of them were merchant seamen serving on ships of the Royal Netherlands Packet Line (KPM). There were also sailors in the Royal Netherlands Navy, members of KNIL and its Military Aviation Division, Air Force Cadets, clerical workers with the Netherlands Indies Civil Administration (NICA), domestic servants, civilian refugees, and later a group of political prisoners and their families were added to the mix.

When the Department of External Affairs first become aware of the novel situation that some of the incoming military personnel were Indonesians it rose to the occasion and alerted the Department of the Interior, explaining that 'the trainees will not all be Europeans' and 'provision for special cooking arrangements will be necessary – some personnel are likely to be coloured or of the Mohammedan religion'.[4] Such a directive must have been a first for the Department.

The NEI administration

Among the first Dutch arrivals was a contingent of senior officials of the NEI Governing Council. There were various accounts of the circumstances of their landing. For instance there is an official record of a flight carrying one or two of them into Sydney on 4 March,[5] while another notes that a group including the Lieutenant Governor-General, Dr H.J. van Mook, and Dr C.O. van der Plas (member of the Council of the Indies), arrived in Sydney on 5 March.[6] On 10 March a number of Australian newspapers, including the *Adelaide Advertiser*, carried reports of the arrival of NEI officials in Adelaide, 'to rally Dutch sentiment and mould it into an effective

Refuge in White Australia

Above: *Indonesian Armed Forces in Australia. Argus newspaper.*
Photo: *Argus newspaper. Collection of Photographs, State Library of Victoria.*

Below: *Indonesian troops landing in Australia.*
Photo: *Penjoeloeh, 27 November 1942.*

striking force.[7] It seems that by some oversight the Australian Prime Minister and Government knew nothing about these arrivals or plans until told of press reports and neither had Prime Minister Curtin received any request from the Dutch for accommodation.[8] Presumably some official contact was soon made because on 25 March, Curtin reported to Parliament that he had extended a warm welcome to Dr van Mook and offered everything in the way of hospitality to him and his people as 'some practical expression of our admiration for the brave fight of the Dutch against overwhelming odds in the East Indies archipelago'.[9] The new relationship between these allies was certainly off to a cordial start.

The first task of the NEI officials was to establish the administration to look after the interests of their people in Australia. This was completed when on 8 April 1942, and before he left for London to join the Netherlands Government-in-Exile, Van Mook announced the establishment of the Netherlands East Indies Commission for Australia and New Zealand, which operated out of 422 Collins Street, Melbourne.[10] In the first instance the Head of the Commission was Dr J.E. van Hoogstraten. His fellow Commissioners included one Indonesian, Raden Loekman Djajadiningrat, a member of the West Javanese aristocracy who was NEI Director of Education. Highlighting the exotic, the *Daily Telegraph* singled him out as 'the most picturesque' of the commissioners, 'a fat little man with a chubby face, vivid black eyes below thick black brows, white brushed back hair and a roguish smile,' who could speak Javanese, Sundanese, Malay, English and French.[11]

The Commission's brief was to work separately from, but in co-operation with, the diplomatic representatives of the Netherlands Government-in-Exile in London, under the Netherlands Ambassador to Australia, Baron F.C. van Aerssen Beyeren van Voshol. Its functions included direction of the Dutch war effort in the Pacific, management of NEI property in Australia and New Zealand, and collaboration in specific NEI matters such as reconstruction, shipping and Civil Aviation.[12] One of its first tasks was the establishment of the Netherlands Indies Government Information Service (NIGIS) to disseminate publicity and propaganda both within Australia and in the NEI. Provision was also made for the entertainment of Dutch and Indonesian servicemen and care in hostels of Indonesian seamen.[13]

'Non-Australian' types

When RAAF officer G. Wallace Campbell first caught sight of Indonesian troops, his reaction was probably similar to that of many Australians at the time: 'I recall the interest I had when looking across to a nearby platform of Flinders Street Rail Station in Melbourne and seeing very small men in strange uniforms – NEI native troops. Any non-Australian type was very noticeable in those days'.[14] At the time, Melbourne was already host to thousands of US servicemen, of whom some 8% were black. The Australian Government had originally been unwilling to accept black troops, but after the Americans insisted on their inclusion, Army Minister Frank Forde reassured the Australian public that 'coloured troops were good soldiers'.[15] Thus the way had been paved to some extent for acceptance of these newly arrived 'non-Australian' types, from Indonesia.

The newspaper reading public of Australia was soon made aware of the presence of the Indonesians in their midst. For instance the Brisbane *Courier Mail* of 10 April 1942 ran a story about Dutch airmen, among whom were 'natives from Java', attached to the Dutch Air Force as ground staff.'[16] The article recounted how the Javanese were causing misunderstanding at the aerodromes because they were acting as sentries, without having a word of Dutch or English 'to their credit.' Readers must have been relieved to read however that, 'with native loyalty they challenge every white man who comes along'. Throughout the ensuing months the press featured photographs of Indonesian troops in battledress, in training or on their way to battle stations. The caption on one such photograph, 'Indonesians Aid Australia,'[17] would have bemused later generations of Australians, but the message was clear: these particular Asians were welcome Allies.

Negative stereotypes

While these positive images were in the public domain in those early days of the Indonesians' presence in Australia, some Australian officials having their first contacts with them were inclined to make racialist value judgements, born of their own ignorance. For example, the Military Police Intelligence Section had as one of its tasks the preparation of Aliens Security Files. This involved interviewing all people then classified as aliens, among whom were three

Above: Indonesian troops in battledress.
Photo: Argus newspaper. Collection of photographs, State Library of Victoria.

Left: Puzzled by rationing, these Indonesians called at the Rationing Commission's Inquiry Office, Dymock's Building, George Street, yesterday to ask how many coupons would be needed to exchange their cotton blouses for warmer clothes. The assistant explained by holding up her fingers.
Photo: Daily Telegraph 19 June 1942.

Javanese women brought to Australia early in 1942 by their evacuee employers, British and Dutch women who settled in Killara, NSW. The Javanese women were employed as nursemaids. After the required interview Constables Barker and Powell wrote to their supervisor that they were unable to find out any details about the women because 'their mentality is that of children'. Nevertheless, they concluded that the women were 'reliable and loyal citizens of Holland'.[18] Apparently the inability to speak English coupled with the trauma of evacuation was equated with a childlike mentality but not with any threat to security.

At the same time, some Dutch officials brought their colonial prejudices with them and often presented these to Australian counterparts as an expression of fact. An example is found in a letter from Mr D Lammers, General Manager of KPM, to the NSW Secretary of the Director-General of Health on 17 June 1942 who described the Javanese as, 'generally speaking of a lower mentality than the Europeans ... The Javanese is essentially a person of sentiment, shy in the presence of Europeans and, one may say, generally speaking inclined to be homesick and indolent'.[19] The reality was that the wealth accumulated by the Dutch in the Indies had come from the labour of those 'indolent' people for over 300 years. However, such generalisations as those above were often accepted by unquestioning Australian officials, at least until the Indonesians themselves proved otherwise.

Comrades in arms

From the time of their arrival in Australia, some Indonesian troops were taking part in dangerous and secret missions gathering intelligence in Java, Dutch New Guinea and the small islands to the north which were part of the NEI. For instance, in July 1942 one such mission was led by KNIL Sergeant Julius Tahija, who had originally been sent to Australia in 1942 as escort for a group of Japanese civilian internees from the NEI. Stranded when the NEI fell to the Japanese, Tahija volunteered for Allied operations. With 13 Indonesian soldiers, he was sent on an intelligence gathering mission to the village of Saumlaki in the Tanibar group of islands some 300 miles north of Darwin. During the course of this operation Tahija and his men were surprised by the arrival at Saumlaki of two Japanese war-

Above: Javanese soldiers visit Melbourne.
Photo: LaTrobe Picture Collection, State Library of Victoria.

Below: Members of Dutch bomber squadron, Northern Territory.
Photo: Australian War Memorial Neg Number 014510.

ships which proceeded to unload troops and equipment. Although heavily outnumbered and armed with inferior weapons the Indonesians attacked the Japanese, killing scores of them before escaping into the jungle. Eventually Tahija and the six survivors of his band, together with some Dutch officials who had been in the village, were given a small boat by friendly villagers, and managed to sail to Darwin.[20] In August 1942 Julius Tahija was presented with the *Bintang Militer Willems Orde*, the highest Dutch award for bravery and equivalent of the Victoria Cross, at a ceremony attended by many dignitaries including the then Governor of Victoria. The other six survivors were also decorated. The local Melbourne press recounted the story of Tahija's exploits describing him as, 'a hero: a black sergeant from the East Indies'.[21]

Tahija's mission was carried out under the auspices of the Netherlands East Indies Forces Intelligence Service (NEFIS), which came under the authority of the Allied Intelligence Bureau (AIB) established by the Allied Commander of the South West Pacific Area, General Douglas Mac Arthur, in July 1942.[22] For the most part, the NEI and Australian forces operated as separate entities, but there were exceptions when Australians and Indonesians saw active service together, such as some of the AIB operations. One of the units of the AIB was the "Z" Experimental Station. Before being sent to enemy territory, members of this unit did much of their training for operations behind enemy lines in Cairns, at a property called "Fairview", which became known as 'The House on the Hill.'[23] Among other activities, they underwent jungle training in the scrub near the house and learnt to use limpet mines in the Cairns swimming baths.[24] A former member of the organisation recalled, 'there was so much activity with Indonesians, Dutch, Englishmen and Australians, you name them – they were there at some time.'[25] 'No distinction of race was permitted or ever crept in,' boasted one historian.[26] A "Z" Unit base was also established at an old quarantine station near Darwin Harbour in December 1942, by a joint Australian-Dutch party. From the inception of the "Z" units in 1942 through to 1945, many dangerous operations were mounted with mixed results that cost Australian, Indonesian and Dutch lives at the hands of the Japanese.

Another example of a co-operative venture between Australian and NEI forces was the No. 18 (NEI) Squadron, which was formed at

17

RAAF Canberra on 4 April 1942. The Squadron gradually acquired 18 B25 Mitchell twin-engine bombers and was manned by Dutch personnel who had been at Archerfield in Victoria, some Royal Netherlands Indies Air Service personnel and a component from the RAAF to make up the shortfall in NEI numbers.

Initial training was carried out in Canberra, while attempts were made by Dutch, Australian and American commanders to sort out problems about equipment, personnel and command structure.[27] The people of the small NSW town of Queanbeyan near Canberra seem to have enjoyed the foreigners in their midst according to a local historian who wrote, 'An influx in the later war years, of Dutch, Indonesian and American servicemen mostly attached to air force divisions stationed at Canberra and Queanbeyan supplemented the population. On a social level the presence of foreign servicemen brought a new air of sophistication to the frequent parties organised for them'.[28] The Indonesians were 'Canberra's first substantial group of resident Asians'.[29] However, in May 1942 the Minister for Air, Mr Drakeford was asked in Parliament whether the Commandant of the RAAF at Canberra had forbidden Javanese airman to dance with Australian girls and whether the Commandant of the WAAF had forbidden girls under her control to meet Javanese airman on terms of social equality. Drakeford denied these allegations.[30] Whether the discrimination implied in the questions was happening or not, the 'colour' question was certainly on the mind of at least one high ranking Australian officer. At a meeting with Dutch Commanders in Washington on 30 September 1942 to discuss matters relating to the 18 NEI squadron, Air Vice-Marshall R. Williams, RAAF, raised objections to non-Europeans (Indonesians) serving with Dutch and Australians and claimed that General MacArthur had similar objections. The Dutch officers were rather mystified by this and one asked whether 'the Australians should have any objections against working with personnel that looks a little bit more sunburnt, if this personnel is civilized and knows its work'?[31] In response Williams insisted that the non-Europeans must do the menial work - 'Asians just have to do the minor work,' and deplored the fact that at the time, Australians were preparing food for non-European personnel.[32]

Despite the objections and ignorance of the Australian officer, in November 1942, at the time of its departure from Canberra to its operational base at MacDonald airfield in Darwin, the squadron consisted of 40 NEI officers, 210 NEI airmen, including 56 Javanese, and because there were insufficient NEI personnel available, 8 RAAF officers with 300 RAAF airmen.[33] The first mission into enemy territory was carried out on 31 January 1943 and in April and May 1943 the squadron moved to Batchelor, a better equipped base closer to Darwin.[34] It was from there that bombing attacks against enemy shipping and land targets were carried out until 1945. Describing the unique features of 18 Squadron a Department of Air press release noted —

> There is much in this squadron that is identical with other Allied squadrons, but many things in every day camp life may appear strange or humorous to the visitor. For instance, there are two saluting bases or parade grounds, two flags, the Australian and Dutch, which are raised during simultaneous parades in the morning and lowered at sunset. There are NEI native cooks, native stewards, and RAAF stewards to provide meals for the three joint messes. As well as the ordinary service dishes such as bully beef and tinned meat and vegetables, they serve a dish called *ryst-taffel*, which the Australians consider a treat.[35]

Jim Gibson's story

The RAAF men were discouraged by the Dutch officers from going to the 'native' section of the camp or mixing socially with the Indonesians. One Australian airman, Jim Gibson, objected to and ignored this advice and befriended one of his Indonesian allies (a Javanese called Djadi) when they were both working at one stage as cooks in the sergeants' mess. A strong friendship developed between the two men and they became 'inseparable' for the duration of the war. Gibson maintains that he was the only Australian from the station to 'knuckle down' and learn the Indonesian language. When Djadi returned to Indonesia after the war the two friends lost contact with each other. However, 53 years later Jim fulfilled a long held dream when he managed to trace his friend and travelled to East Java for an emotional reunion. Djadi died a year later.[36]

Merchant seamen go on strike

The Dutch merchant ships that found themselves in Australian ports at the time of the NEI surrender were chartered to the War Shipping Administration and then to the US Army for the purpose of shipping armaments and personnel to the Pacific region.[37] This was vital and dangerous work for the war effort. Beginning in April and continuing throughout 1942, some 2,000 Indonesian seamen on a number of these Dutch merchant vessels walked off their ships and went on strike. The first public news of this came when *The Sydney Morning Herald* (9.4.1942) reported that 130 Javanese seamen were each fined £10 in default of 20 days hard labour at the Water Police Court for having disobeyed a lawful command of the master of their vessel and refusing to work'. There was no explanation of why they refused to work, but the reason was because they had soon realised that they were working in situations of extreme danger, with wages, accommodation and conditions far inferior to those of Dutch and Australian merchant seamen doing the same job. Their plight has been described as follows —

> The Indonesians ate their food on the deck of their sub-standard accommodation as no tables or chairs were provided. They ate, slept, washed and went to the toilet all in one area in the forecastle. They were expected to sail into the thick of the war zones for £1/10 a month, commanded by Dutch officers who treated them as objects less than human.[38]

Moh Hodrie's story

In 1941 Moh Hodrie from Surabaya in East Java, joined the crew of the Dutch hospital ship *Oranje*. Before the fall of the NEI to the Japanese Hodrie had made two voyages to the Middle East, from whence *Oranje* transported wounded and ill Allied troops to Australia. Back in Sydney, when in March 1942 he and his shipmates heard the news of the Japanese occupation of Java, they wanted to go home to their families. Failing that, they demanded a pay rise, a war bonus and improved amenities so that their wages and working conditions were commensurate with those enjoyed by Dutch, Australian and other seamen doing similar

Refuge in White Australia

Above: Members of 18 NEI Squadron.
Photo: Jim Gibson.

Left: Djadi and Jim Gibson 1943
(Bachelor) and above: 1999 (Java).
Photos: Jim Gibson.

dangerous tasks. The Indonesian seamen were determined not to co-operate unless their demands were met.

Among the senior NEI officials in Australia was Dr C.O. van der Plas. He it was who now boarded the *Oranje* and tried to settle the matter by offering a pay rise of 10 shillings a day and an agreement to pay a 38 guilders war bonus. No mention was made of improved facilities. The seamen refused this offer and were then told that the ship would be departing in a matter of a few hours. At this point Hodrie and 240 of his shipmates walked off the ship and thereby became mutineers in the eyes of the Dutch and illegal immigrants in the eyes of Australia. They were arrested, taken off to face charges of breaching the Australian Immigration Laws, found guilty and sentenced to six months jail or a fine of 100 pounds. Thus Hodrie, an inoffensive young man from Java, found himself locked up in Sydney's Long Bay Gaol. In the following months some 1,200 Indonesian seamen from KPM ships struck in solidarity with the *Oranje* men.[39]

Liewe Pronk's version

Another version of events, some of which substantiates Hodrie's came from Liew Pronk, a former KPM official. He failed to mention the seamen's working conditions but blamed long periods of inactivity due to delays in getting the KPM ships fitted out and armed as the reason for the seamen's dissatisfaction —

> The long period of enforced idleness, coming straight on top of the Japanese occupation of their homeland, took its toll on these loyal but simple people ... they couldn't see the point of going through endless weeks of routine duties on a ship at anchor in Sydney Harbour, when they should have been back home in their kampongs in Java long ago. *"Mau poelang"* (We want to go home.) That was it, we couldn't budge them.[40]

The influx of Indonesian prisoners in Long Bay placed great strains on the gaol and the Premier of NSW, W.J. McKell, wrote to Prime Minister Curtin urgently requesting that they be confined elsewhere or interned, because of severe overcrowding of cells.[41] The situation was relieved when from around July 1942, those sea-

Refuge in White Australia

men who still refused to return to their ships began to be sent to Prisoner of War Camp No 12 located at Cowra in the Lachlan Valley, 300 kilometres west of Sydney. Eventually around 800 of the 2,000 seamen who at some time during 1942 left their ships at ports around Australia were detained there with a KNIL company sent to guard them.[42] Some 60 others were sent to another prisoner of war camp at Loveday in South Australia.

The first Indonesians in Cowra

About the life of the strikers once they arrived in Cowra there are few records. One KPM official, Mr H.B. Barends who visited the camp on 30 July noted that he saw seamen in their quarters and gardening, but, on a second visit in early August he saw the beginnings of a regime of hard labour.[43] In a letter to the secretary of the NEI commission in October Barends confirmed this 'hard labour,' adding that the internees had formed an association of intellectuals and semi-intellectuals, based on their 'way of thinking'.[44] This suggests that what had started out as a strike based on a naive – given that Java was now under Japanese occupation – demand to return home, and on demands for economic justice, may by this time have included political, anti-Dutch elements.

However, later evidence suggested that the main grievance was that the seamen had been promised some pay and war bonus increases to take effect the preceding February, before any strikes had taken place, but the Dutch had never paid this back money. When the Red Cross Official Visitor came to the camp on 15 October to check the welfare of the internees, he was presented with a letter signed by 24 'boys,' wanting to be sent back to Java, and complaining about the non-payment of the money they were owed'.[45] Further evidence of the ongoing discontent in the camp was noted in a military intelligence report for the period 29 November – 6 December with the observation —

> ... as in the case of all Asiatic races, Javanese are easily led by a few fanatics and agitators and those confined in this camp are not exceptions. It is known that amongst the Javanese confinees there is an element of perhaps 20 or 30 which exercises a disturbing influence amongst the remainder, thus creating

Delivering Beer. Eva Cusack (then Sheahan) and her father (Bill Sheahan) with two 'Javanese' internees at Cowra POW Camp Canteen 1942.
Photo: Mrs Eva Cusack.

difficulties in the administration of the compound and preventing likely friendly co-operation with them in the future.[46]

On 30 November two Dutch officers visited the camp to discuss the back pay owing and try to induce the seamen to volunteer to return to service. The Official Visitor's report made a month after this visit noted that in the matter of inducing the Javanese to return to ships, the Dutch 'were entirely unsuccessful, and appear to have encountered a somewhat hostile reception'.[47] He also noted that although the amount offered as back pay had been accepted by the internees, the promised cheque from the Dutch had not arrived, which he concluded was 'unfortunate and likely to be regarded as a breach of faith'.[48] At this time there were still 678 Javanese internees in Cowra.[49]

Outside contact

It appears that the Indonesians in the camp managed to have some contact with Australians. At least one young Cowra woman whose fiance was a switchboard officer there visited the camp on several occasions and conversed with some of the detainees,[50] but there must have been other more clandestine contacts, perhaps with and through Australian army personnel, and these did not please the Military authorities. Concern was expressed in a security report (11-17 January 1943) that Cowra civilians appeared to know the movements of the internees because of leakage of official information and in fact, they knew of these movements several days before they took place. There were also unsubstantiated Dutch claims that some of the Indonesians were in close contact with Japanese prisoners in the camp.[51]

Love story – Pearl and Haroena

The internees were able to send and receive mail, albeit censored, to and from the outside world. A rather poignant example of this remains today in the form of correspondence between Pearl, a young Sydney woman from Darlinghurst, and a seaman called Haroena. The pair must have met and formed a close relationship before Haroena was sent to Cowra. Like hundreds of sailors and their girls before and after these events, they probably met in Kings Cross, in their case in the vicinity of the Belvedere Javanese seamen's hostel, as that was where Haroena was arrested on 16 October 1942. In a letter written to Pearl shortly after his arrival in Cowra he complained indignantly, 'the only reason for my internment is that I've refused to join the vessel which I don't like. But I am not an enemy alien as you know it'.[52] Haroena must have soon decided that going back to sea was preferable to internment as, unbeknown to Pearl, he was one of a number of seamen who agreed to return to service and was released from Cowra on 23 November.[53] Three days later a registered letter from Pearl arrived for him, which of course he never received. Her affection for Haroena was expressed not only in the sentiments of the letter but in the £2 note she enclosed for him, a substantial sum for those days. She told him that 'since you was (sic) here last no boys (Javanese seamen) have been around and I miss you all'.[54] Pearl clearly held no 'White Australia' prejudice in her choice of sweetheart.

Problem solved

While the Indonesian seamen had been walking off their ships the Seamen's Union of Australia had been making representations to the Government on their behalf. When eventually Australian seamen were needed to man the Dutch vessels in place of the strikers, the Dutch were forced to improve working conditions on their ships.[55] In addition, a pay increase was granted to the Indonesian seamen who did return to work, but with the draconian proviso that a portion was to be withheld and paid when the NEI government re-occupied Indonesia and then only on condition that the seamen had demonstrated their loyalty to the Dutch.[56] Some Indonesians accepted this deal, but a large number rejected it. These men could not remain in Cowra indefinitely, so Dutch and Australian officials had to work out what to do with them.

In November 1942 Dutch military authorities came up with a solution, issuing a decree that seamen who refused to rejoin Dutch ships would be required to work in labour camps as militarised civilian labourers who would be subject to 'military provisions for punishment, discipline and military law'.[57] Incredible as it now seems, this decision to apply the military law of another country to its civilians in Australia was supported by the Australian Government.[58] It was deemed necessary to locate the labour camps in Queensland and it was stipulated that the men were not to be employed at any waterfront or place where they might be able to influence loyal Javanese seamen serving on Dutch ships.[59] The Liaison Officer of KNIL, Lieutenant J.P.K. van Echoud, who was responsible for administration and disciplinary matters relating to the soon-to-be labourers, visited Cowra to discuss the important issue of the salary they would receive. He proposed, and the men agreed, that they would be paid 6s 6d per day for their labour, the same amount paid to members of the Australian forces engaged in similar work.

Eventually, with all arrangements finalised for their re-location, in January 1943 the seamen were released from Cowra and sent to commence work at camps at Blackbutt, Toowoomba, Helidon and Wallangarra in Queensland, where they were designated as the 36th Australian Employment Company (36AEC).

The 'boat people' of Port Melbourne

At the same time as the striking seamen were attracting the attention and displeasure of Dutch and Australian authorities, another group of Indonesian seafarers was receiving a very different welcome to Australian shores. In April 1942 a small vessel, probably an inter-island trader or ferry, captained by a Mr Rontalau, berthed at the Victoria Dock in Port Melbourne. On board were some 67 Javanese people, comprising families and a number of single men. They had been living and working in Sumatra, but as the war situation became critical, had been recalled to Java, where the men, who were trained fitters and turners, were required for work in the Dutch arsenal at Bandung. However, the speed of the invasion of Java overtook them and Japanese air and naval attacks made it impossible for them to reach their destination. They continued steaming south and reached Fremantle from where they were directed on to Port Melbourne. Unlike their asylum-seeking successors many years later, these 'boat people' received a kind welcome to their land of refuge.

Dutch officials had been notified of their coming from Fremantle and were there to meet the boat, although they do not seem to have had any plan of how to care for the passengers. Eventually Rev John Freeman, minister at the Port Melbourne Methodist Church and Chaplain to the nearby Royal Australian Naval Reserve establishment, HMAS Lonsdale, was asked his advice about how these refugees should be looked after. Rev Freeman came up with the idea of billeting them in the large Sunday School hall situated next to the church in Graham Street, and after obtaining permission from the Church Trustees, he put this plan into effect with the result that the hall became temporary home to the refugees for the next three years.

With the help of Dutch officials, Rev Freeman set about transforming the hall into suitable quarters for the visitors. Small classrooms were allocated to the families while single men used the main body of the hall. Furniture, household goods, bedding and clothing were obtained from various sources, including the Red Cross. Nineteen of the refugees were Chinese Indonesians so because of religious and dietary considerations they were accommodated separately on the premises of a shop in nearby Bay Street. For the main group a

Above: Outing. Members of Javanese Party provide a bright touch of color walking Melbourne Streets. These young men show their preferences for European costume but retain their colorful sarongs. They always choose bright colours for shirts, ties and jackets. Photo: PIX magazine 6 June 1942.

*Below: Rev J. Freeman.
Photo: Miriam Nicholls.
Right: Doing the washing
in Port Melbourne.
Photo: Miriam Nicholls.*

Refuge in White Australia

Top: In Kindergarten run by Methodist Church, older Javanese children receive special instruction in a class of their own. They happily join with local youngsters in games. Aided by teachers they take part in game, "London Bridge is Falling Down". Photo: PIX magazine 6 June 1942.

Below: Refugee children at Nott Street Public School. Photo: Penjoeloeh 23 July 1943.

communal kitchen was set up and the Dutch supplied bulk foodstuffs such as rice, which Rev Freeman used to pick up and deliver to the hall.

The Freeman family and some of the local Port Melbourne people helped the Indonesians settle in to their new environment. Mrs Freeman took on the responsibility of caring for the women, advising them, arranging their medical needs, assisting them to adapt to the local community, taking them to the city for shopping and entertainment and arranging hospitalisation for the several who gave birth during their stay in Port Melbourne. One child, Amaluddin was claimed to be the first Javanese baby ever born in Australia, in February 1943, and in April one of the woman gave birth to twins.[60] The very young children, together with some local children, attended a kindergarten which was run at the hall, and the older children attended the Nott Street Public School where they soon learned English and excelled at their studies. Rev Freeman helped the men open bank accounts and joined them up in the Metal Trades Union.[61] These men were of particular interest to the Commonwealth Government because of the trade skills they possessed, skills which were in short supply. Accordingly, with the permission of the NEI Commission, they underwent special training at the Beaufort Training School and on completion were employed at the Fishermen's Bend Aircraft factory.[62]

John Guthrie's story
Recounting his first sight of the refugees John Guthrie recalls an excited friend rushing to his house to give him the news of the arrival of a boatload of 'brown people with funny clothes'. The 'funny clothes' referred to were items of traditional Javanese dress: colourful sarongs and sashes and long, close-fitting lace blouses for the women, some of whom were suckling babies; sarongs, jackets, black caps and ceremonial daggers for the men, all of which the passengers had donned before coming on deck for their arrival.

John Guthrie was one of the young local men who befriended the new arrivals took the opportunity to learn something of a new language and culture, and to introduce the refugees to their own, taking them to Australian Rules matches, ice-skating and the theatre. At the time, John based his life on and enjoyed the company of the Indonesians and 'learned to admire and respect them for their generous good nature and natural friendliness'. John and other Australian friends used to enjoy the hospitality of *Roemah Indonesia*, the Indonesian seamen's hostel at the Metropole Hotel, where they tasted foreign food and drank cheap, hard to get, beer. For John Guthrie, these first contacts led to a lifelong interest in Indonesia and to participation in political activity in support of Indonesian independence in 1945.[63]

In May 1942 the *Argus* sent a reporter to the church hall to write about the 'quaint and picturesque' sights at the 'evacuee colony'. It is interesting to note the paternalistic overtones of the article even when in this case, the intent was benign. On a visit to the kindergarten it was noted that there was a gift of a soft ball for a good child. "To whom shall I give it?" asked the donor. Then 'a blue eyed little Australian girl' suggested, 'Give it to the brown children'.[64]

Southern hospitality – the Freemans

This contact with the refugees of Port Melbourne marked the beginning of the ongoing involvement of the Freeman family with many Indonesians in Melbourne throughout the war years, and for some members of the family, of friendships which have lasted to the present day. They welcomed Indonesian servicemen and merchant seamen into their home, held 'Open House' for them on Sundays, and enjoyed new cultural experiences themselves when they were invited to concerts in the Melbourne Town Hall and saw for the first time beautiful Indonesian dances performed by dancers in traditional costume. H. Abdul Rachman, a merchant seaman who enjoyed the hospitality of the Freeman home recalled that it was a home which 'was often visited and offered comfort to Indonesian sailors'.[65] Another frequent visitor was R.M. Roeslan, who later became second-in-command of the Air Force of the new Republic of Indonesia. Roeslan described Rev and Mrs Freeman as his Australian 'mum and dad' who made him and many other Indonesians feel that Australia was their 'second home'.[66] The Freeman sisters learned some of the Indonesian language (Malay as it was called then) and even joined their new friends singing Indonesian songs on a radio show one Sunday. But their openness to new experiences and their lack of racial prejudice was not shared by everybody. They recall the 'dirty looks' they sometimes received when going out with their 'coloured' friends and on one occasion when a visiting Dutch woman saw Mrs Freeman nursing one of the Indonesian babies she informed her that 'we don't even shake hands with them'.[67] The Freemans however described their experiences as 'enriching their lives' in a way they had never previously imagined possible in Australia of the 1940s.

The kindness of strangers

At the same time as the Freemans were caring for the refugees, other Australian families were also welcoming Indonesians into their homes. In Adelaide a Ladies Committee set up to 'do their bit' by entertaining visiting Allied troops was notified that some NEI Air Force cadets training at Parafield were coming and was asked to look after them. The family of Nancy Loan was among those who responded and went to the designated restaurant in Grenfell Street to meet their guests. To their surprise, the first group comprised all 'coloured' men. Their arrival caused a great stir in the restaurant. 'We'd never seen anyone like them, specially as dark as some of the Indonesians were,' Nancy Loan recalled 55 years later. The family's guest book contains entries written by their Indonesian guests thanking them for their hospitality in 1942, before they were sent to Jackson, Mississippi for further training.[68] Also in Adelaide in 1942 the Treloar family entertained Indonesian air force officers and recall the fondness of the men for wearing sarongs on shopping expeditions.[69] In Melbourne at the same time the family of Ted Fryer, RAN, welcomed to their home Indonesian members of the NEI Navy who were at the Flinders Naval Depot,[70] whilst the family of Lilian Perston did the same with some of the KPM seamen, whom she described as 'gentlemen'.[71] In New Farm, Brisbane, where Wendy James lived as a child, a family of Indonesian civilian refugees moved into their street. At the request of a member of the Indonesian community Wendy's mother took the Indonesian children, 'the sweetest and prettiest children,' to school each day with her own children, and friendships were forged.[72]

Spreading the word

By the end of 1942, after nine months in their temporary land, the Indonesian exiles – civilians, military personnel and merchant seamen – were scattered to different places in Australia, particularly, but not exclusively, along the eastern seaboard. The NEI Commission had set up its Government Information Service (NIGIS) in Melbourne, 'to disseminate information regarding political, social, cultural, economic and financial matters' of the NEI to the Australian and New Zealand governments, General MacArthur's Headquarters, the press and the general public.[73] Another aim of NIGIS was the dissemination of pro-Dutch propaganda to the Indonesians in Australia. To this end NIGIS established a Malay language magazine called *Penjoeloeh* (The Torch). This magazine is a useful source of information about some of the day to day activities of the Indonesians as they experienced life in exile in Australia. The first edition of *Penjoeloeh* was published on 21 August 1942, and typifying the tone of the propaganda was the sentiment expressed in the editorial, in which the Indonesians scattered throughout Australia were likened to, '*Lidi jang satoe bersatoe tidak bergoena, akan tetapi diikat mendjadi sapoe.*' (Ribs of palm leaves which are useless on their own but when bound together become a broom).[74] The Dutch, naturally enough, were determined to focus the minds of the Indonesians on the day when the Allies would reclaim their prized colony and its people from the Japanese conquerors and Dutch sovereignty would be restored. From 1942 editions of *Penjoeloeh* we learn of the establishment of the *Roemah Indonesia* hostel for Javanese seamen at the Metropole Hotel in Melbourne, and a Sydney *Roemah Indonesia* being opened at the Belvedere Hotel in July, with a ritual feast, prayers and speeches. In October a feast was held on a Dutch warship to celebrate *Lebaran,* the end of the Muslim fasting month, which was also attended by many Australians, '*memboektikan betapa populer anak-anak Indonesia di Melbourne*' (proving how popular the Indonesians are in Melbourne).[75] In December a *Roemah Indonesia* was opened in Brisbane at the Pacific Hotel in Brunswick Street, and in Melbourne Malay lessons were organised for Australian army officers.[76]

These first months of the Indonesians being in Australia had marked the beginning of people-to-people contacts. Despite the prevailing racialist and colonialist attitudes and policies of the times, genuine and in some cases ultimately long lasting friendships were made at this level. This ability and desire of some Australians and Indonesians to reach out, befriend each other and overcome barriers of communication was to have significant repercussions before the Indonesians' exile was over.

2

Bad Boys and Good Boys

As the Indonesians settled in to their new lives in exile, the NEI authorities were committed to looking after their welfare and also to retaining their loyalty. The Dutch had no doubts that after the war they would reclaim their colony and their sovereignty would be restored. Typical of the propaganda used to implant this idea in the minds of their Indonesian subjects was this excerpt from a teach-yourself-English lesson in *Penjoeloeh*: 'Hitler and Japan will lose this war. Holland and Indonesia will be free again and they will work together for the benefit of their country.'[1] Many of the Indonesians would have accepted these sentiments at this time, but there were soon to be indications that retaining the co-operation and loyalty of all of them might be a more difficult task than the Dutch had anticipated.

The 36th Australian Employment Company

On 15 January 1943 the 692 seamen still detained at Cowra were released from internment and drafted into the 36 Australian Employment Company (36AEC) based in Queensland.[2] The largest contingent, 353 men, were deployed to Wallangarra, a small town straddling the New South Wales-Queensland border on the New England Highway, where there was a break in the rail gauges between the two states. All freight had to be cross-loaded onto the other state's rolling stock and this is where the Indonesians were put to work transshipping, unloading and loading ordnance, ammunition and engineering supplies. Of the remainder, 112 were sent to Helidon where their job was receiving and despatching ammunition at the ammunition dump, 112 to Blackbutt where they had to recondition spent shells, and the remaining 115 to Toowoomba to load engineering supplies. A message from the Brisbane military base on

3rd February reported that the personnel from all locations were doing 'excellent work'.[3] However, shortly after this glowing report, what was to be ongoing discontent and trouble erupted, particularly at the Wallangarra camp.

Six shillings and six pence

The main reason for this discontent was the vexed issue of pay, one of the reasons for the seamen being in this predicament in the first place. As noted earlier, while they were still in Cowra, Lieutenant van Eschoud, the Dutch liaison officer for the 36AEC, had promised the Indonesians that they would be paid the sum of 6s 6d per day for their labour, the same rate paid to Australian Military Forces doing similar work. Unfortunately for the Indonesians, there was a great deal of confusion about this matter. The Australian Army authorities had actually decided to pay them 1s 5d a day but on hearing of the Dutch promise decided to raise this to 3s because, as one official remarked, 'experience with Indonesians has taught us that it is impossible to obtain results if salaries for work already done are paid below expectations aroused'.[4] It was also proposed that the difference between this 3s and the promised and expected 6s 6d per day, would be paid retrospectively, but only for the first three weeks from the date of their arrival from Cowra. Because the Dutch acknowledged Van Echoud's mistake about the amount of pay promised they agreed to cover the cost of this extra sum.[5]

A pay rise from 1s 5d to 3s per day was not enough to placate the unhappy Indonesians. On 19 February, their leader in Wallangarra, Boestami, wrote a letter on their behalf to the 'Dutch Government in Australia' clearly outlining all the details about the promised 6s 6d and expressing their unhappiness that the Australian government had not at that stage even paid the increased rate of 3s per day, let alone the extra back pay for the first three weeks. His letter concluded with a request that all the Indonesians working in 36AEC be paid at the rate of 6s 6d per day promised by Van Eschoud at Cowra, as anything less than that was not enough for the work they were doing.[6] Unfortunately for the seamen, the arrears were never paid and neither was the regular pay ever increased to the promised 6s 6d a day, a fact that was still deeply resented by Moh Hodrie 54 years later as he complained, '... our right to money that has not been paid

Moh Hodrie former striking seaman. Surabaya 1997. Author's photo.

to this day, was based on a promise from Captain (sic) van Eschoud in Cowra Camp that we would be paid 6s 6d per day, but after we worked we were paid 3s per day'.[7]

Trouble at Wallangarra

The first indication of the extent of the Indonesians' resentment came when some of the Wallangarra contingent went on strike. In March, Van der Plas (who was now the NEI Chief Commissioner) sent a telegram to Army Minister Forde informing him that some Indonesians were refusing to work for 3s per day and had been locked up in cells.[8] A breakdown of discipline and an outbreak of pilfering also started around this time.[9]

In an attempt to improve the situation, it was decided on advice from the Dutch Liaison Officer, Van Eschoud, to weed out the 'bad boys' and send them to a camp at Goondiwindi. This transfer of 67 alleged trouble-makers took place on 20 March.[10] However, it seems the discipline problems did not stop there. Complaining to the Director of Labour at Victoria Barracks in Melbourne about inadequate supervision due to lack of appropriate staff, the NEI Security Service Director, Commander G.B. Salm, insisted that these 'bad eggs' in Goondiwindi should be under strict discipline and not free to do what they liked. Although working well they were disobeying orders, going to town without leave and taking rests when they felt like it during working hours.[11]

The 'Javos'

Meanwhile back in Wallangarra, the Indonesians, or 'Javos' as the locals called them, aroused a lot of curiosity. Their camp was actually located on the NSW side of the town (then known as Jennings), where they were housed first in tents, arousing local sympathy because of freezing winter temperatures in the district, then later in fibro or plywood huts, with the camp surrounded by a high wire fence. Local children passing the camp on their way to school were intrigued by the way the 'Javos' went about their ablutions, scooping water from a nearby drain into cups or tins and splashing it over their bodies.[12] After a few weeks the labourers were allowed to walk around the local area at weekends, although some places in town were declared out of bounds, such as the two hotels, the cafe at the picture theatre and the refreshment rooms at the railway station.[13]

People who lived in Wallangarra at the time have common memories of the activities of these men whom most locals thought were actually prisoners of war. These included visiting people's homes to buy vegetables, eggs and chickens to supplement the army diet, hunting rabbits for the cooking pot, making beautiful kites and flying them until they were stopped 'in case they alerted the enemy', visiting the local cinema accompanied by guards, and holding weekly musical evenings in the camp. Another common memory was the Indonesians' fondness for perfumed hair oil purchased from the local shops and the strong scent it exuded as they passed by.[14] Their contacts with the townspeople seem to have been limited to the commercial transactions mentioned above, although there were a few exceptions. For instance they befriended one family from whom they bought chickens and to whom they sometimes brought Javanese food to sample. On one occasion they even gave the man of the house a bag of (probably) stolen vests and braces. As vests particularly were in very short supply due to wartime clothing rationing, this gift was accepted gratefully and remembered fondly by the recipient.[15] There were proven cases where the Indonesians' ignorance of local prices was exploited and they were regularly overcharged at one of the local stores, particularly for cigarettes.[16] This aroused a lot of anger when prices at other shops were compared, causing the Indonesians to complain to their officers. Perhaps their resentment and the fact that the local people thought they were prisoners of war and therefore the enemy, explained the fact that on the whole the two peoples regarded each other with mutual suspicion.

A small group of the 'Javos' also worked in the nearby railway yards at Warwick, on the Sydney-Wallangarra-Toowoomba line to Brisbane. As they were never seen around town and there was no camp for them, they must have been taken there each day from Wallangarra. These 'small, dark-complexioned men,' were of great interest to inquisitive local schoolboys, one of whom recalls, 'this being my first "multicultural" experience in an extremely White Australia, I found absolutely fascinating'.[17] Also fascinating to the boys were the spectacular kites made for them by the Javanese, who introduced them to the thrills of 'the noble art of kite fighting'.[18]

More trouble in the camp

The removal of the 'bad boys' to Goondiwindi had resulted in a few weeks of peace, but throughout May, a number of breaches of discipline occurred which really aroused the frustration of the Australian officers with their Dutch colleagues, who had overall responsibility for administering disciplinary action in the camp. On two occasions, work gangs of Indonesians unloading trucks walked off the job before working hours were finished and refused to obey orders to return. Once an Indonesian flouted authority when he insisted on trying to wash his mess gear in the out-of-bounds sergeants' mess, and became aggressive when ordered not to do so. Another was stopped by an NCO from walking to the European quarters and trying to take water provided 'for the use of white staff.' The offender left the area, but returned shortly after with a bucket which he proceeded to fill, asserting that he would take water from anywhere he wanted to. The Australians became frustrated because when their NCOs reported these incidents, the Dutch ignored them and took no disciplinary action.[19]

Then, on three successive nights in June, large, single explosions occurred in the vicinity of the Indonesian camp area. A check of the

Ammunition Depot revealed that a number of detonators were missing. Military Police were immediately assigned to patrol the camp but were withdrawn when no further incidents took place.[20] Apparently unaware of all this trouble, Major General Stantke, GOC Qld, had recently written to the Allied Land Forces HQ requesting that some of the Indonesian personnel be allowed limited leave in the Brisbane area. He seemed assured that the worst of them had been weeded out as he explained —

> ... the outlook of these people is childlike in that they expect to be punished for wrongdoing. They are just as expectant of reward for good work. The absence of punishment or reward, as the circumstances warrant, is immediately classified as weakness in the former case and an injustice in the latter.[21]

This request had been made in response to a suggestion from Commissioner Van der Plas, so it seems likely that his were the sentiments Stantke was expressing, particularly as Stantke himself probably had no first hand knowledge or experience of 'these people'. Australian officialdom at the time was apt to accept without question Van der Plas's judgements about the character and motivations of Indonesians.

Before any reply to Stantke's request was forthcoming, the next and potentially most serious incident occurred on the evening of 5 July, when a grenade exploded near the tent of an Australian soldier, Private W. Hookeywin, narrowly missing the occupant. The camp Staff Officer who reported the explosion concluded that it must have been an attempt to kill Private Hookeywin, not for any personal reason but simply because his tent was closest. A search of Dutch and Australian NCOs' and Indonesians' kits and tents revealed no sign of explosives, although in the Indonesian camp, 'a quantity of loot of all descriptions' was discovered buried in the bush or hidden in nearby rabbit holes.[22]

As the authorities tried to find reasons for the conduct of the Indonesians, a flurry of reports was sent from officers at Wallangarra to their superiors in Brisbane. The CO of the 36AEC, Captain J.L. Ewing, wrote, 'the conduct, and the discipline of the Javanese is now, after six months, worse than it was when we first arrived in Queensland

and it is rapidly getting worse ... now in my opinion the position here at Wallangarra is worse than before the 'bad boys' were removed'.[23]

Lieutenant K. Lodewycxx, a senior security officer, in his wisdom attributed the deteriorating situation in Wallangarra to various factors: the Indonesian seamen of 36AEC were inferior types morally because of their contact with people who lived in seedy seaport towns in the East and other parts of the world. Because of this poor moral standard, thieving and pilfering was rife. (The writer did acknowledge that some Australian personnel at Wallangarra indulged in the same behaviour). Some of them had had contact with Japanese internees in Loveday camp in South Australia before entering the 36AEC, and had been influenced by anti-Allied propaganda; discipline was lax and control ineffective, with no disciplinary action by Dutch personnel when breaches were reported by Australian NCOs; loss of the Indonesians' respect for some of the Australians who tended to fraternize and become 'unduly familiar' with them; overcharging by certain stores in the township, leading to anti-Australian sentiments.[24] Nobody mentioned the initial cause of discontent and resentment – the broken promise about the 6s 6d which was the root cause of all these troubles.

On 19 July an enquiry into the explosion verified that it was caused by a grenade stolen from an ammunition dump or train where the 'Indianese' were working. Incriminating bare footprints left in the vicinity of the explosion indicated that the culprit was a Javanese. The enquiry concluded that the bombing was an expression, not of personal malice, but of disapproval and political feeling.[25] Subsequently, a man called Asmawie confessed to throwing the grenade and to stealing a quantity of explosives discovered in and around the camp area. He implicated several other Javanese and all were eventually court-martialled by the Dutch.[26] During the hearing when the defendants were accused of being pro-Japan, one of them shouted defiantly, 'Dutch and Australians treat us as dogs and slaves. We are treated worse than the enemy and yet they call us Allies'.[27]

The events at Wallangarra attracted the attention of the Commonwealth Security Service and in a report to the Department of the Army in August 1943, the Director-General, Brigadier W. Simpson, voiced some of his concerns. These centred around the perceived pro-Japanese feelings of the Indonesians, although he acknowledged the likelihood that such feelings were based on fears that the Japanese would win the war, and that they, the Indonesians, would be executed on their return home because they had worked for the Allies. Simpson was also worried about the opportunities that existed for an enemy agent to pass on sensitive information about military equipment passing through the town and about the potential for acts of sabotage. He recommended that the Indonesians be transferred to less important work in a location where there would be fewer opportunities for 'subversive action'.[28]

This recommendation was not followed and it took some time for the situation at Wallangarra to improve. Throughout 1944 there were further wrangles about pay, with the Australian authorities still refusing to pay the 6s 6d on the grounds that the Indonesians were not as proficient as Australians in similar units because 'they are slow of movement and lack understanding' and 'not of strong physique and therefore not capable of handling heavy stores efficiently.'[29] With opinions like this on one side, and ongoing resentment on the other, it was small wonder that there continued to be a hard core of trouble makers among the Indonesians. In November 1944 some of them were accused of 'menacing other personnel in the camp' so at the request of Van der Plas, Lieutenant G. Hough was sent from Brisbane with a detachment of Military Police with instructions to search members of the Company for weapons of any kind, and to escort back to Gaythorne camp in Brisbane for internment any personnel considered to be 'unreliable'. On arrival he found that the camp commander had already compiled a list of 55 personnel whom he and his NCOs believed to be unreliable and pro-Japanese.[30]

Desperados at Gaythorne

On 21 November, the 55 named men were transported by military trucks to Gaythorne, where they were interned. On arrival each man and his belongings were searched, and items considered to be 'lethal weapons' were confiscated. These included knives, many of which were home made, scissors, razors, chisels, a dart, a shanghai, some needles and a skewer. Detective Constable Madsen from the Criminal Investigation Branch of the Queensland Police, who was present at the search, also noted that among the property were large quantities of soap and clothing, 'in such quantities as to suggest that it had not been acquired honestly'.[31]

The sending of these 55 Indonesian 'bad boys' to Gaythorne presented a problem to Australian Army authorities concerned about the legal status under which they were being held. They had actually arrived without the requisite detention orders, in the absence of which they were in fact being held there illegally. The Military authorities were determined not to hold the Indonesians without those orders, which were the responsibility of Brigadier Simpson. Accordingly they proposed that if the orders were issued, the Indonesians should stay at Gaythorne, because 'they would be a nuisance anywhere else', but Simpson would be pressed to consult with the Dutch and work out a plan for their 'ultimate disposal'. If on the other hand detention orders were not issued, the Army would just release them and they would become Simpson's responsibility.[32]

Apparently the necessary detention orders were issued because the Indonesians stayed in internment in Gaythorne until their eventual repatriation at the end of the war. It is interesting to compare the views of the Australian Army officials dealing with them and those of Van der Plas. As noted above, the Army considered that they might be a 'nuisance,' but nevertheless were prepared to release them if it turned out they were being held illegally. On the other hand, following a March 1945 proposal from Simpson to send the interned 55 to Dutch Merauke, in typical fashion Van der Plas demurred vehemently, describing them as 'violently anti-allied and pro-Japan,' and as 'desperados who were even plotting the assassination of Australian officers and NCOs in Wallangarra.' Asserting that 'they were drilled by Japanese internees at Loveday and were in the service of the enemy' he insisted they be detained in Australia.[33]

Some of the Wallangarra labourers in the 36AEC did eventually return to serve on KPM ships again and some were transferred to Brisbane to work in *Roemah Indonesia,* the Indonesian seamen's home.[34] The Dutch also planned the gradual transfer of some of them to KNIL establishments. Some agreed to this but many refused or if they did agree objected to wearing KNIL uniforms, so back to the 36AEC they went.[35] Those who did leave were replaced by men from other sectors of the Indonesian contingents in various parts of the country, until the war ended and the 36AEC was disbanded.

Blackbutt Camp

At Blackbutt, about 114 miles north-west of Brisbane, where there was another 36AEC camp, there were several early attempts at sabotage by some of the labourers working at the ammunition dump. These were relatively minor such as putting water or sand into shell cases and taking cordite packs out of them, and were short lived.[36]

Once this behaviour stopped and things settled down, the Indonesians at Blackbutt enjoyed a better lifestyle than their comrades at Wallangara. Although they had to wear Australian army uniforms dyed prisoner of war maroon for work, when they were off duty they cut quite a dash as they were allowed to don colourful sarongs and smart white jackets and wander freely around the town. The local people were friendly to them and some entertained them in their homes. Because of the severity of the winter cold, many of the local women even knitted pullovers for their Indonesian friends and sewed other items such as pillowcases for them. When paying social visits to local people's homes, the Indonesians still carried out their Islamic prayers at the prescribed times and were considered to be 'right into their religion'. They were also able to go to the local cinema and sometimes played soccer.[37] From Blackbutt, the Indonesians were dispersed throughout late 1943 to Wallangarra, Casino, Melbourne, Brisbane or to KPM ships.[38]

Toowoomba Camp

This camp was located with access to a railway siding, where much of the labour involved loading bags of cement. The strongest memory local people have is of the beautiful kites the 'Javos' made from brightly coloured crepe paper in the shape of birds, flowers and deities. The Indonesians earned money selling these kites to anyone who wanted to buy them, and as a result they started a kite flying craze when local people started copying their methods and designs to the extent that '... it wasn't long before kites were flown all over Toowoomba – in spite of the aircraft overhead'.[39]

Good boys

In contrast to the disgruntled Indonesians of 36AEC who were performing enforced labour and causing trouble for Australian and Dutch military officials, Indonesian merchant seamen still working

Indonesian troops relaxing at a camp 'somewhere in Australia'.
Photo: Penjoeloeh 16 April 1943.

their ships and Indonesian members of KNIL appeared to be passing a much happier time of exile from their homeland. 1943 editions of *Penjoeloeh* show photographs of smiling Indonesian soldiers playing guitars and relaxing in their camps, while others show Indonesian dishes such as *sate* and *nasi goreng* being prepared and eaten by happy people at *Roemah Indonesia* in Melbourne. This food was remembered with relish by Australian guests who had never before seen, let alone eaten such cuisine, which is so commonplace in Australia today. For instance the artist Donald Friend once visited and later recorded in his diary, 'we went upstairs to dine – a wonderful Javanese meal with about 16 dishes, most delicious, though some of them stinging hot with pepper'.[40]

Accounts of activities enjoyed by the Indonesians show that in exile they were preserving their own cultural identity and introducing it to their Australian friends, as well as experiencing and enjoying the culture of their hosts. For example there was a delightful report of a *ludruk* performance held at *Roemah Indonesia*, Melbourne in April, 1943. *Ludruk* is East Javanese folk theatre, including dancing

*Preparing sate at Roemah Indonesia, Melbourne.
Photo: Penjoeloeh 23 July 1943.*

and singing, in which all the parts are played by men. The accompanying photograph showed the costumed cast drawn from the crew of one of the merchant ships in port together with the simple *gamelan* orchestra that was used. The audience comprised Dutch dignitaries, Indonesians working in Melbourne, ships' crewmembers and some Australian guests, including representatives of the press. The guests particularly enjoyed the ardent declarations of love proclaimed by the 'women' of the cast to their suitors. Even though the words were Javanese, the actions made the message clear.[41]

Other activities included parties to celebrate the birthdays of Dutch royals, the success of the first Australian graduates of the Indonesian language course, who were highly praised for their skills, the baptism of four Indonesians in a Methodist church in Melbourne, the formation of a music club in Melbourne and subsequent enjoyment of classical music concerts, film and musical evenings in Brisbane and a soccer match against Australians in Brisbane.[42] On 1 September a new hostel, purchased by KPM to accommodate Indonesian merchant sailors on shore leave or waiting for ships, was opened at the Lido in North Sydney. Some of the local North Sydney population had misgivings about these Indonesians in their midst because 'they used to stare at us as they walked by and spoke their native language'.[43]

Bad Boys and Good Boys

Ludruk performance, Melbourne.
Photo: *Penjoeloeh*, 30 April 1943.

On 14 November 1943, Indonesian and Dutch personnel took part in the Allied Thanksgiving Pageant in Como Park, Melbourne, to commemorate Armistice Day. As well as marching with other Allied forces, the Indonesians contributed to the cultural content of the pageant with performances of traditional dances, songs, martial arts and *gamelan* orchestra.[44]

George Worang's Story

Marching proudly in the front row of the Indonesian contingent at the Thanksgiving Pageant was Private George Worang, an 18 year old KNIL soldier from Menado in North Sulawesi, who typified the 'good boys'. Many of the Indonesian recruits in KNIL came from Menado, a region which, along with Ambon, was traditionally very loyal to the Dutch. Worang was among the KNIL forces who had fought alongside Australian soldiers engaged in fierce guerilla warfare against the Japanese in Timor, before being evacuated to Port Darwin in 1942. From Port Darwin Worang travelled via Alice Springs to Melbourne. Here he threw himself into

47

thorough enjoyment of the wartime Australian way of life, when on leave from his KNIL duties at Bacchus Marsh.

His memories are of friendliness and lack of discrimination from the Australians he encountered. He was invited to homes to stay and enjoyed the company of Australian 'girlfriends.' Among the new skills he learnt or attempted to learn were speaking English, throwing a boomerang, ice skating, eating Australian food, of which there was always too much on the plate for him, and using a knife and fork instead of the spoon and fork or fingers of the right hand which are the norm if eating Indonesian style. He enjoyed riding in trams, going to the races and shopping in Myers department store. In wartime Australia women were performing many of the jobs normally carried out by men, hence George had his first encounter with female taxi drivers, who liked the Indonesians because they tipped generously.

George was transferred to Casino, NSW, in 1943 and later to Sydney where he stayed at the Pacific Hotel in King Street. He recalls visiting Taronga Park Zoo, swimming at Bondi Beach and walking over the Harbour Bridge. Now in frail health and blind, he nevertheless retains a strong interest in Australia and during the interview insisted on singing (in English) old wartime favourite songs such as 'Now is the Hour', 'Lili Marlene' and 'The Hokey Pokey' (with actions) with the author.[45]

The Technical Battalion – Casino

In December 1943, in the northern NSW town of Casino, the Dutch established what was known as the Technical or 'Oil' Battalion.[46] The first intake of one hundred Indonesians from Melbourne were transferred there in December to undergo training in technical skills which could be utilised by the Dutch for the repair of damaged infrastructure, in particular rehabilitation of oil installations, when they reclaimed the Indies after the war. Casino was chosen for its kinder climate for the Indonesians in comparison to the cold of Melbourne.[47] The camp they occupied was located just out of town on the Kyogle Road, and had previously been occupied by Australian forces. When the Dutch took over, the name of the camp (now the site of the Casino Lawn Cemetery) was changed from Camp Carrington to Victory Camp.[48]

Left: George Worang
(front right) Casino 1943.
Photo: George Worang.

Right: at Bandung, Indonesia 1997. Author's photo.

George Worang was among these first hundred Indonesians and took various technical courses including engineering but eventually his English language skills enabled him to become one of the camp interpreters. As they had in Melbourne, he and his comrades entered fully into the enjoyment of life in Casino. With the freedom to come and go as they pleased they enjoyed making friends with Australians and being entertained in their homes, attending church regularly and visiting nearby Lismore and Evans Head where swimming was popular.[49] Speaking of these visits to Evans Head, a woman who used to see the Indonesians there, recalled —

> They had made improvised musical instruments and sang in muted voices very sad and what sounded like songs. We used to take our children to this beach by bus on Sundays and always chose a spot near the group to listen to their music. One day their commanding officer came over and introduced himself and asked permission to give our children some lollies. Thereafter on Sundays he joined us.[50]

The Indonesians were conspicuous around town, dressed in the smart American-style uniforms – tailored outfits consisting of slacks, shirts, ties and forage caps – standard issue for the KNIL forces.[51] Along with other foreign servicemen stationed in the district, they frequented the Monterey Cafe in Lismore, particularly on Sunday afternoons when guitars and piano accordians would be produced to accompany a singsong.[52] They made many friends, were 'wonderful dancers' and used to smuggle rice from the camp for their Australian friends.[53]

Several years ago extensive interviews were conducted with some Casino people who were involved with the Indonesians and these provide a fascinating insight into the impact this particular influx of Asian people had on the residents of what was a typically parochial Australian rural town of the 1940s. The comments show a continuum of reactions ranging from warm acceptance of the strangers – 'they were welcomed into the hearts and homes of Casino residents' – to suspicion and in some cases hostility – 'some people were terrified of anything not Casino, of foreigners.'[54]

On the positive side informants described some of the visitors to their homes as being 'welcomed like family', 'no trouble in town', and 'gentle and softly spoken.' They remembered the wonderful show put on at the camp when 'everyone in town' went and saw 'first class entertainment' – gamelan performances and dances with beautiful traditional costumes. One informant summed the experience up as being like 'stepping into another world ... it was our first taste of elegance'. Commercial interests in town were well served by the visitors with one man commenting, 'The town made a bonanza, they were ripped off with over-pricing. They made a mint out of them'. On the other hand the Indonesians evened the score when some of them indulged in black marketeering, selling hard-to-get and rationed items like liquor, cigarettes, clothing and tinned food procured from the camp.

Most negative comments were racially based, such as the horrified reaction when local families went to the cinema with Indonesian friends or worse still when white girls went out with or had sexual liaisons with or even married 'coloured' men. These girls were given the sobriquet 'Javo Girl'. Some of the women were wives of Australian prisoners of war and when their husbands finally came home

Bad Boys and Good Boys

Indonesian servicemen attending church, Casino 1944.
Photo: George Worang.

and found out they blamed and deeply resented the Indonesians. The husbands also resented the Dutch soldiers and officers who had had affairs with local women and this hostility sometimes led to brawls between them. The Mayor himself reported hearing the Australians telling Dutch soldiers, 'You should go home and take your bloody niggers with you'.[55]

At the camp itself, conditions appear to have been rather relaxed. Local children were fascinated with the newcomers and were allowed to enter the camp where they befriended the Indonesians, and often helped them with English, and in turn learned some Indonesian. Cattle from nearby farms ran through the camp, and some of the Indonesians bought eggs and milk from the farmers and rode their horses.[56] Hank Koolwijk, a Dutchman who served in the camp from March to December 1944, noted that the Indonesians were well-behaved and co-operative, with the same privileges and obligations commensurate with military discipline as the Europeans.[57]

There was however one area where the behaviour of some of these 'good boys' aroused the displeasure of Australian authorities, and that was their dealings with the local Aboriginal population. In November 1944, following a number of adverse reports, a conference was held, attended by the Mayor and Town Clerk of Casino,

51

the CO of the NEI forces in Casino, Police Sergeant Selley and the local Welfare Officer of the Aboriginal Welfare Board. Concern was expressed that the presence of these 'coloured' troops 'had attracted a considerable number of young aboriginal women to the town resulting in immoral behaviour, drinking and gambling'.[58] As a result of this meeting it was decided to place the South Casino area, where most of this behaviour was taking place, out-of-bounds to the Indonesians, and to prohibit coloured Dutch troops bathing in the pools in the town area.[59] How this latter ban would help solve the problem was not mentioned, and may have had more to do with a colour bar and prevailing racist attitudes than with the 'immoral behaviour'. It appears that these measures had some effect for a while, but the following year, the Acting NSW Premier, Mr J. M. Baddley wrote to the Prime Minister reporting that in July the situation had deteriorated again, and that —

> 13 persons of aboriginal blood were convicted on charges of drunkenness, obscene language and resisting arrest, and it has been alleged that one of the main causes of this misconduct is the traffic in adulterated liquor between the Javanese and the aborigines. In the streets after dark and in the picture shows, numbers of aboriginal girls are to be seen in company with the Javanese (and West Indians) although apparently, the same also applies to many white girls.[60]

A request was made that, because the matter was so serious, the only solution was the speedy removal of the troops from Casino.[61] This did not happen. When, some time later, the Indonesian troops were finally removed from Casino, the reason had nothing to do with this particular problem.

R. M. Roeslan's story

Another loyalist 'good boy' was Roeslan, a Javanese trainee pilot who arrived in Australia as a member of the NEI Air Force in 1942 and was stationed at Parafield Airfield north of Adelaide until, after a month's training, he and his companions were shipped to the USA, where he was posted to the NEI Information Bureau in New York. In January 1943, he was transferred back to Australia,

Bad Boys and Good Boys

where he was attached to the NEI Civil Service School operating in Melbourne to train its students to become well prepared assistants of the new NEI anticipated after the war. During his time in Melbourne Roeslan worked actively to introduce his culture and his country to Australians, participating in traditional dance performances and addressing various organizations. He was a frequent visitor at the Freeman home, where the Freeman daughters became his Australian 'girlfriends'. As an Indonesian member of the Javanese aristocracy who had received a Western (Dutch) education he found it easy to adapt to life in Australia, although more so after he learned to smoke, drink and dance Western style a little, none of which 'vices' he had previously.

Although at that stage loyal to the Dutch, Roeslan was very amused by an incident at a function he attended in Melbourne, which demonstrated signs of emerging nationalist sentiments among some Indonesian merchant seamen. In April, 1943, a social evening was organised by the Indonesian crew of the KPM ship *Tasman* to celebrate the birthday of Princess Juliana of the Netherlands. The party was attended by high Dutch officials including the NEI Commissioner Van Der Plas, the Netherlands Minister in Australia, Baron van Aerssen and by Australian guests. The Indonesian organiser made a speech in which he expressed the hope that peace and order would return to Indonesia, and then calmly proposed that everybody stand to sing the *Wilhelmus,* the Dutch National Anthem, then *Indonesia Raya,* (Great Indonesia) the Indonesian Nationalist anthem not recognised by KNIL or the Dutch, and finally the Australian National Anthem. At the time *Indonesia Raya* was identified with the beginnings of the Indonesian Nationalist movement. Its call for the unity of Indonesia had long echoed at Indonesian political rallies before the war, where people always stood in solemn observance. But to have it sung at a function celebrating the birthday of a Dutch royal was unheard of. Naturally, the Australian guests, oblivious to all this, remained standing after the completion of the Dutch anthem, and to their chagrin the Dutch guests were therefore forced to do the same. It must have been an anathema for them to stand as the words, 'Let us all cry for a United Indonesia, Great Indonesia, Free and Independent,' were sung. Van Der Plas quickly made

R.M. Roeslan with Rev Freeman's daughter Bonita.
Photo: Miriam Nicholls.

a face-saving speech in Dutch and English explaining that *Indonesia Raya* was not a national anthem but 'a symbol of the love Indonesians have for their country' and that he had no objections to its being sung that evening.[62]

Roeslan eventually left Australia in 1944 when he was sent to the front and attached to an American unit in Finchhaven, in New Guinea. In July of that year, with the rank of first lieutenant, he became commanding officer of a unit which worked closely with American forces and the RAAF. He returned to Australia for a short time and then went to the Philippines. After the war, as an officer in the NEI Air Force he was regarded with suspicion for some time by the republicans, but eventually joined them and helped to establish the fledgling Air Force of the Republic of Indonesia. He continued to maintain contact with Australian friends, including the Freeman daughters, whom he has visited in Melbourne since the war.[63]

As 1943 drew to a close *Penjoeloeh* reported that the wedding of Freddy Wenas and Emma Lenni Poliy had taken place in November at St Stephens Church in Sydney, followed by a reception at *Roemah Indonesia*. Guests included Indonesians, Dutch and Australians, with

Bad Boys and Good Boys

Hawaiian music group, Casino 1944.
Photo: George Worang.

speeches and congratulations being given in the three languages. This was the first wedding between two Indonesians in Australia. Meanwhile at the Brisbane *Roemah Indonesia*, extra accommodation had been provided for recreational activities and an Indonesian Hawaiian Band was being formed, similar to those already established and popular in Melbourne and Sydney.[64]

The following excerpt from a letter written (in English) to George Worang in Casino in February 1944, exemplifies the enjoyment and life style the 'good boys' were experiencing in Australia while the 'bad boys' were labouring and languishing in 36AEC in Wallangarra. The letter was written by a KPM seaman, Jan Walandouw, who had known Worang in Melbourne and had then moved to Sydney.

> ... Don't worry about me for I am OK. Glad to mention I am having some wonderful times here in Sydney, so don't get jealous George. We are giving parties twice a week (on Wednesday and Saturday nights). I wish you could come over in Sydney and listen to our Minahassa Hawaiian band playing at the KPM boys' club. Fortnight ago we had a big party in Bondi Town Hall on one of our boy's engagement to an Australian girl and everybody

was swinging it. All the Australians love our Hawaiian Band. Oh ya George I am not at the Metropole (Melbourne) anymore. I only stayed three weeks and afterwards I came to Sydney and working in the KPM head office. Oh boy I like it. Really George I like Sydney much better than Melbourne. When I was in Melbourne was a party at Coburg Town Hall so we all went and the NEI Hawaiian band was playing the whole night, but I only stayed till 2 o'clock in the morning. When is it your turn George? You often receive letters from your girl in Melbourne isn't it?[65]

Tilting at windmills

Dutch servicemen also enjoyed hospitality and friendly contacts with ordinary Australians. At official levels however, after a good start, relations between the two allies were often difficult. It is not intended here to examine the problems in depth but some aspects are an essential part of this story. One early source of tension was the difference between Australian and Dutch views about the role Australia might have in post-war NEI. The fledgling Australian Department of External Affairs was seeking to capitalise on the position in which Australia found itself as host to the NEI administration and to the new influence it expected to have in the region after the war.

In an address delivered at Holland House in New York in April 1943, the Minister for External Affairs, Dr Evatt, left no doubt as to his ideas about Australia's role when he said, 'Australia regards Australian Dutch relations as being vital ... The NEI and Australia *can* become great partners in developing and bringing a better way of life to the peoples of Indonesia.'[66] Not surprisingly, the Dutch were unimpressed with these views and the Netherlands Minister to Australia, Van Aerssen, quickly informed Prime Minister Curtin that his government, could not agree to any power, becoming a 'partner' in the process of developing and assisting the Indonesian people.[67] Curtin promptly defended Evatt's statement saying it implied only 'that there should be friendly collaboration and co-operation as regards the territories in which our two countries are especially interested.' Further he explained that the word 'partner' denoted 'a close association imbued with high ideals for the prosecution of a great purpose and a great cause', and that Evatt was in reality paying the Dutch a great compliment.[68] Dutch concerns about Australia's ambitions were not allayed by this detailed explanation.[69]

In October and November of 1943 the Netherlands Government-in-exile in London started a process of reorganising the NEI administration in Australia in preparation for resumption of power after the war. Whether this move and its timing had been planned all along or whether it was prompted and hastened by unease caused by Evatt's statements is not known, but nevertheless, moves were afoot. The first step was the appointment of Major-General L.H. van Oyen as Commander-in-Chief of the Netherlands forces in Australia, with the added task of being in charge of post-war reconstruction in the NEI after liberation.[70] This development was followed by a decision to send Dr H.J. van Mook, at the time in London as Netherlands Minister for the Colonies, to Australia as Lieutenant-Governor designate of the NEI. When he learnt of this plan Evatt immediately wrote to the Australian High Commissioner to the UK, Mr S.M. Bruce, urging him to contact the Netherlands Government and 'strongly discourage notion of sending Netherlands Indies Governor to this country. In the present situation appointment would be most embarrassing.'[71] We can only speculate on what this embarrassment might be. Perhaps it was because of the reception Evatt's own comments had received from the Dutch or perhaps it was because he did not want Australia to be seen as providing a base for an administration bent on preserving its pre-war colony. In any event, the Dutch were not deterred. On 3 December, Bruce cabled Evatt to confirm the Dutch intention to send Van Mook to Australia as Governor-General designate of the NEI.[72]

Evatt tried everything he could to pressure Bruce into persuading the Netherlands Government-in-exile to defer the implementation of this plan, insisting that it was 'quite inopportune' at the time to formally set up a 'gubernatorial regime' in Australia, whatever might happen in the future. Evatt's pleas were to no avail for on 18 December, Bruce informed him that matters were now out of his hands as the Dutch were about to make official representation to the Australian Government to make arrangements for Van Mook's appointment. Events then moved swiftly. On 24 December, Baron van Aerssen wrote to Prime Minister Curtin to announce the forthcoming arrival of Van Mook, stating that, 'my government plans to establish a Netherlands Indies government organization to replace the NEI Commission for Australia and New Zealand,' and that Van Mook was coming to discuss this with the Australian government. Van Mook's visit took place during February and March 1944 and in meetings with Prime Minister Curtin and with Evatt it was explained that a Lieutenant-Governor and a Council of Heads of Departments would be appointed, but that the relationship with the Commonwealth would not change, as the Minister for the Netherlands would continue to be the accredited representative of the Dutch Queen Wilhelmina to the Commonwealth, the Netherlands and its colonies.[73]

The *Sydney Morning Herald* (7.3.1944) reported Mr Curtin's announcement after these meetings under the headline, 'No New NEI Rule From Australia.' Curtin said, 'The office of the Lieutenant-Governor of the NEI and the Executive Council for the Administration of the NEI will be domiciled temporarily in Australia as the Commonwealth is a convenient location for carrying on their administration, but they are not going to establish a Government in Australia'. Whatever the Dutch intentions were, it seems that the Australian Government had little choice but to co-operate, however reluctantly, and when Evatt wrote to Van Aerssen on 5 April, 'I am glad to inform you that the Australian Government welcomes the proposal,'[74] the capitulation was complete.

The relationships between the three protagonists in this story – Australians and Indonesians, Indonesians and Dutch, Dutch and Australians – were now evolving and changing as they all adapted in different ways to their new found involvement. The people to people relationships between Australians and the 'good boys', such as those Indonesians in the forces, the loyal merchant seamen and the well behaved ex-merchant seamen in 36AEC continued to flourish. It was a different story with the 'bad boys'. The merchant seamen turned labourers in the 36AEC, who had been obedient servants of their Dutch employers when they arrived in Australia, changed after they became aware of the injustice of their working conditions compared to those of their Australian counterparts. From then on, it was what they perceived as on-going economic exploitation of their labour and Dutch breaches of faith which transformed them into strikers, troublemakers and in some cases, hardened rebels. For some of them, resentment about economic issues widened into resentment about the political issue of Dutch overlordship in general. Their defiant actions and demeanour in Wallangarra did not endear them to most Australian military personnel and civilians there, or to their Dutch superiors. At the same time, small cracks born of different expectations began appearing on the surface of the Australian-Dutch relationship at official levels.

3

The Coming of the Nationalists

One freezing winter's day in June 1943, a steam train pulled in to Cowra railway station in south-west NSW, and a group of bewildered and apprehensive Indonesians – men, women and children – alighted and stood shivering on the platform. Their circumstances were far different from those of their compatriots who were already in the country. These people were political prisoners, some with their families, who had been evacuated to Australia from their place of internment in Boven Digul, in what was then Dutch New Guinea. The NEI Government had interned them because of their activities in the 1920s or 1930s, in one or other of the various Indonesian political movements or nationalist organizations which began to emerge early in the 20th century. These political prisoners were to have a significant impact on Indonesian and Australian affairs. Because of this significance it is pertinent to include here a brief sketch of the development of Indonesian nationalist aspirations and organizations, and how the Dutch colonial government dealt with them prior to 1942.

The impact of Dutch colonial rule

The Dutch presence in the Indies began early in the 17th century and lasted for some 350 years. For the first 200 years their main interest was trade conducted through a trading company, the VOC. At the end of the 18th century the VOC was taken over by the Dutch government, which, apart from a brief British interregnum, ruled for another 150 years.

Dutch colonial rule was marked by phases, each of which heavily impacted on Indonesians, particularly Javanese, and their traditional societies. The exploitation of land and labour in the 19th century yielded enormous profits for the Dutch and left most of the Javanese peasantry impoverished. Around the end of the 19th century, some ex-colonial administrators and visitors, appalled by the plight of the peasantry, protested on their return to Holland and publicised abuses in the press. These two factors gave rise to the decision that alongside the commitment to making profits, a more humanitarian concern for the welfare of the peoples of their expanded colony was now a necessity and responsibility of the colonial government. This concern was manifested in what was called the Ethical Policy, introduced as official government policy in 1901. It focused on a number of reforms, with its instigators envisaging that under Dutch leadership and tutelage the Indonesians might eventually aspire to becoming citizens of some sort of self-ruling province in a Netherlands Kingdom.[1]

But despite these reforms, the overall impact of Western capitalism with its corrosive and disintegrative effects on their society had left most of the peoples of the NEI not with ideas of becoming any kind of united entity, but with a desire to shed foreign domination and return to their traditional social structures and ways of life. This desire motivated the initial resistance to the colonial government, which took the form of localized (and eventually unsuccessful) uprisings or tribal revolts at different times during the nineteenth century.

The first phase of Indonesian nationalism[2]

The period 1908-1928 was a period of transition from the localised revolts mentioned above to an independence movement based on the concept of a larger Indonesian society. During this time the first large scale people's movements emerged, the most significant of which had ideologies based on Islamic principles on the one hand, e.g. *SI* (The Islamic Union), or Marxist principles on the other e.g. PKI (The Communist Party of Indonesia), whose initial aims were principally to influence the colonial government to address the grievances of the people and improve their material welfare.

The colonial government meanwhile, despite its Ethical Policy, remained repressive. In 1918, in response to growing restiveness, it made one of its greatest concessions to its Indonesian subjects in establishing an advisory body, the *Volksraad* (People's Council), some of whose members were appointed and some elected. About 40% of the seats were allocated to Indonesians. As far as they were concerned however, the *Volksraad* was an ineffective vehicle because any reforms they proposed were either ignored or outvoted.[3]

The Coming of the Nationalists

In late 1926 and early 1927 PKI-instigated violent rebellions erupted in West Java and West Sumatra. But because they were ill-conceived and prematurely launched against the orders of the senior leadership of the party, and did not have enough mass backing, they were quickly and harshly repressed by the Dutch. However, as one scholar correctly says, 'the memory of the revolt gave the communists the reputation of super revolutionaries so dangerous to colonialism that the party had to be banned and its leaders exiled ...'[4] This dubious reputation was to be a significant factor some years later in Australia.

The slogan of these early movements had been *Kemerdekaan* (Freedom). This did not necessarily mean total freedom from Dutch sovereignty nor conceive of a political entity encompassing all the territories of the colony. However, in the next period of struggle, the slogan of the nationalists exemplified their broader aim: *Indonesia Merdeka* (Free Indonesia).[5]

The nationalist movement

The nationalist movement was characterized by two kinds of organisations, those prepared to co-operate with the Dutch to achieve their goals and those who would not. The co-operators believed that because the colonial rulers would not tolerate open nationalism, more could be achieved by not antagonising them. On the other hand the non-co-operators insisted that co-operation only strengthened Dutch rule, with the result that the colonial government regarded them as disloyal extremists.

After 1928 secular nationalist parties emerged, the main one being the PNI (Indonesian Nationalist Party), of which Soekarno, later the first president of Indonesia, became leader in 1929. The PNI called for a free Indonesia, which it hoped to achieve through non-cooperation with the Dutch, and collaboration between all existing political parties.The government acted swiftly against the party: its leaders, including Soekarno, were interned and the PNI was outlawed.

Throughout the 1930s a number of nationalist parties emerged representing socialist, Islamic or secular ideologies but all calling for a free Indonesia. In 1931 the New Indonesian National Education was formed, not to urge revolution, but to promote nationalist ideals by providing education about politics, economics and history to its members.[6] Other influential parties of the 1930s advocating non-co-operation, were the Party Of Indonesia (led by Soekarno after his release from prison), Young Indonesian Communist Party which, with Party of the Indonesian Republic was a clandestine offshoot of the banned PKI, Union of Indonesian Muslims and Party of Indonesian Islamic Union.

'The Green Hell of Tanah Merah'[7]

The Dutch dealt harshly with rebels and nationalists whom they perceived as a threat to the colonial status quo. Executions of some ringleaders had followed the failed PKI rebellions of 1926 and 1927 and hundreds of people of all nationalist persuasions were eventually imprisoned or exiled throughout the 1920s and 1930s. Among the latter were those Indonesians who found themselves shivering on Cowra railway station so many years later.

A week after the 1926 revolt in West Java, the Dutch took steps to establish 'a special place' for the mass internment of the captured rebels. The Governor General, de Graeff, convened a special meeting of the NEI Council putting to it his view that arrest of the 'dangerous communist leaders' would only be a stop-gap measure, as they would soon be released through lack of evidence to support prosecution, and so would be free to continue their activities. He proposed that the way to stop this happening would be by 'interning the principal communist leaders on a large scale'.[8] Shortly afterwards the category of potential internees was widened to include 'communist leaders,' and also those deemed to be 'propagandists,' as a means of eliminating the possibility of further anti-Dutch activities. It was to be left to the arbitrary decision of local heads of regional administrations to nominate just who these communists and propagandists were.[9] In other words anyone could be interned at the whim of a local leader and no one faced any legal charges or trial.

The place decided upon as perfect for the mass internment camp was in an administrative district called Boven Digul, on the upper reaches of the Digul River in then Dutch New Guinea. It was considered perfect because of its isolation in dense jungle and its comparative inaccessibility. The centre of this district was called Tanah Merah, located some 450 km upriver from the mouth of the crocodile infested Digul River at Merauke, and it was here that the camp was

The Coming of the Nationalists

situated. The Governor-General declared that it was to be called an 'isolation colony,'[10] where the inmates would 'create a little peaceful Indies, an outpost of civilization in the dark island, insulated from the outside world, undisturbed politically, and closely monitored by the state, where the internees could do something more useful and should not waste their life for the sake of untenable political dreams'.[11] Internees' families were allowed, and indeed encouraged, to accompany them into exile.[12]

We catch a glimpse of some of these first exiles in a photograph in the nationalist newspaper, *Bintang Hindia*, (12.2.1927). It shows the 'first communists' bound for Boven Digul, embarking on a ship at the port of Tanjung Priok in Jakarta, on the initial stage of their journey. Tanah Merah was later called a concentration camp in some emotive propaganda, but in the sense of Nazi concentration camps and all that they implied, this was inapt. However, there is an eerie and sinister quality in this photograph, evocative of Nazi deportations of Jews, which shows jack-booted Dutch military and police personnel holding swagger sticks, together with some civilian officials, gathered around the gangplank as internees embark. The time is midnight, and the prisoners, alleged communist men and women, have been transported to the ship 'secretly,' according to the caption.

An account in the pro-Dutch newspaper *Pandji Poestaka* tells us that on arrival at Tanah Merah, the internees were taken to the barracks which had been built for them and given foodstuffs as well as items such as kettles, bed sheets, mosquito nets and kerosine. The next day the men were handed tools and told they must work for their own and the general good. Each man or family would receive land on which to build a dwelling with timber cut from the jungle, and land for farming. As well as their own houses they had to start building more accommodation for incoming internees who would follow them. When the ship which had brought them departed on 17 March (on what was to be one of many such voyages) to pick up more 'communists' from Java, there were 105 internees together with 95 wives and children in Digul. Perpetuating the idea of the 'outpost of civilisation' the newspaper enthused that 'Tanah Merah which was formerly a lonely place has now become a bustling village'.[13]

There have been a number of accounts of life in Digul, which are naturally coloured by the experiences and allegiances of the writers.

First communists boarding ship for Boven Digul.
Photo: Bintang Hinda 12 February 1927.

One of the earliest damning criticisms appeared in 1929 in the nationalist paper *Indonesia Merdeka*, written by Mohammad Hatta, who was then studying in the Netherlands and who was himself to be interned in Digul in 1934. He quoted an extract from a letter smuggled out which illustrated the grim reality of the place —

> Death grins at us continuously. Digoel is no longer a place. It has become a heap of consumptives, and malaria sufferers, neurotics and semi-lunatics, under the scorching heat of the merciless tropical sun, surrounded by unhealthy marshes in the midst of deep, impenetrable forests.[14]

A year later, in *De Socialist*, Hatta commented on a report by Mr Hillen, a member of the NEI Council, following an inspection visit. One of his tasks was to determine whether any of the internees should be released if they had been wrongfully interned. In fact, when Hillen visited in 1930, the population of the camp had reached its peak, with 2,000 occupants, of whom 1,308 were internees.[15] On the basis of interviews he concluded that there were quite a number of former peasants and small traders in the camp who knew nothing

The Coming of the Nationalists

about communism, and should never have been interned. On his return (suffering from malaria himself) Hillen recommended that 412 of those innocent people should be released. Governor-General de Graeff agreed, but only to the extent of releasing 219 of them.[16] However, during the 1930s waves of new internees kept arriving as the Dutch clamped down on nationalists of all ideological and political persuasions.

Life in Digul

Of the first person accounts of Digul the most comprehensive was written by IFM Chalid Salim, a communist nationalist interned there from 1928-43. He recorded that the internees were divided into four groups according to their willingness to co-operate with the authorities. The first group, the majority, were those willing to work at all sorts of tasks for low wages. The reason for the popularity of being classed as willing to work was that these people had a chance of being selected for release. The second group were those who chose not to work for the Dutch but for themselves, as fishermen, fruit and vegetable growers, or running small businesses. They received no wages but were given 15 kilos of rice per month until they were self-supporting. The third group were people too disabled, mentally or physically ill to look after themselves and so were provided for entirely by the Dutch. The final group comprised men who refused to acknowledge that they were criminals and so would not work or co-operate in any way, as a matter of principle. Provided with a ration of foodstuffs, they were left to supply all their other needs themselves. Kept under constant surveillance by some of the internees who worked as spies for the Dutch, they manifested their continuing hostility by demonstrating against the injustice of their detention whenever important officials visited the camp.[17]

From the very early days of Tanah Merah, a second camp had been established for the recalcitrants or hard liners, some five hours further upstream at a place called Tanah Tinggi. Many of the non-co-operators were eventually sent there, where conditions were much worse than Tanah Merah, for varying periods of time. Initially there were about 125 occupants, including women and children, but gradually the number decreased due to deaths – particularly from malaria – escapes, and some fights between inmates which also proved fatal.

Nationalists at Boven Digul.
Photo: Siti Chamsinah.

There was no hope of repatriation for these people. The best they could hope for was being returned to Tanah Merah because of illness or in a few cases by repenting and declaring themselves willing to work.[18] There were three communist 'cliques' in Tanah Tinggi in the mid-1930s, based on opposing interpretations of communist ideology, who pledged, despite their antagonism towards each other, not to capitulate to the Dutch. But in 1937 two of the groups repented and asked to be transferred back to Tanah Merah, leaving 25 hard liners who were still there when the camp was evacuated in 1943.[19]

As the years passed, physical amenities improved and Tanah Merah assumed the appearance of normal village life.[20] But this facade of normality disguised the miserable reality of existence for the internees. The relentless attacks of malaria (despite the quinine which was issued regularly) and other diseases both physical and mental, steadily took their toll. A Dutch official who visited the camp in 1943 wrote, 'Men of twenty seven, after ten years of internment, are grey and broken, and stricken in years. Complete wrecks turn out to be men younger than fifty'.[21] Clearly, de Graeff's 'outpost of civilization' came at a terrible cost to many of its inhabitants

The population of Digul
As a propaganda ploy, the Dutch tended to label all of the Digul internees as 'communists,' irrespective of their ideologies. Indeed

there were some leading PKI men there, including Sardjono, chairman of the PKI when the revolts took place. However, from its inception, Digul was used by the Dutch to isolate anyone at all whom they considered to be a threat to their regime. Accordingly, throughout the 1930s, prominent leaders and members of the various nationalist parties of the time were interned there. The inmates represented a virtual 'Who's Who' of the nationalist movement. A notable absentee was Soekarno, who was incarcerated elsewhere, but Sjahrir and Hatta were both arrested and sent there in 1935, along with other prominent nationalists from a variety of parties. This ensured a volatile political mix which included some communists who had received their indoctrination in Moscow. Most of the internees were from Java, Sumatra or Sulawesi but there was one notable exception, an Ambonese called A.J. Patty. Ambon was certainly not known for its nationalist sentiments, in fact quite the contrary. In 1920 Patty had established an organization called the Ambon League, in an attempt to 'bring Ambon into the mainstream of the nationalist movement'.[22] His political activities led to his arrest in 1924 and his eventual internment in Boven Digul in 1930, the only Ambonese to be interned there.[23]

Siti Chamsinah's story – Part 1

Among the people on Cowra railway station that freezing June morning was a young girl called Siti Chamsinah. She had arrived in Tanah Merah as a two year old, when her mother and 4 siblings followed her father, Mohammad Amin, into exile. He had been arrested in 1926 for his activities with the Islamic Union. Her father was a non-cooperator, and supported his family by selling to other internees the corn, cassava and onions that he grew and the fowls he raised. Because of his status, the family was watched constantly by the military and by spies.

When Siti was old enough to go to school, her father first sent her to the Dutch style Standard School for Natives. She learnt reading, writing, maths and history, 'but of course not Indonesian history,' and Dutch was compulsory. The teachers were internees, as they were at the other, 'wild' school, which did not follow Dutch lines, refused to teach Dutch and substituted English as the second language after Indonesian. Siti's father later took her out of the Dutch school and moved her to the alternative school. However, this stage of her education came to an abrupt halt one Labor Day, when her teacher was making a political speech to the class. Suddenly soldiers burst in and started wrecking the school, the teacher was arrested and the children ran away or hid in terror. After this the only form of education available to children who did not go to the Dutch school was classes held in the homes of the internees, including Siti's. Even so, the Dutch allowed no more than three families to gather at a time in one house being used for classes, and often raided homes to enforce this rule. Three more children were born to Siti's mother during the 15 years the family spent in Tanah Merah before they were evacuated in 1943.[24]

Nationalist response to World War II

Isolated away in the jungle, the inhabitants of Tanah Merah and Tanah Tinggi would probably not have known much about what was happening in the outside world let alone imagined the drastic impact that the Pacific War would have on their own lives. When Germany invaded the Netherlands in May, 1940, the Indonesian nationalists in the NEI had decided to 'subordinate their demands to the interests of democracy at large'.[25] In this spirit they co-operated with the Dutch and some parties even helped their war effort financially. But when in 1940 the Dutch members of the *Volksraad* dismissed three reformist motions introduced by moderate Indonesian members, nationalists perceived that no concessions would be made in return for their co-operation. Dutch insensitivity had let an opportunity to build goodwill slip though their fingers.

Dashed nationalist hopes were re-ignited when Queen Wilhelmina made a radio broadcast in May 1941 implying that there would be more opportunities for some sort of autonomy for the Indonesians after the war. Their optimism seemed justified when the Dutch Government-in-Exile in London endorsed the Atlantic Charter later in the year. One of the principles of this important blueprint for the post-war world was support for the rights of peoples to choose their own forms of government.[26] However hopes were dashed again when the Dutch Minister for Foreign Affairs clarified his government's position —

The Coming of the Nationalists

We have to be careful that we do not thoughtlessly project Western ideas into a situation to which they are not, or at least not yet, adapted. It is in this sense that we have to interpret President Roosevelt's words that the Atlantic Charter applies to the whole world. The Charter is an instrument for good and as such is to be applied intelligently. Viewed in this light, Dutch colonial policy is in keeping with this Charter.[27]

With the Dutch unwavering in their determination to hold on to the colony on their terms, the nationalists saw little reason to hope for change and in the last few months leading up to the impending Japanese invasion, relations between the two were at an all time low.

The end of 'the outpost of civilization'

When the Dutch surrendered to the Japanese the effects were felt in Digul very quickly when supply ships from Ambon (which had fallen to the Japanese) could no longer reach the camps, resulting in severe food shortages. Between June and September 1942, the Dutch moved some of the internees to the Merauke district in the south of the island in the hope that they would be able to plant enough crops for their own needs. On arrival they were given land and left to fend for themselves.[28] For those remaining in Tanah Merah a new threat arose in February 1943, when the Japanese launched bombing and strafing raids in the Tanah Merah region.[29] Air raids like this were usually the precursor of the arrival of troops, and this possibility was of great concern to the Allies, particularly after Japanese marines occupied Hollandia (now Jayapura, the capital of West Papua).

These concerns were first expressed in a secret report written on 27 January 1943 by Dutch Liaison Officer Lieutenant Colonel J.B. Sandberg. Following an inspection of the Merauke area he noted that Operations Command in Merauke saw the presence of the internees as a danger because, 'in case of action by the enemy, they may be able to assist the enemy or in some other way create unrest and chaos'.[30] He mentioned that Colonel Langford and Sir John Laverack of the Australian Army were of the same opinion and considered that removing these prisoners to Australia as soon as possible was a necessity.[31]

When Sandberg returned to Brisbane he met Dr van der Plas,

the NEI Chief Commissioner, who strongly agreed with the plan to evacuate the internees, and asked for an official request from GHQ to arrange for the evacuation of these prisoners. This 'official request' was made on 4 February by the Commander-in-Chief of the South-West Pacific Area, General Douglas MacArthur, who informed Van der Plas that he agreed with the desirability of evacuating the political internees, 'as their presence there might be the cause of unrest and fifth column activity,' and asked him to pursue the matter with Australian authorities.[32] Van der Plas wrote to Colonel W.R. Hodgson, Secretary of the Department of External Affairs noting off-handedly that although the proposal to evacuate the internees to Australia had a pre-eminently military character, 'it would appear that the Australian Government as well had to be consulted'.[33] The letter was accompanied by a memorandum apprising Hodgson of who the internees were and the nature of their 'crimes'. Van der Plas described the Tanah Tinggi inmates, of whom 21 plus one wife and four children remained, as 'extremely dangerous psychopaths,' and listed acts of arson, murder and desecration of sacred religious sites, which they had allegedly committed 'in order to prove themselves real and conscious communists'.[34] He made no mention of nationalist aspirations as the political motivation for any of their actions and said there were practically no 'intellectuals' in the group. The 250 men with 53 women and 126 children remaining at Tanah Merah were described as 'less dangerous psychopaths, asocial people and probably a small number of communists'.[35]

The Department of the Army was less than enthusiastic about the evacuation proposal, concerned about the 'many problems associated with the holding of native families of this type (including criminal elements) because of their habits, language, diet and medical condition,' and suggested that because of these problems the evacuation go ahead 'only if imperative for operational reasons'.[36]

On 2 March Van der Plas left Australia for Merauke and Tanah Merah to discuss arrangements. When he addressed the internees and told them of plans to evacuate them to Australia because of the danger of the situation in Digul, he promised that on arrival they would be free to work for an appropriate wage, but it was their choice to go or otherwise. Some of the non-co-operators and intractables did not want to face the dangers that such a journey would entail and argued strongly against the plan, but in the end they really did not have a choice and it was only a handful of very elderly or sick people who were left behind.[37]

In a memorandum written from Merauke on 13 March, Van der Plas showed himself to be a man who was genuinely concerned about the physical welfare of the internees, but with little sympathy for the ideals that had sent them to internment in the first place: rather, he regarded their nationalist beliefs as a kind of illness, which could be cured with the right treatment. He described most of them as being 'not quite reliable, but a long way on the road to social and moral recovery'.[38] He wanted them sent to camps in a subtropical climate, with the idea that 'healthy therapy of work in a good climate will make it possible to regenerate this group'.[39]

There had already been an amount of scepticism about the whole proposal in some Australian army circles, and this is seen again in a minute paper written by Brigadier D.J. Urquhart on 5 March 1943. He raised a note of caution, suggesting reasonably enough that there was not much likelihood of the Japanese going 250 miles up the Digul River and even if they did, they had plenty of people under their control who could be more useful as guides or anything else than the internees would be. He believed that even though the internees were undesirables, the cost and extent of resources necessary to bring them to Australia was not commensurate with the risk they posed. But approval had already been given by the Minister for the Army to accept these Indonesians for internment in Australia on the same basis as other classes of aliens accepted for internment on behalf of other Empire or allied governments. It was decided that they would all be accommodated in the prisoner of war camp at Cowra NSW where the striking seamen had been held earlier, with the 'dangerous group' segregated from the others.[40]

During March and April, Dutch and Australian officials began negotiating the logistics of the evacuation and settlement of the internees, often disagreeing over details. Van der Plas strongly objected to the plan to intern them at Cowra, his main concern being that they might see or converse with Japanese prisoners-of-war.[41] Together with the 'criminal types', who would be gaoled or detained separately, the internees would now total 523 people. It was agreed that they would be subject to Commonwealth law (although there was no intention to prosecute a 'Muhammedan' who might have two wives) and the Dutch would repatriate them immediately after the war.

Further negotiations between various government departments confirmed that the Tanah Merah people would all be accommodated in compound 12B at Cowra, and the 'criminals' from Tanah Tinggi would also be in Cowra (not Long Bay as Van der Plas requested), accommodated in compound 12C.[42] As well as the internees, the Dutch intended at the same time to evacuate some 170 wives and children of Ambonese members of the Dutch militarised police at Tanah Merah and settle them in Mackay in north Queensland.

Before any of the internees could enter Australia it was necessary for the Australian Government to issue detention orders under the National Security Act of 1939-1940, to validate Australia's support for the move. On 17 May, John J. Dedman, Minister for War Organization and Industry, acting on behalf of the Minister of State for Defence, signed a document which delegated powers to Colonel Harold Redvers Langford who was at that stage of negotiations to take custody of the internees once they had been transported from Merauke to Thursday island. The document read in part —

> ... I, John Johnstone Dedman ... do hereby delegate to Colonel Harold Redvers Langford, an officer of the Australian Military Forces, the powers and functions conferred on me by regulation 26 of the National Security (general) Regulations in so far as the exercise of those powers is necessary for the purpose of making orders for the detention in Australia of those persons who have been sent to Australia from Dutch New Guinea for internment in Australia.[43]

The issuing of this order, and its legal basis, were to have significant repercussions. It sanctioned for the only time in its history, the detention on Australian soil of political prisoners of a foreign country.

Farewell to Digul

Finally, late in May 1943, all the arrangements were finalised, and the evacuation from Digul began. The first group of internees was taken in small boats down river to where a Catalina aircraft lent by

The Coming of the Nationalists

the Dutch Navy to NEFIS was moored. Salim described his mixed feelings as he saw for the last time, the place where he had lived for the past fifteen years —

> Besides the worry about the dangers that threatened us during our journey to Australia I felt sad to be leaving my house and especially the books which I had collected with great difficulty ... and as a criminal at the time of leaving his cell behind looks longingly at his sleeping mat, so too I felt sad when I saw my house and its garden for the last time.[44]

Confusion exists in the various accounts about which island in the Torres Strait group the Indonesians were actually flown to. Officials were talking about Thursday Island, and this is often mentioned as their destination. However, it appears that it was actually Horn Island, adjacent to Thursday Island, which became the mustering point from where they would be shipped south. The proof of this is found in the flying log of the Dutch pilot, Floris Bloos, who the flew the Catalina for eleven shuttle flights between Tanah Merah and Horn Island between 25 May and 6 June.[45] The flights were also used to transport Australian soldiers, notably the 26th Infantry Battalion, to Tanah Merah. Some of these soldiers were actually the first Australians to have contact with the internees.[46]

The exiles spent about a week on Horn Island, waiting for the various parties to arrive, and were accommodated in tents or houses.[47] Eventually all the internees and civilian evacuees were assembled and preparations were made for the next stage of the journey. Personal belongings were packed up ready to be shipped to Australia separately. Amazingly, given the circumstances of the evacuation, these belongings included the instruments of a *gamelan* orchestra made from found objects some sixteen years previously by a Javanese master musician interned in Tanah Merah, instruments which remain in Australia to this day.[48] Finally everything was ready, and on 1 June, the first contingent, comprising the civilian evacuees – the wives and children of the Ambonese policemen staying behind – and the Tanah Tinggi 'psychopaths'[49] set sail southwards on the merchant ship *Katoomba*, together with all the baggage. Shortly afterwards the remainder were embarked on the KPM ship, *Both*.[50] The journey to Australia had begun.

The decision to move the internees from Digul to Australia turned out to be a tactical blunder for the interests of the Dutch, a blunder which was to lead to tensions between Australian and NEI officials, and was to eventually give a significant group of experienced Indonesian political activists the freedom to pursue their nationalist agenda. But for now, after so many years of isolation, hardship and enforced political inactivity in Digul, their destination was the New South Wales country town of Cowra.

4

Cowra and Beyond

As the *Katoomba* and the *Both* steamed southwards, we can imagine the conflicting feelings that the passengers must have had: for the political prisoners and their families relief at being out of Digul, some after sixteen years of exile; for the families of the Ambonese military police, distress at being parted from husbands and fathers; and for all of them, apprehension about the unknown fate that awaited them in the alien land of Australia.

Katoomba

The *Katoomba* passengers comprised 190 civilian evacuees, as well as the 'criminals' from Tanah Tinggi and a Dutch official.[1] The 'criminals' were immediately handed over to an Australian military guard but despite this felt some sense of pleasure at being 'freed from the clutches of Dutch authority,' to which they hoped never to return.[2] The first port of call was the northern Queensland town of Mackay, where the civilians and the official were disembarked on 7 June. Mackay already had 'a slight Asian sprinkling' in its population mix, a legacy of the indentured Javanese cane workers who had worked in the area in the late 1800s.[3] The evacuees settled in well and during their time there had an amicable relationship with the local community who 'extended a generous north Queensland welcome to strangers from another land.'[4] However, this generosity did not preclude such dubious witticisms as this in the *Mackay Mercury* shortly after the Indonesians' arrival —

> Considerable interest has been taken in the arrival of a dusky baby, which increased the number of Mackay's small foreign community shortly after its mother's arrival here as a temporary visitor. At the hospital the baby's unfamiliar name proved

to be too much of a mouthful for busy nurses so the infant was given the simple, descriptive title of 'Jungle Juice,' in strictly unofficial moments.[5]

Having disembarked its civilian passengers *Katoomba* continued its voyage to Sydney, arriving on 16 June, whereupon the 'criminals' were taken under guard to the Liverpool military camp to spend the night. There they were issued with the dyed maroon-coloured army uniforms which were actually standard issue for prisoners of war, before being taken by train to the Cowra POW camp, previously occupied by the striking Indonesian seamen. Any hopes they had of enjoying a greater degree of freedom had been quickly dispelled and they later lamented that from the moment they set foot on board the *Katoomba* until they arrived in Cowra they were strictly guarded, because it was as 'dangerous prisoners' that they had been transferred to the Australian authorities'.[6] An Australian Intelligence Report written shortly after the arrival of these 'dangerous prisoners' clutching the meager worldly possessions they managed to bring with them after their 15 or 16 years of extreme privation in jungle exile, gives us a snapshot of them —

> ... These internees, who seem to be all old men, appear to be quite friendly and of a happy disposition, and seem far from being 'dangerous criminals'. They also seem to have a higher degree of intelligence than the Javanese previously confined in this camp, although not nearly as clean or well dressed. The Indonesians brought with them a great quantity of personal belongings, mainly junk. Upon being searched they were found to be in possession of clothes, cooking utensils, jungle knives (machetes), sheath knives, tomahawks, hoes and other tools. All dangerous weapons were taken away from them. The majority of these internees had large quantities of reading matter written in Dutch and English. Some literature appeared to be political whilst some other reading matter comprised grammar books and romances.[7]

These were the men Van der Plas had claimed were uneducated and the 'dangerous weapons' of course were simply the tools needed for survival in Tanah Tinggi. They were interned in compound 12C to await what fate had in store for them and as we shall see, to try to influence that fate.

Both

Meanwhile, the *Both*, escorted by two cruisers, steamed towards Brisbane. At night, with the fear of attack by the Japanese ever present, a strict blackout was maintained and the passengers had to sleep below decks in the hold.[8] After a refuelling stop at Bowen, the voyage continued and finally the *Both* arrived safely in Brisbane on 22 June. The original plan had been to take the Indonesians all the way to Sydney by ship, but arrangements changed at the last minute and they were disembarked in Brisbane.[9]

From the port they were taken under guard by truck to a field where they found a jumbled heap of warm clothing awaiting them. The men were issued with long-johns and the maroon coloured army trousers, jackets and overcoats which incorrectly designated them as prisoners of war – a fact which they bitterly resented when they later found out the significance of the colour. For the women and children there were skirts, shoes, stockings (but nothing to hold them up with), jackets and dresses of all shapes and sizes to choose from, but mostly too big for the small-statured Indonesians.[10] The sartorial effect of this attire was later noted with amusement —

> Clothes having been issued in Brisbane, a comical spectacle being (sic) presented by native women and girls wearing semi-high heeled shoes, particularly one girl with shoes much too large and worn on the wrong foot.[11]

Then everyone was loaded back onto the trucks and driven to the railway station to entrain for the long, cold journey to Cowra. During the trip an incident occurred which demonstrated that despite all they had endured, the nationalists had not lost their fighting spirit. On 24 June, a communist railway worker who happened to be standing at Newcastle station described this unexpected encounter with them that day —

'... a special train from the north, heavily guarded by Australian soldiers, entered. As the passengers were of foreign origin (coloured), especially dressed as prisoners of war, I was eager to talk to them, due to their nationality. So I approached the wagon and asked some questions. To my astonishment one of them pushed his head through a window and said in perfect English, that they were Indonesian communists'.[12]

The railwayman was even more astonished when a letter explaining the facts about Digul and the reasons for the Indonesians' internment there was thrust into his hand and he was asked to pass it to a newspaper in the hope that it would be published and read, 'especially by Australian comrades'.[13] Clearly the communist internees at least were ready to resume their political activities at the first possible opportunity.

Many hours later, as the train pulled into Cowra railway station, waiting to receive the new arrivals on that freezing winter day on 25 June were an intelligence officer and some camp guards. All were amazed as the shivering passengers alighted and the new intake of anticipated 'prisoners of war' was revealed to be not only men, but also women – some still in sarongs – and children. At that stage the Australians had no idea who these people were, but could see they were different from the Japanese, Korean and Italian prisoners who were already in the camp. Quickly the women and children, together with the elderly or sick men, were loaded onto trucks to be driven to the camp, while the fit men were lined up for the hour long walk.[14] Thus, in a period of about four weeks, these Indonesians had exchanged a life of privation in a hot, steamy, jungle encircled camp in New Guinea for internment in a barbed wire encircled prisoner-of-war camp situated in a country town on the south-western plains of New South Wales, in the middle of winter.

Dire beginnings

The first night in camp was terrible. The bewildered internees were given a typical Australian meal of those days, huge helpings of meat and potatoes, which unaccustomed diet made many of them ill. Their luggage had not yet arrived, so all they had were the clothes they had been given in Brisbane and a few blankets. There were no

Lionel Boorman 1999. Former intelligence officer Cowra POW Camp. Author's photo.

heaters in their quarters on that first night and everybody suffered terribly from the cold. The toilet blocks were a long way from where they were sleeping and everyone prayed not to have to use them. Nauseous and cold, families slept huddled together for warmth. In the morning they heated water to warm their frozen feet, before going outside when the sun came up to wait for their baggage, which finally arrived late that afternoon.[15]

The barracks in compound 12B were divided into cubicles for the women and children, while the men were allocated huts or cubicles and provided with palliasses, straw and blankets. There was a separate ablution block for the women, for whom plunge baths were provided. Thankfully more appropriate rations, especially rice, soon became available after consultation with Dr van der Plas.[16] The number of internees immediately increased by one when the wife of the Ambonese nationalist A.J. Patty gave birth to a baby girl in Cowra District Hospital on 24 June. This birth gave an opportunity for another woeful Australian witticism: 'despite one birth report states that whether or not Javanese babies have blue bottoms is not yet confirmed.'[17]

However, the joy of this birth was overshadowed six days later when the bitter cold and pre-existing illnesses began to take their toll and the first of the nine internees who passed away in Cowra between June and September 1943, Soengeb Al Kartomidjodjo, died from pneumonia.[18] The dire health situation was demonstrated by the fact that in the first couple of weeks the average number on sick parade was 45 of a total of some 500 internees, while 23 were in hospital. An intelligence report in early August highlighted how even more critical the situation had become by then: 'Sickness is steadily increasing among the internees. There are presently 130 in hospital suffering various complaints mostly influenza and pneumonia and it is feared an epidemic of measles has broken out among the children'.[19]

James Baillie's story

For the Australian medical staff and orderlies working in the camp hospital, 'very few of whom had any knowledge of these polite, dusky folk, except that they were Javanese,' it was the plight of the children that was the most heart-rending. James Baillie, a sergeant in charge of the theatre block who sometimes also worked in the ward, gives a graphic description of the conditions when the Indonesians arrived and of the sickness that followed —

> Cowra in mid-winter can be very cold and almost as soon as the Javas arrived, a week of bitter weather, with rain and black frosts hit the place. You may well imagine the devastating effect this had on an already frail people, straight from the tropics to southern New South Wales, at a time when the weather is at its most bitter. One had the impression that whoever was responsible for the decision to send them there at that time, didn't care much ... there was an outbreak of German Measles, followed by its most common complication, bronchial pneumonia, an unfortunate combination which proved too much for their almost defenceless bodies. The children were the worst affected and, despite round the clock efforts by every member of the staff, there were losses ... and the orderlies, no strangers to patients in their last hours, had great difficulty in handling a dying child, especially if the child had been in hospital for about a week and you got to know the curly black hair, the big white eyes and the flashing instant smile as he called, 'Tuan, Tuan' as you walked by.[20]

In September Justice Davidson, one of the International Red Cross Official Visitors to the camp expressed his deep concern over the number of deaths, urging that the Indonesians be moved as soon as possible to a warmer locality.[21] Four children, two women and three men died and were buried in unconsecrated ground in Cowra cemetery, (next to the graves of four Indonesian seamen who had died there in the preceding year) with fellow internees carrying out appropriate Muslim rites as well as they could in the absence of an Islamic cleric.[22]

Despite their illnesses, some of the internees maintained a defiant attitude towards the Dutch, as displayed on one occasion when a Dutch delegation arrived to inspect the compounds and the hospital. The patients were forewarned by the Dutch doctor accompanying the delegation that they should stand at attention beside their beds if well enough, or otherwise to lie at attention in bed, when the dignitaries came by. But when the VIPs came in, the patients showed their contempt by either turning their backs to them or rolling over onto their fronts, all rigidly in the 'attention' position.[23]

This visit was a precursor to some bad blood between the Dutch and Australians because the former made a string of complaints about the conditions in the hospital, one of which was that there were no sheets on the beds. According to Baillie, these had been removed at the request of the patients who found them too cold. The Dutch doctor, J. van Leent, refused to believe this, which led to an angry exchange between him and the Australian medical officer in charge of the hospital. When Van Leent threatened to report the Australian doctor, Major John Digby, to the Minister for the Army, Digby's memorable reply was, 'You can report it to the bloody Pope for all I care'.[24]

However it does seem that in the first two months when epidemics of measles and influenza were at their peak, resources were definitely strained and some of the complaints about inadequate facilities and food and the lack of any Malay speaking nursing staff were justified.[25] At the time Van der Plas was appalled to discover that conditions in compound 12C, where the former Tanah Tinggi men were interned, were better than those in 12B. Unable to conceal his unwavering hostility toward these rebels Van der Plas complained, 'the reason for this discrimination in favour of people, one of whom is a murderer and the rest psychopaths, has not been ascertained.'[26]

A month after this visit, it seems that improvements had been made, a Chinese Indonesian doctor had been added to the staff and the Dutch could now find no fault with any of the arrangements for accommodation and care of the internees.[27]

Camp life

Gradually the newcomers settled into the routine of camp life, where they did their own cleaning and cooking, and established a school for the children. Apart from this, there was nothing much to do, and boredom and inactivity became a problem. The tedious, daily routine consisted of being woken up each morning by reveille, followed by breakfast, roll-call, wandering around behind the barbed wire, lunch, more wandering or lying down, dinner then bed. This inactivity led to widespread apathy.[28] The boredom was alleviated a little when a friendly Australian guard, (internees reported that many of the guards were sympathetic and ignored orders not to mix with them) got into the habit of passing newspapers to one of the internees, Bondan. After he was given the day's paper Bondan would lock himself up and read it and then later in the day translate the contents to an ever-growing audience. In this way, the Indonesians were able to catch up on news of the war and the outside world.[29] Initially at least, there seems to have been no contact with the civilian population of Cowra, most of whom would have had no idea of the existence of these new inhabitants in their midst. Wartime censorship ensured that no mention of them was made in the local town newspaper.

Brigadier Simpson v Commissioner Van der Plas

While the internees were settling in, some incidents connected with them were taking place outside the camp, one of which revealed the way Commissioner Van der Plas often achieved his own ends by manipulating the Australian officials with whom he was dealing. Shortly after their arrival, he informed the Director of Prisoners-of-War and Internees, that because of a breakdown in communication, 12 well-educated men who were not internees had been wrongfully interned in Cowra, and requested that some of them

Above: Internees at Cowra 1943.
Photo: Siti Chamsinah.

Below: Teachers with pupils.
Photo: Australian War Memorial Neg Number 030151/4.

should be released immediately because they were needed urgently for NEI service in Melbourne.[30] Among the names listed were those of two of the leading nationalists, who had been interned in Tanah Merah since 1935. The others on the list too had all been interned in Tanah Merah, including Moenandar, who was for a long time one of the camp leaders. Therefore, for Van der Plas to say that they were 'non-internees' was a lie. Perhaps after all his talk of 'psychopaths' and 'asocial' types he wanted to reassure the Australian authorities that they would have nothing to fear if these particular men, whom he needed for his own purposes, were released. At the same time Van der Plas revealed that the wives and children of the internees were in fact free people – the first knowledge the Australians had of this.'[31]

Van der Plas seemed to be under the impression that he merely had to say the word, and anyone he chose could be released forthwith. But the Director-General of the Australian Security Service, Brigadier W.B. Simpson, whose job it was to sign release orders for internees, had other ideas. Mentioning his unease in a letter to the Adjutant-General for POW and Internees on 23 July, Simpson wrote, 'This matter becomes more complicated and less understandable as time proceeds.'[32] 'This matter' to which he referred was the whole question of interning these Indonesians in Australia in the first place and secondly, the assumption that he would sign release orders and let them be absorbed in the community on a simple request. 'That is incorrect,' he stated, 'I am not prepared to act simply as a rubber stamp.'[33] Simpson stipulated certain criteria by which he would sign release orders, such as provision of details about the internee's identity and security risk. Despite this nine of those on Van der Plas' list were released to work for the Dutch at NIGIS in Melbourne.[34] This was the first of a number of wrangles over Indonesian affairs between Van der Plas and Simpson.

An unjustifiable use of a great power
In fact by August, the question of the release of all the internees was being discussed more widely. Some of this discussion was prompted by the action of the Indonesians themselves, in particular the 'psychopaths' of compound 12C. This action did not take the form of physical violence but of representations made to a Red

Cross Official Visitor, Mr Justice A'Beckett Terrell, both in interviews and in two lengthy petitions. During his official visit to the camp on 3 and 4 August, 15 men from compound 12B, including some of the well known nationalists such as Sardjono, A.J. Patty, I.A.C. Salim and Jahja Nasution, as well as 6 men from compound 12C, sought interviews with him to voice complaints, all of a political nature. In a special report to the Deputy-Director of Security NSW, Justice Terrell summarised the complaints as follows —

> 1. They objected to being moved from Dutch New Guinea at all.
> 2. They wished to be informed of their exact legal position, i.e.
>   (a) were they still under the control of the NEI Government, and if so, had the Commonwealth Government surrendered its sovereign rights so far as they were concerned, or
>   (b) were they under control of the Commonwealth Government in which case their merits should be judged by the standards obtaining in Australia, and not by those obtaining in the NEI.
> 3. As they preferred democratic ideals and were anti-fascist in sympathy, they objected to being put in a POW camp with Axis enemies, i.e. Italians and Japanese.
> 4. Many of those in 12B complained that though they had shown unswerving loyalty to the Dutch Government, others, who did not have such a good record, had been released.[35]

Although Justice Terrell explained to the internees that the main purpose of his visit was to enquire into conditions in the camp, a confidential report he made reveals that he had serious misgivings about the legal basis for their detention, a matter they themselves had raised with him. Recapitulating his understanding that the majority of the men had been exiled because they were communists or guilty of subversive political activities, and that the wives and children voluntarily accompanied the men, he stated —

> From the internal evidence of the Internment Order itself, it is evident that Col. Langford did not satisfy himself that it was necessary for the safety of the Commonwealth to make an internment order. He did so merely because the NEI Govern-

ment had sent these men, women and children to Australia for internment. He therefore did not exercise any discretion in the matter ... if this view is correct, all the orders are *ultra vires*.[36]

Justice Terrell was particularly concerned about the position of the wives and children, who were all free citizens and should never have been detained by the Commonwealth when the NEI Government itself did not consider them to be a political danger. He concluded that the Camp authorities, 'would have no answer to proceedings for Habeus Corpus in the case of the women and children and probably none in the remainder of the evacuees.'[37]

Two carefully detailed petitions addressed to the International Red Cross were written in the High Malay used by well-educated Indonesians and signed by 19 men in compound 12C. These fascinating documents described among other things their views on Dutch imperialism in the Indies, attempts at resistance, internment and suffering in Tanah Tinggi and the circumstances of their forced removal to Australia. The legal questions raised must have given Justice Terrell much food for thought. For example they made the point that they had been banished to Digul on the basis of Article 37 of the NEI Government, but as this government no longer existed the sentence of banishment was now void. They also said that in Australia the Dutch had to recognise the laws of Australia, and pointed out that they themselves were neither prisoners of war nor Australian political prisoners, so should be granted, 'a little more freedom and happiness'. One petition included a request for assistance to procure a translator and a solicitor to help establish the legal status of their internment in Cowra.[38] These documents gave the lie to Van der Plas' often repeated prejorative comments about the lack of intelligence among the 'criminals'. Australian Army officials charged with having these documents translated wryly noted that because of the Dutch interest in these Indonesians it would be better to employ a translator not connected with the Dutch, and that the petitions should be kept confidential.[39]

Justice Terrell's report and his conclusions that the detention orders were *ultra vires*, as well as the possibility now raised of an appeal by the Indonesians, were of particular interest to Brigadier Simpson who wrote to the Solicitor-General asking his advice about the Indonesians' right of appeal against the orders. He made the important point that according to the Detention Orders made under Regulation 26 of the National Security Regulations and signed by Colonel Langford, the justification for making an internment order for each Indonesian was to prevent that person acting in any manner prejudicial to the public safety or defence of the Commonwealth.[40] Simpson's own view was that because no order for their internment had been made in New Guinea prior to their arrival, the only evidence upon which the detention orders were made was the fact that they had been sent to the Commonwealth to be interned, and that from a 'strictly legal' point of view, Justice Terrell was correct in his assessment that the detention orders were *ultra vires*.[41] Simpson pointed out that because the Indonesians were in the custody of the Department of Army, the questions raised by Justice Terrell were not the immediate concern of the Security Service, but would become so in the event of appeals being lodged against the detention orders, since these were administered by the Attorney-General through the Security Service. Furthermore, if the Attorney General granted appeals he, Simpson, would not oppose release of the internees unless the Department of the Army could ascertain that there were 'reasonable security grounds for continuing detention'.[42]

While these legal niceties were being debated in high places, support for the Indonesians' release began coming from other quarters as word eventually leaked out about the detention of Dutch political prisoners on Australian soil. It appears that one source of these leaks was some of the Australian guards and hospital staff. Four internees wrote clandestine letters to the Cowra Branch of the Australian Labor Party and these were smuggled out of camp by friendly guards who were also spreading the word about the Indonesians to their own friends.[43] One of the orderlies, Private Taylor, contacted the Communist newspaper *Tribune* with the story, whereupon Mr A. Ely of the Communist Party of Australia (CPA) was sent to Cowra to investigate. During the three days Ely spent in Cowra, unsurprisingly he was not permitted to enter the camp, so relied on Pte. Taylor as his link with the detainees. Ely wrote a comprehensive report of his findings, incorporating such colourful flights of fancy as, 'Comrades, the most significant thing in the life of these heroic exiles is their unbroken spirit – the song that is sung by the men, women and children every day and all day is "The International"'.[44] However, leaving aside the communist rhetoric, his report was a fairly accurate account of the internees' history, and was accompanied by letters written by some of the Indonesian 'comrades'. Private Taylor was passing copies of *Tribune* to the men inside, and commented that 'the capitalist press has been very silent on the plight of these great men.'[45] This contact at Cowra was probably the beginning of the strong link that was soon to be forged between the CPA and the Indonesian nationalists, in particular the communists, which later played such a significant role in the propaganda war on behalf of Indonesian independence.

Mrs Laura Gapp of the Civil Rights League was a great activist on behalf of the detainees. Her efforts included protesting to the Attorney-General, Dr H.V. Evatt, about the treatment of the internees, 'raising a storm' at the Dutch Consulate in Sydney and gate crashing a Dutch run medical clinic to demand treatment for some sick prisoners at Liverpool.[46] In fact there is good evidence that it was Mrs Gapp who at least indirectly first brought the matter of the internees to Dr Evatt's attention. Writing to Brigadier Simpson in November, Evatt mentioned that he had heard about a letter (written by Mrs, Gapp) being circulated by the Australian Civil Rights League which revealed that Dutch political prisoners were being interned in Australia. Subsequently Evatt received a full report about the internees from Simpson, which he was at pains to maintain was the first he had heard about the whole affair as he had been in London when the internees had arrived in Australia. He was clearly appalled by the situation and told Simpson, 'sufficient appears from your report to show that there is no satisfactory ground for the further detention in internment of the Indonesians ... statements ... suggest not only illegality but an unjustifiable use of a great power, which should only be exercised in the clearest of cases.'[47] Concerned that the affair reflected badly on the reputation of Australia, particularly in light of the deaths that had occurred at the camp, Evatt instructed Simpson to take the matter up with the Army authorities, without 'an hour's delay' ... 'so that their detention should be terminated at the earliest possible moment'.[48]

Where to next?
Releasing the internees from Cowra was one thing, but working out where to send them next presented a problem. While the Department of the Army and Simpson tried to negotiate the legal aspects of the inevitable release, Van der Plas and Mr J. van Holst Pellekaan, Secretary of the NEI Commission, were discussing with the Department arrangements for the internees' future once they were freed. As was often the case with Australian-Dutch negotiations, a number of complications and changes of plan slowed down the process.

For their part, the Dutch did not use the term 'internment' but rather 'quarantine' to describe the reason for the Indonesians' detention. From their perspective, this was a reasonable description in the light of Van der Plas' original proposals. He had never actually wanted them to go to Cowra in the first place, but to stay for a short time in a warmer place in Queensland for the purpose of medical checks and quarantine. So it was perfectly natural that as early as August Van der Plas had been discussing with the Department of the Army plans for the release and incorporation of a good number of the men into employment companies as soon as the medical authorities agreed.[49] At that stage he envisaged that wives and children would accompany the married men and some single men to the 36AEC camp in Helidon, the majority of the single men would go to Toowoomba and some older boys would be sent to technical training courses, probably in Casino. As he was most insistent that the ex-Digulists not mix with the rebel merchant seamen, he wanted the seamen to be moved out of any location before a new intake from Cowra came in. An elaborate Dutch plan was put forward in September which would see the Cowra people and the rebel seamen being transferred like chess pieces from one camp to another, to ensure that they would all end up in separate places in Queensland.[50] Then in November Simpson came up with a proposal, approved by the Department of the Army and Dutch authorities, that some of the Indonesians, particularly families and some unmarried men not considered a security risk, be sent to work on an agricultural project at Home Hill in Queensland, while 200 single men would join an employment unit under Dutch military control. Accordingly Van der Plas sent to the Commonwealth Director General of Agriculture a long list of conditions and requirements for accommodation, food and so forth.⁵¹ A few days later Simpson convened a conference in Melbourne for representatives of all the parties hoping to reach final agreement and effect the release from internment no later than 13 December but to his frustration even more changes of plans were proposed from the Dutch side.

The next day the NEI Commission received a letter from Mr Brian Fitzpatrick, secretary of the Australian Council for Civil Liberties, asking whether Indonesians in Cowra had been released and employed by the Dutch Government in Melbourne, and whether there was any prospect of the remainder being released if their anti-fascist attitudes were established.⁵² Dr van der Plas, writing to Dr Evatt, referred to this as, 'a letter couched in courteous terms,' which he would not ignore, although he was very annoyed by the attack on the Cowra internment from the Civil Rights League. He expressed his delight that Evatt was taking up the matter and also opposed the internment of the Indonesians on Australian soil. The wily Dutchman did not tell Evatt of his involvement in the decision to bring the internees to Australia in the first place.

Van der Plas then implied that the responsibility for the problems lay with the Australians: instead of Queensland the Indonesians were sent to Cowra because it was the only camp with adequate sewerage; Dutch efforts to get people, especially women and children away from Cowra failed because the War Department refused to have workers with families assigned to labour camps; the Home Hill plan was fraught with problems. Then he proposed yet another plan: to send 23 young people to Melbourne for further education, to send 160 men to 36AEC in Queensland and to send the families to Mackay to replace the families evacuated there on the *Katoomba*, contingent on returning these wives and children of the Ambonese police to Merauke, now safe from the threat of Japanese attacks.⁵³

Simpson's annoyance spilled over in a letter to the Department of External Affairs, shortly after he became aware of Van der Plas' claim that he had been trying to get the Indonesians out of internment since June. Simpson pointed out that it was not the Dutchman but he himself who had been doing everything possible to achieve this. One of the sticking points all along had been the problem of accommodation of the wives and children. Neither side had been able to reach agreement on this and to cap it all the Dutch had now 'unofficially' abandoned the Home Hill plan. All of these frustrations led Simpson to deliver his ultimatum: on 7 December he would release the single men to join the 36AEC, leaving 121 men, 72 women and 139 children in Cowra still awaiting release. As all efforts made to accommodate these people in line with Dutch requirements had failed, Simpson would release them all on 13 December, and the Dutch themselves would have to provide them with accommodation.[54]

The Toowoomba contingent

So it was that after almost 7 months' internment in Cowra, on 7 December 160 of the single men found themselves free men again, some of them after 16 years of detention. Of course, they were not entirely free, as they were sent immediately to Toowoomba to begin their new lives as militarised labourers in 36AEC.

Upon arrival in Toowoomba they were kitted out in Australian Army uniforms, much too big for them to everyone's amusement, then put to work. One man commented wryly that his first job as an upholder of democracy in the world was loading heavy rolls of barbed wire onto trucks. When work was finished for the day, the Indonesians were free to visit the town and mix with the local people, who impressed them with their friendliness and lack of the racial prejudice which they had feared might confront them. Friendships were made and for the Indonesians, after life in Digul, Toowoomba was 'heaven on earth'.

It had been agreed that they would be paid 3s a day, but it seems that this was 4s less than soldiers performing equally heavy labour were now receiving, and the Indonesians protested to Mr van Holst Pellekaan, Secretary of the NEI Commission. This concerned him as he was sure that the Indonesians would 'find means of attracting public opinion to this case, as most of them have communist tendencies and relations even in Australia.'[55] He was also concerned that if an increase were given in Toowoomba, the Indonesians in Wallangarra would hear about it and cause more trouble than they already had about the issue of pay. At this time the Dutch were trying hard to attract Indonesians into the NEI forces, so Van Holst Pellekaan proposed to Army Minister Forde that 15 Indonesians willing to co-operate should be released from Toowoomba and enlisted into the NEI force at Casino, where they would immediately receive 7s per

93

day, in line with army pay. This scheme, he suggested, could be used as a kind of 'propaganda' to the 36AEC men and the ex-Digulists in order to eventually attract as many as possible of them into NEI organizations.[56] This incentive must have worked as 36 ex-Digulists did finally join the NEI force in Casino.[57]

After about a year the 36AEC camps were phased out because much of the danger to Australia had passed, so they were no longer needed. The ex-Digulists were dispersed to different places with some, including Bondan, and Sardjono, the former PKI Chairman, initially being taken into NIGIS in Melbourne and others going to Sydney or Brisbane, where at last they had the complete freedom of movement that had been denied them for so long.

Farewell Cowra

Back in Cowra, for the families and the few single men remaining, time dragged on while the wrangling between the Australians and the Dutch continued. Simpson's ultimatum about turning them out of the camp in December for the Dutch to deal with was not enforced.

A camp intelligence report of early 1944 reported that the Indonesians appeared to be quite happy and were making no complaints about anything. They were being treated to screenings of motion pictures 'of a good moral type' and had expressed their appreciation in letters to the camp commandant. Two more babies, one called 'Cowra' and one called 'Parkon' (after the orderly room sergeant) had been born, bringing the total of children born at that stage to 10.[58] Despite the motion pictures 'of a good moral type,' the prolonged confinement and frustration may have contributed to another incident reported at the same time, that is, a case of assault where one man attacked another with an axe, causing serious wounds. 'The motive', said the report, 'is age old (*cherchez la femme)* and appears to be the culmination of a quarrel that has been going on for some time. A single man being accused of making advances to the wife of another man, who, after the manner of his people, adopted the time-honoured method to eliminate the source of his annoyance'.[59]

Simpson was frustrated too. He had signed orders for the release of the remainder of the internees on 20 December, but ended up asking the military authorities to defer taking action because accommodation had still not been found for them. Then he had persuaded the

Department of the Army to accommodate them in Casino, with the Dutch meeting the costs and the Australian Government providing appropriate building materials. Van der Plas was informed of these plans and politely undertook to move the internees immediately. But by the time Simpson was reporting all this to the Department of External Affairs on 4 March 1944, still nothing had transpired, and it had become clear to him that the Dutch had made up their minds to ignore the Australians and to follow Van der Plas' plan and keep the families in Cowra until they could be sent to Mackay. All these delays troubled Simpson, who, concerned that winter and its inherent dangers to the Indonesians was approaching again, considered that the situation was very embarrassing because the Government would have no answer to any charges that these people were being held in an internment camp without just cause.[60] When he received a letter from the NEI Commission informing him of their intent to transfer the Indonesians around 20 March, he concluded, 'I can be excused for not accepting this with much confidence because promises of action in the immediate future have been going on now for some months.'[61]

It must have been a great relief then to Simpson when the stalemate was finally broken and the civilian evacuees in Mackay were finally shipped back to Merauke on 1 April, leaving the way clear for the Cowra families to take their places.[62] Five days later, the remainder of the internees, with their wives and children, were released from Cowra and sent to Mackay, arriving there on 9 April.[63] Before leaving, the families of those who had died were taken to the Cowra Cemetery for a last visit to their graves.[64] This poignant poem entitled *Selamat Tinggal Cowra* (Farewell Cowra), was written by one of the internees to mark the end of this chapter in their lives —

> We who still remain in Cowra,
> Three hundred souls, men, women
> Young and old, all thought
> We would not be here for long.
>
> Now the time has come
> To head for Queensland and try a new life,
> In Mackay, not Toowoomba.
> We leave Cowra with sorrow and sadness

Above: Old graves of Indonesian internees, Cowra Cemetery.

Left: Indonesian Ambassador Wiryono at renovated graves 1997.

Both author's photos.

> For yonder, outside of town,
> Nine lives, yes there were nine,
> After pain and suffering
> Ceased, were lost and closed their eyes.
>
> Oh Cowra, place of mountains,
> We will always remember you
> And leave you with the thought
> We will likely never meet again.[65]

The graves gradually fell into disrepair and were neglected for many years until in 1997 they were identified and subsequently renovated by the Indonesian Government. At a ceremony at the site attended by officials from the Indonesian Government and Cowra Council, the 13 Indonesians buried there were rightly acknowledged and honoured with the official designation, *Pejuang Kemerdekaan*, Freedom Fighters.

The Mackay contingent

Enjoying their revised status as free evacuees, the new arrivals quickly settled into life in Mackay, a town whose climate was much more suited to them. For the most part they occupied the houses in Tay Street, Kenilworth Street and Palm Street formerly inhabited by the evacuees who had returned to Merauke.[66] Others were concentrated in Goldsmith Street, and Cremorne.[67] Some children attended Mackay Central School though most went to North Mackay State School, where they were remembered as being 'obedient, friendly and intelligent' pupils who played happily with their Australian friends after school hours.[69] There was also a special Saturday School where the children studied English and Dutch and some of the Indonesian arts.[69] The NEI Commission paid rental and utilities costs, medical expenses and a small allowance to the families. To meet all their other expenses many of the adults found work in local industries such as engineering or agricultural machinery firms, while others worked in the sugar industry.[70] Close friendships were formed between some of the Indonesians and their neighbours, which in some cases continued long after the Indonesians were repatriated in 1946.[71]

Siti Chamsinah's story – continued

When she was released from Cowra, Siti was 17 years old. Her family went to Mackay, but she and her younger sister, along with some other young girls, were sent to Melbourne where they were enrolled in the Emily McPherson College to undertake a course for nurses' aides. Some of the training involved working in a hospital, where they were put to work scrubbing floors and peeling vegetables. The Dutch paid their expenses and they stayed in a boarding house in St Kilda, located opposite a park. The girls spent much of their recreation time in this park, and met Australians there, some of whom became their friends.

After the girls had been in Melbourne for about a year, the NEI authorities told them they were to be sent to Hollandia (in Dutch New Guinea) to help look after wounded Dutch soldiers. The girls indignantly rejected this proposal, having no interest in caring

Left: Siti Chamsinah at Emily McPherson College, Melbourne 1944.
Photo: Siti Chamsinah.

Right: with sister and nephew Chasni Cowra, (born at Cowra POW Camp) Jakarta 2000.
Author's photo.

for soldiers of the colonial power responsible for interning their fathers. Thereupon they were threatened that if they continued to refuse they would receive no more education or financial support, and would have to join their families in Mackay. None of the girls relented, and they were all sent to Mackay.

Siti's memory of relations between the Indonesians and some people in Mackay differs somewhat from the positive recollections mentioned above. She recalls that some were quite suspicious of the Indonesians and insulting, racist remarks were sometimes heard. She decided that one way to 'educate' the local people was to display some of the Indonesian culture. So she and her friends collected together examples of arts and crafts such as *batik* and *songket* cloth, *krises* – anything the Indonesians had managed to bring with them – and held a display for the townspeople. Apparently this was so well received, that some of the Indonesian women set up a small *batik* making enterprise in town and found plenty of customers for their work. Siti did not get paid work but helped her mother at home and, along with her parents, also became involved in political activities.

In September 1945, she was married to the political activist, Jahja Nasution, to whom she had become engaged in Cowra.[72]

The 'criminals'

The occupants of compound 12C, that is the men from Tanah Tinggi, and one or two other hard liners, had been excluded from all the foregoing plans for release, even though it had been their petition which first challenged the legality of the detention. In September 1943 they had been transferred from Cowra to the internment camp at Liverpool.[73] A military report from Liverpool in May, 1944 revealed that 17 of them were causing trouble, refusing to carry out orders, refusing to cook, and apparently living on nothing but bread and jam for the previous two months. These troublemakers had been segregated from the others and were 'embittered and sullen'.[74]

When Van der Plas was informed of this he wrote to Brigadier Simpson, who in the meantime was assessing whether they should be released like the others and wanted evidence that the men really were a security threat to Australia. Van der Plas admitted that no records of their crimes in Java actually existed, although he, Van der Plas, remembered some of the cases, including murder of fellow internees at Tanah Tinggi. He identified seven men whom he said should not be released, but suggested that the others could perhaps be sent to Brisbane and encouraged to accept employment in NEI organizations there.[75]

Once again, as their captivity continued, the Indonesians appealed to the International Red Cross, in the form of another petition, written on 16 June 1944, which was handed over via the District Censor in Sydney to Delegate Mr George W Morel.[76] Not surprisingly, there was a different slant on events in Liverpool from the Indonesians' perspective. They claimed they had refused to work 'in slavery' cultivating vegetables and chopping wood for 1s a day, and accused the Camp Commandant of treating them no better than Dutch planters treated their contract coolies. In their rather purple prose they described themselves as 'martyrs to hunger and cold,' of which they expected to die at any moment. Great surprise was expressed that the Australian Government would collude with the Dutch in this mistreatment, particularly as they considered that the NEI no longer existed and would never exist again. Finally, perhaps as an act of desperation, they asked the International Red Cross, on their behalf, to ask Dr Mohamad Hatta, Yogyakarta, for 'clothes, cigarettes, books and other necessities to relieve our sufferings, caused by our mental and physical privations, deprived of the most essential things, which a civilized person cannot do without. And all this in spite of our innocence'.[77] One wonders at their seeming loss of touch with reality in expecting Dr Hatta, in Japanese occupied Indonesia, to even be contacted, let alone fulfil their request.

The District Censor was unable to find anyone to translate this letter, so Mr Morel in his wisdom, asked Mr Pennick, the Consul-General for the Netherlands in Sydney to do the job. As could be expected, Pennick used the opportunity to feed some propaganda to the naive Australians by informing them that Dr Hatta was 'an unfavourably known Indonesian', and that the criticism about the NEI was 'certainly unjustified'.[78]

Nothing more was heard of the petition, but Brigadier Simpson persisted doggedly in his attempts to deal fairly with the question of the internees' detention. Frustrated by Van der Plas' inability to provide reliable evidence that the 18 men still held at Liverpool were guilty of violent crimes, Simpson took the matter into his own hands and arranged for them to have an appeal heard by the Advisory Committee in NSW under Mr Justice Pike. By the time the appeals were heard in July 1944, one of the men had died. Each of the remaining 17 was questioned (through an interpreter) about the reasons for his detention in Tanah Tinggi, his behaviour in Liverpool camp and his preparedness or otherwise to now don a Dutch uniform and join the Dutch battalion in Casino.[79] The finding of the Committee, with which Simpson and the Dutch agreed, was that four of the Indonesians now willing to work for the Dutch in Casino should be released. The remaining 13 were to remain in detention, the official reason being that because of their bitterness at the treatment they had received, the trouble they had caused in the camp and their lack of English, they could cause trouble if they were at large in the community. They were all willing to work in any capacity for the Australian Government but were adamant they would not work for the Dutch. Every one of them had been interned following the failed rebellions in 1926 and 1927 and every one of them claimed to have taken no part in the violence but to have been arrested because they were self proclaimed communists.[80] Reporting all this to Dr Evatt, Simpson suggested that the Dutch might be urged to remove these 13 men back to Dutch New Guinea.[81]

Van der Plas rejected this idea because he considered that there were still opportunities in Merauke for these 'completely intractable psychopaths' to plot against the Allies, and wrote to General MacArthur to tell him so.[82] As had been the case throughout all the preceding attempts to resolve this issue, wheels turned slowly, and the Indonesians were still interned at Liverpool in March 1945 when, writing to the Department of the Army, Simpson explained that in his view, despite the 'bad record' the internees had with the Dutch, there was insufficient justification for continuing their detention in Australia.[83] Again his frustration with Van der Plas was clear as he noted that for a long time there had been no action in response to his many requests for the Dutch to agree to remove the internees to Dutch controlled territory. Simpson was relieved then when General MacArthur approved the transfer. Van der Plas had no choice but to agree that they would be returned to Tanah Merah, via Merauke, where he would instruct his people to take the necessary measures 'to safeguard the interests of the Allied Forces'.[84] Just what threat these old men would be after all they had been through during the previous 19 years is hard to imagine, but their story disappears from the records when they were shipped back to Tanah Merah before the end of the war.[85]

Through its policy of isolating so many nationalists away from the rest of the NEI, the Dutch had actually concentrated in Digul many of the most experienced political leaders and activists in the colony. Then, thanks to their decision to bring them to Australia for 'quarantine,' and then later release them into the wider community, the ex-Digulists were now at liberty to work for the cause for which they had been interned in the first place – Indonesian independence.

5

Battle Lines are Drawn

The NEI officials and personnel in Australia were utterly convinced that it was only a matter of time before the Japanese would be defeated, and they would be able to reclaim their colony and re-establish themselves – perhaps gradually guiding their Indonesian subjects to some degree of self-rule in the future. True, there had been some trouble from the striking merchant seamen, but that had not been motivated by any political aspirations, and certainly those Indonesians serving in the NEI forces were loyal. The hard liners from Tanah Tinggi were safely under lock and key in Liverpool POW Camp and the release of the ex-Tanah Merah people from Cowra did not seem to pose any threat. Most of them either went to work for the NEI or the war effort in some capacity, while the families settled into civilian life in Mackay.

However, what the Dutch failed to appreciate was that the release of the nationalists from Cowra injected a new political element into the Indonesian population mix in Australia. The long years of exile in Tanah Merah and the hardships of Cowra had not extinguished the revolutionary spirit of the ex-Digul men and women. They were united in their desire for an independent Indonesia, although because of their own differing and sometimes conflicting ideologies, they were by no means united in their ideas about how that should be achieved. Nevertheless, despite these differences, it was the common thread of commitment to independence that they took with them to Melbourne, Casino, Mackay, Sydney, Helidon, Toowoomba, Brisbane and wherever else they found themselves. This was eventually to have significant repercussions for their compatriots, for the Dutch and for their Australian hosts. But first, they had to get organised.

SIBAR

The August 1944 edition of *Penjoeloeh* reported that a new Indonesian association had been born on foreign soil in Melbourne. This was the New Indonesia Association (SIBAR), formed with the full approval of the NEI Commission, who felt 'there was a need for such a group to plant awareness of democracy in the hearts of Indonesians.'[1]

There was a certain irony in the fact that the chairman of this Dutch-approved association was the ex-Digulist Sardjono, chairman of the PKI at the time of the 1926-1927 uprisings and interned at Digul for his involvement. After their release from Cowra or later, from Toowoomba, a number of these ex-Digul nationalists, including Sardjono, were employed by NEI agencies such as NIGIS, the official disseminator of NEI propaganda. Sardjono and other communists who held office in SIBAR had seemingly performed an amazing *volte face* in deciding to co-operate with the Dutch. However, there was a reason for this. Sardjono had quickly established relations with the Communist Party of Australia, with the aim of illicitly re-establishing the PKI. The CPA supported this but wishing to maintain its own authority as representative of world communism in Australia, it instructed Sardjono to call his new party the 'Foreign Section of the PKI Operating Among Indonesians in Australia'.[2] Following the Nazi invasion of the Soviet Union in June 1941 the latter had joined the Allies, with the result that the CPA was ordered by Moscow to oppose the Axis powers. Consequently when Sardjono was free to take up political activity again he in turn was instructed to co-operate with the Dutch. Thus when SIBAR was formed it was not surprising that the core of both its leadership and membership in Melbourne, and eventually in other branches, came from the clandestine PKI.[3]

The stated policy of SIBAR was to co-operate with the Netherlands Government in liberating the NEI from the hands of the enemy and to prepare the basis of a new and democratic Indonesia along the lines of Queen Wilhelmina's speech.[4] Branches were also established in Sydney, Casino, Brisbane and Mackay.[5] This enabled the ex-Digul SIBAR members to establish contacts and disseminate nationalist ideas among a cross section of Indonesian members of KNIL, particularly in the Technical Battalion in Casino, and among KPM merchant sailors in the capital cities.

The formation of SIBAR came to the attention of the Australian Security Service branch in Melbourne, prompting a report to Brigadier Simpson in Canberra. Particular note was made of the role of the 'known communist,' Sardjono, and of other communists.[6] A report also came from Lieutenant K. Plumb, liaison officer for the Commonwealth Security Service with the NEI Security Service, NEFIS, explaining that it too was suspicious of SIBAR, aware that some of the members were ex-Digul communists.[7] NEFIS admitted that prior to the Pacific war there was a tendency in the NEI to label as communists anyone who opposed or often even criticized the administration, but explained that the men interned at Tanah Merah were indeed 'dangerous revolutionaries', and anyone now referred to as a communist really was one.[8]

Van der Plas informed External Affairs Minister Evatt, of SIBAR's formation, taking pains to clarify the political nature of the organization, and explaining that the leadership had asked him to ascertain whether the Australian Government's permission was needed for them to work openly among Indonesians in Australia. As was Van der Plas' practice, on this occasion too he tried to manipulate Australian officialdom to his own way of thinking. He told Evatt that SIBAR had originally been sincerely committed to furthering the war effort.[9] This was probably his opinion when he had been steering one of his own protégés towards the leadership of SIBAR. But when this did not eventuate, Van der Plas once again raised the communist bogey, warning that the communist ex-internees from New Guinea had seized the leadership after establishing contact with the CPA. Clearly trying to undermine SIBAR he asserted that it was not right to establish and operate political organizations in a foreign country without that country's approval.[10]

Once again, Brigadier Simpson, found himself drawn into Dutch/Indonesian affairs when Evatt asked his opinion. After his previous dealings with Van der Plas, Simpson was clearly not prepared to take everything he said at face value. He told Evatt that although he had been informed that the Tanah Merah internees had been dangerous revolutionaries, 'whether their revolutionary activities were inspired wholly by Communism or partly by nationalist aspirations,' he was not prepared to say.[11] Nevertheless he felt that the CPA interest in SIBAR, plus the predominant ex-Digul membership, could lead it to becoming an 'anti-Dutch organization under communist direction', and therefore concluded that it should not officially be recognised or approved.[12]

Officially recognised or not, as a Dutch-sanctioned political organization, SIBAR provided a valuable front for the activities of the PKI, and its policy of co-operation with the NEI authorities led to some of its members taking employment in NEI and KNIL agencies and thus gaining access to documents and information which could be used to their own political ends. Three months before the end of the war, with victory in sight, the executive of SIBAR decided that the time was coming to disband the organization, and this decision was put into effect in the weeks immediately after the Japanese surrender, when any co-operation with the Dutch came to an end.[13]

PARKI

In Mackay, the liberated internees took advantage of their newfound freedom to make contact with the union movement and with the local CPA branch.[14] Many of them, described as 'Trotskyist and Muslim activists as well as orthodox communists,' also attended evenings of political discussion and debate held at Mr Jock Burnett's bookshop, and some, with communist union help, were even able to attend conferences in Brisbane.[15]

Although a branch of SIBAR had been established in Mackay, a number of the ex-Digul nationalists there were totally opposed to it because of its policy of co-operation with the Dutch. They felt that this co-operation was contrary to the ideals for which they had been exiled to Digul in the first place. Accordingly, in March 1945 this group formed its own party, The Indonesian Independence Party (PARKI).[16] The principle aim of PARKI was 'the recognition of Indonesia as an independent nation'.[17] As a consequence of its total opposition to any form of co-operation, PARKI was naturally also opposed to any future form of government in Indonesia which involved the Dutch. One of their first actions was to draw international attention to their struggle for independence. In April 1945, the executive sent a cable to the United Nations Conference for International Organization in San Francisco, asking it to consider declaring that Indonesian independence should come into effect as soon as the war ended.[18] This may have been the reason why on 16 August, (one day after the Japanese surrender) the members of the PARKI executive were summoned to the NEI headquarters in town and told that they, their families, and all PARKI members were being sent back to New Guinea immediately and would be re-interned in Tanah Merah if they displeased the Dutch authorities.[19]

The PARKI executive decided to fight this order and immediately sent petitions and protests to the Australian Prime Minister, the British Prime Minister, the US President and the USSR leader Stalin. Closer to home they appealed for aid from the CPA and the Mackay Trades and Labor Council, basing their appeal on their conviction that they would be re-interned at Tanah Merah, and their claim that they had previously been promised freedom and repatriation by the Dutch to their place of origin when the war was over. It appears that their fears were well founded since the Australian Security Service received information that because PARKI was considered to be a seccessionist movement whose members were regarded unfavourably by the Dutch, it was intended to re-intern them all. In fact the NEI authorities intended to send to New Guinea and re-intern 'all politically troublesome Indonesians'.[20]

Fortunately for the Indonesians their protests succeeded. After an investigation by a Government official and representations from the Trade Union movement in Mackay an agreement was reached between the Australian government and NEI authorities that the decision to return the PARKI members to New Guinea would be rescinded.[21] This decision left these hard liners free to pursue their agenda of gathering support for the cause of independent Indonesia, particularly after this independence was proclaimed on 17 August, 1945. They appear to have been very active in supplying information and lobbying various interest groups to their cause, particularly through a pamphlet periodically published in Mackay. The contents of the November 1945 edition showed the range of issues they addressed including a detailed critique of statements about the Indonesians and the virtues of Dutch rule made in a speech at the Mackay Rotary Club by the wife of a Dutch official and a response to the Australian 'Hands Off Indonesia Committee' in Western Australia which wanted a description of the Indonesian flag.[22] PARKI, together with another organization formed by ex-Digulists in Mackay, the Indonesian Political Exiles Association, (IPEA), continued to be active until February 1946.

SARPELINDO

As we have already noted, early in 1942 Indonesian seamen on KPM ships took strike action and walked off their ships, not for any political motive, but in a bid for better wages and conditions. Because they had no union of their own at the time, the Indonesians' claims were advanced and backed by the Seamen's Union of Australia. The strikes and subsequent trouble at Wallangarra had not endeared the seamen to the NEI or Australian authorities dealing with them. It was rather a bold move then when early in 1944 Maramis, an Indonesian petty officer employed in the accounts section of KPM in Sydney, applied for permission to publish a monthly periodical to be known as 'The Indonesian Seamen's Journal'. Mr Barnwell of the Commonwealth Investigation Branch looked into the matter and found that Maramis, 'who was coloured', was considered to be well behaved and efficient, and wanted his magazine to 'stimulate a spirit of solidarity amongst Malayans (sic) in opposition to the Japanese occupation of their land'.[23] KPM itself apparently had no objections to this publication, but NEI officials had other ideas, stating that *Penjoeloeh* was already stimulating a spirit of solidarity and there was no need for any private news sheet. Accordingly, Maramis' request was refused. The suspicion felt towards the seamen was manifested in an official's comment, 'No good purpose would be served by this paper. There is a possibility of it being used for expressing views of disgruntled seamen'.[24]

However, there was soon to be a way for the seamen to express their solidarity far more effectively than they could through any journal. Given Sydney's position as the largest port in Australia, much of the Allied shipping was located there, including a number of Dutch ships whose Indonesian crews were quartered at the Hotel Belvedere. It was here, in 1944, that the seamen had their first contact with ex-Digulists, in particular Soeparmin, interned at Digul in 1938, and Mohamad Senan, among the first intake of internees at Digul in 1927. Upon their release from Cowra, Soeparmin had worked with the Employment Company at Helidon for 3 months before going to Sydney to work in administration at the Hotel Belvedere. Senan was sent to Casino as an instructor in the Technical Battalion for a few months before he too left to join Soeparmin at the Belvedere.[25] Both men were members of SIBAR and neither had been in the PKI.

Battle Lines are Drawn

Soeparmin and Senan organised weekly meetings with the seamen and became aware for the first time of their poor working conditions and wages compared to those of their Australian counterparts, particularly in light of the dangers of enemy attack whenever they put to sea. Gradually the Digul men started raising the seamen's awareness of the injustice of their position and at the same time planting the seeds of nationalist ideals within them. From these meetings the idea emerged of forming an organization especially for Indonesian seamen in Australia.

A meeting was held at the Belvedere in November 1944 at which the seamen formed a union and named it *Sjarikat Pelajar Indonesia*, (SARPELINDO), the Indonesian Seamen's Union. When the time came to elect the executive of the new union, they unanimously appointed Senan as chairman and Soeparmin as vice-chairman, even though neither of them were seamen. The first secretary was a Javanese seaman, Toekliwon, who later became chairman after Senan and Soeparmin were repatriated to Indonesia. The treasurer was an Australian businessman with strong connections to the labour movement and the Labor Party, Mr C. H. Campbell, a director of United Lubricants. The use of the word 'Indonesian' in the name of the union was an indication that although it was mainly concerned with the welfare of the seamen, there was also an underlying nationalist agenda. In common with other non-Seamen's Union of Australias of the time, SARPELINDO officially affiliated itself with the Seamen's Union of Australia, and branches were formed Melbourne and Brisbane.

One of the first disputes between SARPELINDO and KPM took place in May 1945 when KPM authorities decided to cut the wages of Indonesian petty officers and seamen in their employ. The plan was to retain the amount of 25 guilders per month per man, (which had been set aside and earmarked as deferred pay after the agreement made in the wake of the first seamen's strikes in 1942) and not pay it until after the Japanese were defeated in the NEI, and then only to those seamen who had given uninterrupted, satisfactory and loyal service.[26] When the petty officers employed at KPM headquarters in Sydney received this news from their employers they immediately went on strike. Most likely at Dutch instigation, almost immediately two of the ringleaders, Max Soeprapto, vice-president of the Indonesia Club, a social club for Indonesian petty officers, and Will

Pande Iroot, the Secretary, both of whom were SARPELINDO officials, were arrested under the Commonwealth Immigration Act, and taken to Long Bay Gaol. In June, The *Guardian* reported that they had been taken under guard to Brisbane by train, and then deported to Dutch New Guinea – possibly to Tanah Merah.[27] The Communist press fiercely denounced this 'railroading' of the two men. The Secretary of the Seamen's Union of Australia, Mr E. V. Elliott, protested to the Australian Government and accused it of assisting the Dutch in denying democratic rights to the Indonesians and using the Immigration Laws illegally, adding that Tanah Merah had been re-opened to take all the Indonesian political activists in Australia.[28]

In May 1945 (just before the arrests of Soeprapto and Pande Iroot) the member for Eden-Monaro, Mr Fraser had expressed in Parliament his concern for the members of SARPELINDO. His attention had been drawn to their fears about their fate after the Dutch regained possession of the NEI, particularly as trade unions had not been permitted in Indonesia prior to the war. He said —

> ... having gained some measure of freedom of expression and enjoyed reasonable standards of living ... they say they have cause to fear that they will soon have to return to the extremely unsatisfactory conditions under which they existed prior to the war, and, moreover, that action will be taken against those who have shown any progressive political spirit during their stay in Australia.[29]

The action taken against Soeprapto and Iroot showed that these fears were justified. Despite this, as we shall see, it was not long before SARPELINDO was to take a leading role in resistance to the Dutch in Australia.

KIM and CENKIM

The most important and influential political organizations established by the expatriate Indonesians were the Indonesia Independence Committees (KIM). Initiated by the ex-Digulists, these were formed in Brisbane, Sydney, Melbourne and Mackay soon after the declaration of independence on 17 August, 1945. The Brisbane Branch became the Central Committee and was known as CENKIM.

Not surprisingly the KIM and CENKIM came under the scrutiny of the Australian Security Service and the NEI authorities, and also unsurprisingly most of the office bearers were labelled in official reports as 'communists,' whether they were or not. Their activities will be discussed in the following chapters.

The Australia-Indonesia Association

To this point the focus has been on organizations formed by Indonesians in 1944 and 1945. However moves were also afoot among Australians who wanted to form some kind of an organization through which they could learn about and become more involved with these visitors to their country. The best known of these was the Australia-Indonesia Association (AIA), which, with some breaks in continuity, is still active to this day, with six separate state or territory branches.

The impetus for the establishment of the first AIA, in Sydney, came from a woman whose name eventually became well known to hundreds of Australians and Indonesians (and between 1944-1948 to the Commonwealth Security Service), the indefatigable Molly (Mary) Bondan (nee Warner). The idea arose from discussions she had had early in the war with friends who shared her view that something should be done to establish an organization to 'improve the woeful isolation of so many Australians,' by promoting an interest in Asia, through cultural relations and education. Although nothing was done immediately, the idea was not forgotten. As the war started swinging the Allies' way it was resurrected, with the suggestion that Indonesia (which at that time they were calling the Netherlands East Indies) should be the country chosen, not because the group knew much about the country or the nationalists' aspirations for independence, but because it was the nearest Asian country to Australia. Accordingly Molly and her friends decided to contact a broad range of organizations including the Council of Churches, the Housewives Association, the Civil Rights Association, Sydney University, the NSW Trades and Labour Council and others, inviting their members to attend a luncheon to discuss the formation of the new organization. The lunch was held in November 1944, and the 30 representatives of the various organizations who attended agreed to start working to form an Australia-Indonesia Association, (this time using the word Indonesia), as someone had heard that this was the name for their

Friends of Australia. Mrs Laura Gapp and Indonesian anti-fascists at an Allied Unity function.
Photo: *Tribune* 16 November 1944.

country used by the Indonesian people.[30]

Shortly after this meeting, Molly found the opportunity to meet Indonesians for the first time, when she was told about a social club in Sydney which had been formed by Indonesian petty officers from KPM. This was the previously mentioned Indonesia Club, which operated from premises near Chinatown. The club was attended by the petty officers, sometimes by ordinary seamen, and by Australians, some of whom were the wives and girlfriends of the Indonesians. Although the activities of the club were social – dancing, picnics, making music and conversation – it was here that Molly first heard criticism of Dutch colonial rule and evidence of nationalist sentiment revealed in scepticism that things would improve after the war. In following visits to the club, she heard much stronger sentiments in her discussions with former Digulists such as Soeparmin and Senan.[31]

After some delays, during which Molly had tried unsuccessfully, and perhaps naively, to persuade the NEI Consul-General to become Patron, the Australia-Indonesia Association (AIA) was officially formed on 3 July 1945, at a public meeting which 'packed to capacity' the Oddfellows' Hall in Castlereagh Street, Sydney.[32] In her report on the proceedings, Molly showed herself and her friends to be way ahead of their time in their understanding of the changes wrought to Australia's place in the world brought about by the war. She wrote, 'Australia is a Pacific country, not an appendage of Europe,' and the AIA had been formed 'in order to promote a friendly relation with a region of which Australians have little knowledge, yet a region that will play an important part in Australia's sphere of foreign affairs in the post-war world'. [33]

The invitation Molly sent to the Indonesians revealed similar enlightened though perhaps idealistic sentiments —

> Your stay in Australia has made it possible for you to build a wide circle of acquaintances and close friends: at the same time you have awakened amongst Australians an interest in your homeland and people. Not only has the war made this possible: it has also been responsible for the growing realisation among Australians that a better understanding and a greater concern for the well-being of one another in the past might have had vastly different results in meeting the Japanese aggressor.[34]

Membership was open to Australians and associate-membership to Indonesians (on payment of 2s 6d) and the list of officers of the Association reveals a diverse range of people. The President was Professor A. P. Elkin, first Professor of Anthropology at the University of Sydney and Vice- presidents included Mr Clarrie Campbell, the above mentioned first treasurer of SARPELINDO, Bishop Cranswick and Dr A. Capell with Molly herself as Honorary Secretary. There were two other noteworthy office bearers. One was avowed Communist Gerald Peel, an Englishman and descendant of British Tory Prime Minister Robert Peel. He became an active propagandist for the Republic of Indonesia and wrote a pamphlet 'Hands Off Indonesia' which became a widely used propaganda tool. The other was Mrs Laura Gapp, from the Civil Rights League, who had worked for the liberation of the Cowra internees. Described as 'a well-off middle class lady from Narrabeen, with strong socialist beliefs, she worked tirelessly for the welfare of the Indonesians, particularly merchant seamen and then for the cause of the Republic, as long as there was a need. Commonwealth Security Officers kept her under scrutiny all the time she was active.[35]

Although when the idea of forming an association was first discussed there had been no political motivation, in the interim things had changed, as demonstrated by this expression of AIA philosophy —

> This Association believes that to implement the spirit of the Atlantic Charter, including the principle of freedom of determination of their own future in a democratic way, is the surest guarantee of a progressive and prosperous Indonesia.[36]

Further, their aim had broadened from, 'promoting an interest in Asia through culture and education,' to the far more radical one of, 'meeting Indonesians on the same basis as it does all the peoples of the freedom loving world, and on this foundation of equality the Association aims to cultivate friendly, cultural, social and trading relations'. These aims were to be achieved through ambitious programs of public lectures, publications, displays of Indonesian art, music and dancing, and exchanges of students, sports people, cultural bodies, academics and technical personnel.[37]

The AIA cultural program got off to a good start when performances of Indonesian dances, music and singing were presented at a meeting of the NSW Arts and Crafts Society, leading Molly Warner, at least initially, to be very optimistic about the Association's future.[38] However, after the proclamation of Indonesian independence, the AIA experienced problems which led her to conclude that it was organizationally incapable of the (political) support it might otherwise have been able to give, and that 'as an organization it was to turn out a failure'. The main problem arose when, in accordance with its stated support for the terms of the Atlantic Charter, it came out in favour of self-determination for the Indonesian people. Apparently some of the office-bearers who also held public office, feared that this would be interpreted as an anti-Dutch stance and resigned from the AIA, leaving it organizationally weakened.[39] Nevertheless, it seems that the Commonwealth Investigation Branch regarded it with enough suspicion to keep an eye on whatever activities it did manage to pursue. Reporting to his superiors on 28 September 1945 about a circular issued by the AIA, Inquiry Officer W. H. Barnwell noted that, 'C. H. Campbell is an active Communist and Mr (sic) M. Warner is also regarded as a Communist'.[40] Molly Warner had been watched by Australian security officers since the AIA was formed and was regarded by them as 'a strong communist and constantly in the company of Indonesians, said to be engaged in assisting the Indonesian Republican Movement, learning Indonesian and training Indonesians in the Communist movement'. In later years her brother strongly denied that she or any member of the Warner family had ever been a communist but the label stuck to her.[41] The NEI authorities too regarded the AIA as a pro-Communist organisation, particularly noting the involvement of Communists Guy Anderson, a Sydney businessman, and Molly Warner.[42]

Another report on 5 October noted a forthcoming meeting to held by the AIA in the basement of the Sydney Town Hall, 'to muster public support behind the Indonesians', and that, 'developments in this matter will be watched and reported'.[43] The meeting, held on 15 October, was attended by some 500 people, two thirds of whom were Indonesians, and was indeed 'watched and reported' by a C.I.B. Inquiry Officer who acknowledged that at no time was there any 'communistic talk,' in the speeches but noted that whenever a reference was made to the Soviet Union, 'there was great acclaim from the audience'.[44]

When the AIA wound up this phase of its life in Sydney is not clear, but it was still active in 1946.[45] Perhaps it lost some of its momentum after Molly Warner moved to Brisbane early in 1946. Despite Molly's disappointment that it was not able to achieve all of its aims, its significance has been justifiably acknowledged as 'the first public organization of citizens ever to arrange contact and exchanges with Asians aspiring to end colonial rule'.[46] A pro-Republican newspaper in Indonesia praised the AIA as a sign that 'the ties of friendship between Australians and Indonesians were strong, with mutual respect and understanding increasing as time went by'.[47]

An Australia-Indonesia Association whose stated aim was to help foster friendship between the two countries was also formed in Melbourne, in August 1945.[48] Early records of the Melbourne AIA are sparse but the 1947 files show that despite a small membership, which included the Australian wife of an ex-Digulist, Mrs Jean Zakaria, Eric and Elizabeth Marshall who had strong ties with and helped many different Asians in Melbourne during the war, including Indonesian seamen, ex-Digulists and pearlers,[49] and future Labor MP Jim Cairns, it was very active organising public meetings and lobbying the Australian Government in support of Indonesia's independence. This first AIA in Melbourne lasted until about 1949. [50]

We see then that the nationalists released from Cowra lost no time establishing organisational structures by which they could politicise their compatriots and wage propaganda and political warfare on behalf of the cause of independence from the Dutch. At the same time some of their Australian supporters had their own structures in place in support of the same cause.

The Netherlands East Indies Government

During 1944, significant regrouping was also taking place in the NEI administration in Australia. On 23 October Dr H. van Mook arrived back in Australia to take up his appointment as Lieutenant Governor-General, and the Netherlands Indies Government, operating on Australian soil, became a reality.[51] The Netherlands Indies Commission was dissolved and the new administration preparing to reclaim power in the NEI when the Japanese were defeated, moved to Camp Colombia, Wacol, in Brisbane, which was seen by the Dutch as their temporary seat of government.[52] Former Chief Commissioner van der Plas, was appointed to the important post of Director of the Interior and Chairman of the Board of Department Heads. Agencies such as NEFIS transferred to Camp Colombia, leaving a small contingent in Melbourne.

Large numbers of Dutch army and airforce personnel also moved to Brisbane bases. The number of NEI personnel in Brisbane, not counting merchant seamen, swelled to some 2,000 people, the majority of whom were Indonesians.[53]

The souring of Australian and Dutch relations

While this restructuring was taking place two particular issues emerged during 1944 and continued into 1945, which increased the tension between Australian and NEI authorities. One involved the latter's complete disregard for Australia's immigration laws, and the other concerned a Dutch plan to accommodate and train in Australia a force of about 30,000 troops from Holland, ready for use in the NEI after the war.

The first recorded incident of the Dutch flouting of immigration laws had actually occurred as early as December 1943, when Dutch 'aliens' from New Guinea arrived in Queensland without any proper documentation or reporting to Australian officials. An angry Director-General of Security Simpson had then insisted that, 'there is no excuse for Dutch Authorities not being conversant with this (National Security Aliens' Control) regulation'.[54]

Despite assurances that the problem would be rectified, in July and again in August 1944, there were further unauthorized arrivals, this time of 21 Indonesians who, under Dutch orders, flew into Queensland and then made their way to Dutch naval or air force establishments. They had no documents and by-passed Australian authorities.[55] Similar breaches occurred at intervals right through 1944 and 1945 until the end of the war, despite all protestations to the Dutch. In June 1945 Simpson's exasperation led him to threaten 'to arrest the next unauthorized NEI personnel who landed in Australia,' and to urge the Department of External Affairs to lodge an official protest to the NEI Legation.[56] It seemed that Australian authorities saw the Dutch disregard for their law as a sign of 'arrogance and contempt,' while the Dutch saw 'Australian red tape,' as hindering their legitimate activities, and therefore they did their best to circumvent it.[57]

If this issue caused friction, it was the second matter, a proposal to train a large number of Dutch military personnel in Australia, which was to cause a serious rift between the two allies. From as early as December 1943 and into the first months of 1944, the NEI Army Commander, Lt-General L. H. van Oyen, and Netherlands Minister, Baron van Aerssen Beyeren, had been negotiating with Australian Army High Command to increase the number of NEI Army personnel in Australia. The first plan to achieve this involved bringing more Indonesians into Australia but it transpired there was no source of Indonesians available.[58]

When it became apparent that the tide of the war in Europe was turning against Germany, the Netherlands authorities proposed an ambitious new plan. On 16 August 1944, Baron van Aerssen Bayeren wrote to the Department of External Affairs explaining that after the liberation of Holland a force of 30,000 troops would be sent to the NEI after training, and requesting that the Commonwealth Government grant permission for them to be accommodated, maintained and trained in Australia.[59] Prime Minister John Curtin submitted the proposal to the Advisory War Council for consideration and on 21 September the Council recommended, with the approval of the War Cabinet, that the Australian Government should agree with the proposal in principle, and be willing to provide such facilities and assistance as practicable, taking into consideration any other existing or prospective commitments.[60]

The Netherlands Minister was informed of this decision, but any pleasure he took from it evaporated when nine months later, in June 1945, he was informed by the Acting Minister for External Affairs, that due to recent heavy demands on resources and manpower in Australia leading to a 'drastic review' of the war effort, the Commonwealth was unable to accept the obligations necessary for meeting the requirements of the proposed 30,000 Dutch troops.[61] The acrimony with which the Dutch received this decision showed that they believed the agreement was watertight. That it was not, soured their relations with the Australian Government for the rest of their time in Australia and beyond.

The brunt of their displeasure was borne by Mr J. B. Chifley, who, following the death of John Curtin, had been chosen in July 1945 as Leader of the Labor Party and therefore Prime Minister. Some unidentified Dutch authorities vented their anger by leaking information to the Leader of the Opposition, R.G. Menzies, and to the press. When Menzies raised the matter in Parliament, Chifley's response was quite dismissive, either because he was not fully briefed on the latest developments in this issue, which could have been possible in the flurry of his recent assumption of the Prime Ministership or at worst, he was careless. His reply to Menzies was —

> There was a suggestion made, I think some time last year, that the Dutch would be likely to bring to Australia certain forces ... but there was nothing very concrete about the proposal ... I do not want to go into the matter in detail. I know of no particular file on this subject.[62]

The whole affair moved into the public domain when the press used the information leaked by the Dutch, and Chifley's weak response to Menzies, to launch attacks on the Government's decision, describing it as, 'a serious breach of faith'.[63] Chifley was then forced to release a press statement outlining the reasons for the Government's decision, but also expressing his displeasure at Netherlands officials for their public criticism of the Government's decision and for leaking the content of private official correspondence.[64] Baron van Aerssen, immediately assured Chifley that the leaks did not come from him or his officials, which may have mollified the Prime Minister, but did not make any difference to the final outcome.

In a detailed explanation to Van Aerssen why the Australian Government did not in the end have the resources to accommodate and train the Dutch troops, Chifley quite correctly pointed out that the original agreement had been *in principle*, and that it 'did not involve a definite commitment,' but depended on 'whether our capacity could meet this additional strain'. He reiterated Australia's gratitude to the Dutch for their wartime assistance and expressed his wish that 'this decision should not lead to any impairment of the excellent relations which have always existed between our respective Governments'.[65] An opportunity to mend fences seems to have been lost when Van Aerssen invited five Government Ministers, both Speakers and six parliamentarians to a reception to celebrate Queen Wilhelmina's birthday on 25 August. In what looked like a deliberate snub, only one member of parliament attended. Van Aerssen, perhaps tongue in cheek, dismissed the incident as normal behaviour and not evidence of ill will.[66]

Despite this papering over of cracks in the relationship, these incidents were symptomatic of the entrenched cultural differences in operating styles between Australian and Dutch officials, which caused much mutual frustration, and as events unfolded after the war ended, a real deterioration in the 'excellent' relations between the two governments.

The end of the war and the declaration of Indonesian independence

According to the strategy the Indonesian nationalist leaders had agreed on when the Japanese occupied Indonesia in 1942, Soekarno and Hatta carried on the struggle overtly by co-operating with the conquerors in return for a promise of self-government, while Sjahrir worked covertly and organized an underground political network of *pemuda* (youth) groups.[67] The Japanese military set up a committee with Soekarno and Hatta to handle arrangements for the handover of independence, but the Japanese defeat and surrender overtook them before any action was taken. Two days after the surrender, following a bizarre set of circumstances which ended in *pemuda* impatient for the declaration of independence temporarily kidnapping Soekarno and Hatta, in an attempt to force the issue, the proclamation was made on 17 August. A group of supporters gathered outside Soekarno's house to hear him read the momentous words —

> We, the people of Indonesia, hereby declare Indonesia's independence. Matters concerning transfer of power and other matters will be executed in an orderly manner and in the shortest possible time.[68]

Soekarno was proclaimed President and Hatta Vice-President of the new republic. The announcement was quickly broadcast throughout Java and then by short wave radio transmitter to the outside world by young Indonesians trained as radio operators by the Japanese.[69] The Republic was born but it still had to be won from the colonial masters.

The news reaches Australia

In all the euphoria surrounding the Japanese surrender, it is no surprise that the news of this event, in a country about which they knew so little, did not immediately reach the Australian public through the media. According to one source, The Department of External Affairs picked up news of the proclamation through a short wave radio broadcast on 19 August, but kept the information quiet,[70] probably waiting to see whether this was a significant event and how widespread was the support for the Republic in Indonesia itself. The NEI government in Brisbane also knew about the proclamation, but they hushed it up too, no doubt concerned about the effect it could have on the Indonesians in Australia.

However, it did not remain a secret for long. There are a number of accounts of how news of the proclamation was made known.

Battle Lines are Drawn

One comes from Mohamad Bondan, the former Digul internee who became one of the foremost Indonesian leaders in Australia. Bondan had gone from Cowra to work with 36AEC in Toowoomba, then on his release had joined other nationalists employed by the Dutch at NIGIS in Melbourne. It was here, on 18 August that he heard a secret report about the proclamation, from a friend operating the Dutch service monitoring radio broadcasts from Indonesia.[71]

Bondan immediately began spreading the word among his compatriots and sympathetic Australians. As the news was surreptitiously circulated among the Indonesian nationalist community in Melbourne, NIGIS became suspicious of some of their Indonesian employees, including Bondan, whom they soon transferred to Camp Colombia in Brisbane. On the way north he stopped off in Sydney to pass the word to trustworthy friends and it was agreed they would start making preparations to 'defend' the proclamation and await the signal for action from Brisbane.

Bondan described Camp Colombia as a Dutch and Indonesian village complex. The occupants were both civil and military personnel who worked in a variety of occupations inside and outside the camp. Among them he met up again with former Digulists, some of whom he had worked with in Toowoomba. Thus he found a group of men ready and willing to join him in planning strategies, including enlisting the support of Australian citizens and organizations to the Republican cause. On 20 September it was unanimously agreed to form the Indonesian Independence Committee (KIM) with Djamludin Tamin (a prominent nationalist/communist leader from Digul) as President and Bondan as Secretary.[72] As mentioned earlier, KIM were also formed in Sydney, Mackay and Melbourne, each with ex-Digulists in leadership positions. Because of the large numbers of Indonesians in Brisbane, the Brisbane branch was designated to co-ordinate all KIM activities and became the Central Committee for Indonesian Independence, known as CENKIM.

Thus, as the location of the NEI Government representing Dutch interests, and of CENKIM representing the interests of the Republic, Camp Colombia became in effect a kind of microcosm of the NEI in Australia, where the respective battle lines in the propaganda war were drawn. A foreign revolution was about to be fought in part, on Australian soil.

6
___

The Indonesian Revolution Comes to an Australian Country Town

The unlikely setting for the first overt act of rebellion by Indonesians in Australia in support of the Republic, and against the Dutch, was the peaceful, northern NSW beef-producing town of Casino. The Indonesian soldiers who had first arrived there in December 1943 to form the Technical Battalion had given no trouble and rebellion was the last thing on their minds as they trained hard on work days and enjoyed the pleasures of life in a country town during their free time. But as new forces came into play with the proclamation of the Indonesian Republic, the peaceful co-existence between the Dutch, the Indonesians and the town of Casino was shattered.

Victory Camp Casino

By the time the war ended, the Dutch establishment known as Victory Camp had expanded to consist of the Technical Battalion, a Militia Labour Battalion and a contingent of personnel from Dutch colonies in the West Indies. Among the Indonesians were a number of former Digul internees who had soon established contact with communist and unionist sympathisers in the town and also with the Queensland Trades and Labor Council.[1]

As mentioned earlier, to this point the Indonesians had enjoyed the freedom to come and go as they pleased for leisure activities in Casino and nearby towns, and had been befriended by many of the local citizens. Nevertheless, a blatant expression of racialist attitudes apparently held in some quarters was revealed in an item in the *Daily Telegraph* (22.9.1945) on the reaction of the Casino Council to a rumour that 2,000 Javanese were to be evacuated to Victory Camp to recuperate from war related problems. The Mayor complained —

Indonesians from Technical Battalion with friends, Casino 1943.
Photo: George Worang.

> We've had a Javanese camp here for the past two years under Dutch control. There are still about 1,000 Javanese here and we'd rather be without them. The Javanese are well behaved but they are from the coolie class and we are not happy about having that type of person here ...²

In fact it turned out there was no truth to the rumour, but an interesting outcome of the affair was the outspoken reaction of Indonesian merchant seamen in Sydney, who suggested that the Mayor's comments would have 'a serious effect on the wonderful impression other Australians had created on Indonesians'. They pointed out that Australians had treated them with great kindness but that they no more wished to stay in Australia than Australians on their islands wished to stay there.³ The *Daily Telegraph* also took the citizens of Casino to task with its editorial comment —

> Regarded as coolies, Javanese evacuees are unwelcome in Casino, which has a camp of them and dislikes the prospect of having more. They are not here because they like it but because the Japanese have driven them from their own country. One test of our right to participate in the council of civilised nations

is our treatment of war victims, whatever their colour. If the Casino attitude is representative we are failing.[4]

Little did anyone foresee that events following the Proclamation of Independence would keep the town very much in the public eye and tarnish its reputation further for quite some time to come.

Mutiny and 'Little Belsen'

First news that the Republic had been proclaimed reached Victory Camp via a manifesto drawn up by CENKIM on 1 September, calling on Indonesians everywhere in Australia to defy the Dutch.[5] Disgruntled men in Victory Camp lost no time in complying. On 10 September the CO of the Technical Battalion received a letter signed by 183 former KPM seamen, now drafted into the Militia battalion, many of whom had been transferred to Casino after the 36AEC was disbanded. The letter recapitulated the whole affair of the promises made to them when they were interned in Cowra back in 1942: they would be released from Cowra and drafted to work for the war effort in 36AEC at a wage of 6s 6d a day and would be sent back to their homeland as soon as the war was over. Then came their ultimatum, a demand to be repatriated as soon as possible and when working in Indonesia again to receive the same wage as they did in Australia. In the meantime they wanted to be discharged from the militia and allowed to return to civilian life with immediate payment of the disputed deferred wages. They gave the Dutch a week to comply with their demands or they would refuse any orders relating to repatriation.[6] Although they had made no mention of the Republic, on 12 September when the CO reprimanded them and made it clear their demands were futile, the 130-140 men who immediately came out on strike declared that they were no longer under Dutch jurisdiction. CENKIM asserted that they did so 'in support of the Republic'.[7] Whatever the case, retaliation was swift. The strikers were incarcerated in a compound hastily erected in the middle of the camp and encircled by a high barbed wire fence. Watchtowers were situated on the four corners of the compound which was floodlit at night and the guards were armed.[8] One local who lived near the camp commented, 'It happened overnight, one minute there was no compound, then there was, and the Indonesians were like caged animals, their personal belongings scattered all over the place'.⁹

As the first sketchy accounts of the 'Java Natives Bid to Form a Republic' - as the *Sydney Sun* put it - began to appear in the press, so too did word of this strike. The *Sun* commented that locals and Dutch authorities in Casino were concerned at the 'restiveness' of the Indonesians, with one official betraying his ignorance by suggesting that the Javanese were being 'spoilt' by high wages and contact with white people.¹⁰

Over the following months, as Indonesian servicemen from other NEI camps in Australia mutinied, they too were transferred to the Victory Camp compound for detention. As word of its existence spread, a war of words erupted over conditions in the compound with claims and counter claims being made by the Indonesians and some of their Australian supporters on the one hand, and NEI and Australian authorities on the other. For example, Trade Union and Communist sympathisers dubbed Victory Camp with epithets such as 'Horror Camp,' 'Little Belsen,' 'The Black Hole of Casino' or 'Hell Camp.'¹¹ The Secretary of the Queensland Trades and Labor Council (TLC), Mr Mick Healy, went so far as to allege that, 'in the quiet democratic town of Casino there existed a horror surpassed only by that of the German and Japanese prison camps,' describing the conditions for sleeping, medical treatment and sanitary arrangements as 'truly appalling'.¹² But following a personal inspection of the camp and interviews with some of its occupants, a correspondent from the Lismore *Northern Star*, refuted Healy's claims saying, 'to describe the Indonesian camp at Casino as a "miniature Belsen" is completely absurd'.¹³

Meanwhile, with the exception of a handful of soldiers and technical trainees, all remaining Indonesian regular soldiers in the camp also went on strike during the first weeks of October and were detained in the compound pending court martial.¹⁴ In Melbourne at the same time 53 Indonesian servicemen from the NEI army who mutinied, were arrested, held in custody in Melbourne Goal and then entrained to Casino.¹⁵ The arrival of these mutineers brought the number of prisoners in the compound to about 400.¹⁶ A *Sun* reporter sent to the town to investigate the situation reported that the Mayor blamed 'pamphlets circulated by Brisbane Communists' for the refusal of duty by the Indonesians, while a Dutch officer said dismissively, 'Today they give one reason, tomorrow another'.¹⁷

The Indonesian Revolution Comes to Town

However, the Indonesians themselves made their reasons very clear in a letter to the Prime Minister on 29 November, requesting that an Australian lawyer be appointed to represent them in their forthcoming court martial. Describing themselves as 'responsible Indonesians of Casino Concentration Camp,' they stated that they were refusing to obey the Dutch because the war in the Pacific was over, they were Dutch subjects no more and regarded the Dutch Government as non-existent and any Dutch-run court martial as null and void.[18] Accordingly they asked the Prime Minister to remove them all from the Dutch 'concentration camp' to an Australian camp if possible at the earliest possible moment.[19]

The hoped-for independent legal representative was never provided, and when the court martial took place, one (Dutch) officer represented the defendants.'[20] Reporting the results of the court martial to his superiors, an officer of the Commonwealth Investigation Branch noted the severity of the sentences compared with Australian standards.[21] Protests at this severity were sent to M.P. Mr E. Ward by an organisation of local supporters called the Casino Indonesian Defence Committee.[22] Repeating the now familiar allegations of ill-treatment, the letter drew attention to the court martial and claimed that sentences ranging from one to five years had been imposed. The committee asked some valid questions about the legality of the Dutch conducting a court martial on Australian soil, the denial of independent legal defence for the Indonesians and the prospect of Australia becoming a jail for the Dutch if the sentences were worked out in Casino.[23]

These allegations of ill-treatment began to attract the attention of a wider section of the Australian public. For example Brian Fitzpatrick, Secretary of the Australian Council for Civil Liberties, expressed concern to the Prime Minister at reports he had received about this alleged ill-treatment and asked whether the Commonwealth had made any representations to NEI authorities about it. Equally disturbing to Fitzpatrick was a statuatory declaration he had received from Mr Robert Cooper, a railway employee of Casino, making two serious allegations against the Dutch. One was that one evening when he had been visiting the Victory Camp (not the compound), as he often did to chat with friends, he had been summoned out of the tent where they were sitting by Dutch soldiers and taken by jeep under armed guard to the local police station to be identified. Cooper dramatically claimed —

> Constable J Mackinnon duly identified me and expressed surprise that an Australian should be treated in such a manner for no apparent reason. I am definitely under the impression that had I not been duly identified the Dutch soldiers would have carried out their threats to shoot me.[24]

The second was that one evening armed Dutch provosts had entered a private home in North Casino, where a large number of local residents and some Indonesian servicemen were present. The Dutch allegedly threatened to shoot someone, before they left taking one Indonesian with them and ordering the others to make their way back to the camp. Apparently the next day the Dutch Sergeant Major had apologised for his mistake in entering an Australian home in such a way.[25] The Commonwealth Investigation Branch made a half-hearted enquiry into these allegations after receipt of a complaint, but dismissed them by referring to a claim made in the *Sunday Mail* that the Casino police had heard nothing of such incidents. The investigating officer concluded, 'It would appear to me that these incidents were manufactured by the Trades and Labor Council for the purpose of bringing discredit to the Dutch to bolster their fight for the Indionese (sic)'.[26]

In January 1946, the Sydney AIA also took up the matter of alleged ill-treatment when Molly Warner wrote to the Prime Minister requesting a thorough inspection of the camp and steps to alleviate the poor conditions if they were found to exist. 'It is felt', she wrote, 'that a foreign power should not be permitted to impose conditions on Australian soil that would not be tolerated by an Australian Government in respect of its own nationals'.[27]

Following these protests, the Commonwealth Investigation Branch did conduct a comprehensive investigation of conditions at the compound. The investigating officer inspected the camp and interviewed various Australian army personnel who had served there (but no Indonesians) and again reached the conclusion that the allegations of ill-treatment and bad conditions 'were not based on fact'.[28]

The first death

On 17 April 1946, tension in the compound increased when an Indonesian prisoner was shot dead by a Dutch guard. This was reported in a small paragraph the next day in the *Sydney Morning Herald* and in the *Northern Star*. CENKIM immediately wrote to the Acting Prime Minister, Mr F. Forde, requesting a full investigation into the matter and also that their countrymen be transferred to an Australian-operated camp from Casino, where they 'are confined to too close quarters, ill-fed, and badly treated and now they are to suffer without redress and pay with their lives for the sake of the brutalities of a government not of their choice'.[29] In response Mr Forde passed the buck and claimed he could do nothing about the treatment of Indonesian internees at Casino because they were under the control of NEI authorities. At this early stage of the Indonesian/Dutch dispute the Labor Government was maintaining a strictly neutral political stance.[30]

There was a swift reaction too from many trades unions around NSW (alerted by the AIA) who all sent letters of protest to the Prime Minister.[31] At the same time the Casino supporters of the Indonesians made their fellow townspeople aware of what had happened in no uncertain way. The *Richmond River Express* reported how Communists were 'flooding the town with propaganda aimed at discrediting the Dutch and furthering the Indonesian independence movement'.[32] Mr Ken O'Hara of the local branch of the Communist Party distributed to letterboxes pamphlets proclaiming. 'Dutch Gestapo Murder Indonesian in Casino Camp, ... their murderous rifles hurled a rain of lead into a crowd of unarmed defenceless men'.[33] A large sign was painted on the road in front of the town's popular hotel, the Royal, with the message, 'Down with the Dutch. Get Rid of Hell Camp. People of Casino our town is known Australia Wide as Little Belsen.' Another large sign in the same vein, bearing a swastika, was hung on the overhead bridge near the railway station.[34] The people of Casino could not have failed to be aware of the trouble in the camp and the notoriety, justified or otherwise, that it, and by association their town, was gaining.

Tribune weighed in with its version of events, accusing the Dutch of 'cold blooded murder'.[35] Although *Tribune* slanted its story to suggest that the whole town was outraged by events at the camp and that there was a groundswell of support for the Indonesians, this was clearly not the case. Some residents just wanted all of the NEI personnel, Dutch and Indonesians, to be sent home as soon as possible.

A preliminary report on the shooting was made by a CIB investigator on 24 April. According to this, the camp CO ordered the Indonesians in the compound to erect some extra tents and then some of the inmates occupied them without permission. When told to vacate the tents they refused, and the CO punished them by delaying their upcoming meal by two hours. They reacted by pushing food containers through the barbed wire separating the kitchen from the compound, which delayed the food preparations even further. In this atmosphere of confrontation and frayed tempers, the prisoners, led by Tarsan, the man who was killed, rushed towards the entrance, daring the Dutch to shoot them. The guard called the CO, who ordered warning shots to be fired over the prisoners' heads. When the NCO in charge of the guards went to the watchtower to see the prisoners better, 'a Dutch guard with rifle at his hip accidentally fired ... no aim being taken'. This was the shot that struck and killed Tarsan.[36] A full investigation conducted on 24 May, found that accounts of the shooting, 'were many and varied,' and offered no definitive conclusion other than the fact that only one bullet had entered Tarsan's body.[37] That was the last official word on the incident.

This investigation included a report on public opinion about the camp and predictably found a town divided. People who were friendly with the Dutch were against the Indonesians, those friendly with the Indonesians were against the Dutch, the pragmatic business people were not against anyone and the recently returned Australian ex-servicemen were antagonistic to both parties, particularly over the issue of their relationships with Casino women. The Inquiry Officer pronounced the communist propaganda 'very blatant and totally misleading,' in the main mostly ignored by the townspeople, the majority of whom liked neither the Dutch nor the Indonesians and concluded —

> Taking everything into consideration, it is felt that the people of Casino would be more satisfied if the camp were disbanded. There is no antagonism because of the shooting in the camp

and the alleged bad conditions. Further, the people are very concerned with the bad publicity being given the town, which the communists are presenting to the rest of Australia and which they say is wholly unwarranted'.[38]

Unfortunately for the townspeople, there were to be 7 more months of 'bad publicity' before the camp was closed.

Going around in circles

When, in May, 200 striking Indonesian servicemen detained at Lytton camp near Brisbane were sent to Casino after the Dutch allegedly told them they were being sent home, the number of Indonesians in the camp rose to 567. CENKIM informed Immigration Minister Calwell of this development and pointed out that because of this the Indonesians in the camp did not trust the Dutch and would therefore resist any further moves to repatriate them unless a member of CENKIM or Mick Healy from the Queensland TLC was present at negotiations.[39] The AIA too was lobbying the Government, suggesting that because conditions had deteriorated so much the camp should be abolished and the Indonesians freed until such time as they could be repatriated.[40] Similar protests deploring the use of any part of Australia as an internment camp by a foreign power were sent to the Prime Minister by numerous trade unions.[41]

The Casino situation was soon vexing the minds of the Departments of External Affairs, Immigration, and Army. It seems that as far as these departments were concerned, the right hand sometimes did not know what the left hand was doing. For example an internal note to the Secretary of the Department of External Affairs (June 1946 – more than four years after the Dutch arrived) reveals that some officials there were not even sure of the circumstances under which Dutch forces were allowed to enter and be maintained in Australia in the first place. Someone else suggested that because the war was over, Australian authorities could now have the Dutch military personnel withdrawn at any time and should intervene if needs be in cases of ill-treatment of natives by the Dutch. There was even discussion about whether the Dutch did still have any authority over the Indonesians.[42] This was a different line from that taken by the Department of the Army earlier when it had refused to intervene in such matters.

The Dutch meanwhile were proceeding with their own plans for withdrawal from Casino. The Secretary of the Royal Netherlands Legation, Mr J. A. de Ranitz, informed Mr Calwell in July that the NEI military guards at Casino were needed for other duties (presumably in Indonesia) and would soon be withdrawn. Pursuing this matter with the Department of External Affairs, de Ranitz claimed that Calwell had proposed that when the Dutch withdrew, the Commonwealth Government would take over the responsibility for detaining and guarding the mutinous Indonesians until their sentences expired, an arrangement that suited NEI authorities provided that the serving of the sentences was 'in accordance with NEI Army regulations.'[43]

This set in train another instance of an apparently straight forward solution to a problem involving negotiations between Australian and Dutch authorities being thwarted by misunderstandings, stubbornness and high handedness. When Army Minister Forde asked Calwell to clarify his offer to provide Australian guards at the camp, Calwell claimed that de Ranitz had totally misunderstood his suggestion. What he meant was that after the Dutch withdrew their guards the Indonesian detainees should be placed on their word of honour not to leave the camp pending repatriation, and that a Commonwealth Investigation Branch officer should be appointed as civilian camp commandant with Commonwealth Peace Officers to assist. Calwell's priority anyway was to repatriate the Indonesians as soon as possible, irrespective of any sentences they were supposed to serve.[44]

On learning this, de Ranitz informed the Prime Minister that the NEI authorities were prepared to accept the Peace Officers taking control, provided that the detainees served their full sentences. Further pressure was put on the Australians when de Ranitz stressed that the matter was now urgent because the withdrawal of Dutch guards, which had already started, had affected the 'efficiency of the surveillance of the camp,' and further withdrawals were imminent.[45]

Despite this veiled hint of potential trouble in the camp as a result of inadequate surveillance, the Australian authorities stood their ground, informing the Netherlands Minister that the Commonwealth Government would definitely not detain the Indonesians in the camp until their sentences expired, but only until arrangements could be made for their repatriation. Clearly fed up with the long delay in resolving the issue, the Australian officials asked as a matter of urgency what date the NEI authorities would hand the Indonesian detainees over to control of the Commonwealth so that the matter could be finally resolved.[46] But before this could happen, there was more violence in the compound.

The second death – murder or suicide?
On 11 September 1946, the dramatic headlines of the *Richmond River Express* announced, 'Indonesian Hanged at Casino'. The paper reported that an Indonesian military prisoner was murdered, having been found hanging by a rope from a tent pole after receiving a blow on the head. Dutch authorities claimed that the victim, Emod, had been murdered by 'reactionary political elements,' to prevent him leaking information about 'undercurrent activities'. It was reported that two days earlier another prisoner had been stabbed (not fatally) and Emod had been charged with this attack. The Dutch C.O., Captain Sleeborn, together with senior Dutch and Australian officers visiting the camp had decided to hand Emod over to the local police the next day to be charged. National dailies also reported the hanging, describing it as a 'mystery death' (*Sydney Morning Herald*, 12 September) or 'murder' (*The Age*, 12 September). However, after investigation the local police, who took a number of the Indonesians to the police station for questioning, discounted the murder theory and found that the death of Emod was suicide while of unsound mind. The Dutch were not convinced of this and continued to maintain that Emod was murdered, but despite the publicity and conflicting ideas about this hanging, no official enquiry was ever held into its cause.[47]

The third death
The next day, 12 September, there was more violence: one Indonesian was killed and two wounded when guards opened fire on them. 'The Indonesian, Soerdo, who was shot dead by Dutch tommy guns, died shouting "Long Live the Indonesian Republic," with 13 bullets in his back,' claimed *Tribune*, with its familiar predilection for purple prose.[48] As presented by the local newspapers, the facts were that guards had entered the compound to remove a man called Lengkong, whom they wanted to question about the earlier stabbing

and the death of Emod the previous day. He had foiled a previous attempt to remove him by hiding among the other prisoners and among the closely packed tents in the compound. The guards then called a parade and had the prisoners march in single file past the gate, where a guard was waiting to seize the wanted man. Lengkong managed to elude him and a hostile demonstration broke out. Warning shots were fired over the prisoners' heads and most flattened themselves on the ground. Some, including Soerdo, 'defied and menaced the guard,' who opened fire and allegedly pumped 13 bullets into Soerdo's body. Two other prisoners, one of whom was Lengkong, were wounded when attempting to shelter behind Soerdo.[49]

The news of this shooting was taken up by metropolitan newspapers such as the Sydney *Sun* (13.9.1946) which claimed that the camp was 'seething with unrest' and that fearing a riot and a breakout of the prisoners, the townspeople wanted the camp closed. The talk of 'riots' leading to death and woundings attracted the attention of the Department of External Affairs, which expressed to the Department of the Army its concern about the treatment received by the Indonesians while negotiations were going on with the Dutch about their withdrawal. An urgent request was made for full details of the incident and how the casualties occurred.[50] The Department of the Army again distanced itself from the incident, declaring that as it had no responsibility at all for the custody of the Indonesians in Casino it was unable to supply any information about the incident.[51]

As would be expected CENKIM too reacted swiftly, requesting an enquiry into the conditions and treatment of prisoners at the camp. Their version of the incident was that following the police finding that Emod's death was suicide, 'the Dutch authorities were apparently not satisfied with Australian impartiality, but preferred to seek some motive to chastise and punish other members of the compound'.[52] The AIA too was active on the case, informing unions and community groups all over the country of the incident. This led to a stream of telegrams and letters pouring into the Prime Minister, with expressions of outrage at the violence and demands to close the camp, from representatives of a diverse collection of unions ranging from boilermakers, builders, transport workers and miners to nurses, teachers, housewives and university students as well as concerned individuals.[53] One such individual, Mr E. Helsby from Ade-

Prisoners' compound at the Dutch Military Camp near Casino.
Photo: Northern Star 18 September 1946.

laide, compared the treatment of the Indonesians to that meted out by the Germans and Japanese, concluding, 'That any foreign power can use Australian soil to perpetuate such treatment is to cast the same blot on ourselves'.[54]

In the context of the ongoing negotiations about withdrawal of the Dutch from Casino, the Commonwealth Investigation Branch conducted yet another enquiry into the camp (but not into the shootings) and uncovered a new development: the Dutch C.O. of the camp had separated 12 of the Indonesians and placed them under special guard. The reason given was that the Dutch had identified these men as ring leaders whom they alleged had been involved in the hanging of Emod, despite the fact that they been cleared of involvement by the Casino police. They were being held under armed guard in a barbed wire encircled hut about 1,200 yards from the compound.[55] Despite the findings of the local police, the Dutch clearly refused to accept that Emod's death was suicide.

Mr Barnwell, the enquiry officer, ventured an opinion that was beginning to dawn on some Australian officials: although all the Indonesians under sentence were convicted of mutiny, they were not criminals but were in fact political prisoners because they were supporters of the Indonesian Republic. Barnwell noted that the prisoners he saw in the compound itself looked to be 'average type Indonesians' and that Australians had little to fear from them as far as camp discipline was concerned.[56]

Barnwell again canvassed local opinion about the camp and his findings suggested a softening attitude towards the Indonesians. He sensed that in town there was a new 'silent sympathy' towards them because the local people felt they were not being fairly treated by the Dutch, who were 'not well regarded'. There was no concern about the camp remaining, but no support either for an open camp which would allow the Indonesians free access to the town. Barnwell's conclusion therefore was that if the Commonwealth took over the guarding of the camp, the discipline that the Dutch maintained by 'resolute, determined, well-armed guards prepared to shoot if necessary,' would be eased, and it would then be impossible to keep the Indonesians contained. With the possibility of their presence in town causing trouble, Barnwell's opinion was that their guarding by the Commonwealth was 'inadvisable'.[57]

A few days later a public meeting was convened in Casino by the Richmond and Tweed Rivers TLC to discuss the whole issue. After a variety of opinions were expressed ranging from, 'It appears that the guards do not value the lives of their prisoners,' to, 'It was their own fault they were shot down,' a motion was passed protesting the continuation of the Dutch Armed Forces at Victory Camp and demanding a public enquiry into the recent deaths.[58]

Stalemate

In the meantime the stalemate between the Australian and NEI authorities continued. The Dutch would not agree to the Indonesians being released before the expiration of their sentences and the Australians would not agree to guard them for this length of time.

In October 1946, a discussion took place between Mr Calwell and NEI forces Commander, Colonel Moquette, who pointed out that military law and reasons of discipline made it impossible to release the prisoners until they had served their sentences. The sentences of about 228 of them were due to expire on 18 October, and the Dutch had decided in principle to release these men from the Army at that time, provided the Australian authorities would be responsible for them. If the Commonwealth would not undertake to guard the

The Indonesian Revolution Comes to Town

remaining 340 until their sentences expired in 1948 and 1949, the only solution was to ship them all under guard to Morotai in Dutch New Guinea and imprison them there.[59]

Reporting this discussion to the Prime Minister, Calwell said that he had given Moquette his personal view that the Australian Government would not agree to the shipping of the Indonesian prisoners to Morotai under armed guard. If Australian authorities took responsibility for the Indonesians it would be on condition that they were treated as prohibited immigrants (not military prisoners) and guarded by state prison warders or Commonwealth Peace Officers until their repatriation to Indonesia on an Australian ship. Given that Dutch authorities would not agree to this course of action, Calwell pressed Chifley to deal directly with the Netherlands Minister, Baron van Aerrsen, to resolve the impasse.[60] What Calwell wanted was for the Dutch to suspend the sentences so that the prisoners could be released and then treated like other free Indonesians in Australia awaiting repatriation. He was probably also aware that there had been protests from various sectors of the Australian community who believed that the Indonesians were being held for political, not criminal reasons and were badly treated, and this was providing fuel for increasing anti-Dutch sentiment being expressed in some quarters.

The first releases

In anticipation of the expiration of sentences of 228 of the Indonesians due on 18 October, Mr F. Kearns, an officer from the Department of Immigration, in company with Mr Hay from the Commonwealth Investigation Branch, went to Casino to take charge of the released men and arrange for their transfer to Brisbane. When they arrived, to their annoyance the C.O., Captain Sleeborn, turned them away, telling them he had received no orders about the release and until he did he would not even discuss the matter.[61] The orders must have come through because on 21 October Kearns and Hay returned to finalise arrangements with Sleeborn, who dourly refused the Australians permission to explain matters to the Indonesians or to enter the compound. Instead he had the Indonesians come out a few at a time to be processed, fingerprinted and registered by the Australian officers, under Aliens Control Regulations. When this process was complete, he addressed the men himself and told them of arrangements for their release the following day.⁶²

On 22 October, the Indonesians were released, handed over to Kearns and Hay and each man was given a certificate of discharge from the NEI Army. Then, with the assistance of the local police, they were transported to the railway station for entrainment to Brisbane where they were met by the Commonwealth Migration Officer, Mr Bird, and transferred to the open Chermside Camp where they stayed happily for about a month until their repatriation in November.⁶³

Great abuse of hospitality
Frustrated by the refusal of the NEI Authorities in Australia to remit the sentences of the remaining Indonesians, the Department of External Affairs cabled the Australian Legation in the Netherlands and the Australian Political Representative in Batavia asking them to take up the matter directly with the Netherlands and NEI Governments respectively. Acknowledging concern about public opinion, the Department pointed out that due to the killings, the widespread conviction of many Australians that the Indonesians were political prisoners and the fact that the continuation of the Casino Camp as a foreign detention centre fourteen months after the war had ended was 'an obstacle to harmonious Dutch-Australian relations,' the Netherlands Government should be pressed to terminate the remaining sentences and repatriate the Indonesians on the ship due to leave on 16 November.⁶⁴ Nothing came of these overtures, and the prisoners were still in Casino when the ship left. The Netherlands Legation however, did inform the Department of External Affairs that the NEI Army intended to withdraw all of its guards from Casino on 15 December.⁶⁵

Before this happened an even greater 'obstacle to harmonious Dutch-Australian relations' arose from some information Calwell received from CENKIM on 23 November. After thanking Calwell for his efforts for the release and repatriation of the first group of Indonesian rebels from Casino, Bondan dropped the following bombshell —

> We wish to bring the following information to your attention, obtained from two entirely different Indonesian sources, who had no opportunity to consult with each other. Both sources state that they were told by some Dutch official or officials that

on the night of November 7th, 13 Indonesians were secretly removed from Casino prison camp by Dutch Authorities to be transported to Timor. The thirteen were: Gazali, Kamirin, Woworoento, Kamagi, Tala, Toela, Karto Praitno, Dengah, Moestari, Sahja, Lengkong, Jadi and Lantang.[66]

These were the same men whom Barwell had seen; those segregated and accused by the Dutch of being the murderers of Emod. Bondan concluded dramatically, 'We are afraid that these 13 men have gone to almost certain death, but would plead with you to use your influence on their behalf, if it is not already too late'.[67]

When the Netherlands Charge d'Affairs, de Ranitz, was informed of this allegation he admitted not only that it was true but that the plan to do it had existed for a long time because those Indonesians 'were the source of so much trouble,' including 'riots,' 'disturbances,' and the death of Emod. Further he revealed that the men had been taken by air to Jakarta where they were to face trial on charges of murder.[68] Enraged by this high-handedness, on 7 December the Department of External Affairs again contacted the Australian legation in the Hague asking them to press the Netherlands Government to intervene. The wording of their cypher left no doubt how strongly the Australian authorities felt —

> ... the incident is regarded by the Australian Government as a great abuse of hospitality, in view of the great assistance rendered to NEI forces in training, accommodation and services during the war. No Australian authority was informed of the movement of 7 November although the future of the camp and its detainees was under active discussion at the time. This failure to inform the Australian Government can only be construed as a deliberate attempt to circumvent the Australian Government in a matter which the Netherlands authorities well knew was of grave concern to us. This action is bound to react most unfavourably against the interests of the Netherlands and to prejudice the development of good relations between Australia and the Netherlands. The only solution which might repair the situation is the return of the thirteen prisoners from Batavia to Casino.[69]

While the Australian authorities fumed about this issue the NEI Army went ahead with its plan to withdraw from Victory Camp. Having apparently decided that they had no choice but to remit the sentences of their prisoners, on 14 December the remaining 319 Indonesians were discharged from the Dutch Forces, handed over to the care of a Commonwealth Immigration Officer and immediately left Casino for Brisbane and Chermside Camp. The officer reported that 'throughout the whole movement the conduct of the Indonesians was exemplary'.[70] On 16 December The *Richmond River Express* reported their departure with the headline, 'Dutch Camp at Casino Cleared of Prisoners.' As the Dutch personnel had also left at the same time, the citizens of Casino must have heaved a collective sigh of relief.

Although the sojourn of the Indonesians and the Dutch in Casino was over, the Dutch subterfuge in secretly removing the 13 prisoners continued to prejudice relations with Australian authorities for almost two years after the event. Throughout December telegrams went back and forth between Canberra and the Hague, with the Australians becoming increasingly frustrated by the lack of response from the Netherlands Government authorities. This reticence continued throughout 1947 and was commented on by Mr Calwell in a telegram to the Australian Minister in the Hague on 23 June when he said he 'gravely regarded Dutch violation of our sovereignty and abuse of our hospitality in kidnapping 13 Indonesian members of their army from Casino and the studied refusal of the Hague to even reply to our protests in this matter of December last'.[71]

It was not until August 1948 that the matter was finally dropped, with the Dutch having the last official word. A telegram to the Department of External Affairs from the Australian Minister to the Netherlands related that he had at last had a report on the matter from the Netherlands Ministry of Foreign Affairs, which he paraphrased as follows —

> It appears that all prisoners concerned except one have been released some considerable time ago and sent to Republican Territory – the one exception, Wararunto, was convicted of particularly serious offences including being a Japanese agent. The Army authorities state that they have questioned closely all the

Netherlands officers concerned and are satisfied that no one of them realised that the Australian Government considered that an undertaking had been given to return all Indonesians. They regret the incident – which was due to the overzealousness on the part of the officer concerned – and the Ministry of Foreign Affairs trusts that it can now be considered closed.[72]

There was nothing further that the Australians could do but they were in no way mollified by this explanation as we see from a comment scrawled on this telegram by an Australian official who noted that the explanation was unsatisfactory, and that because Colonel Moquette of the Dutch Army, 'a typical Prussian,' had uttered 'veiled threats' when told that the Australian Government would not repatriate the Indonesians to Dutch controlled areas of Indonesia, he believed that the abductions were premeditated.[73] This incident was another instance of the Dutch not respecting Australian decisions that were not in accordance with their own wishes, and therefore, ignoring them.

The Indonesian presence in Casino between 1944 and 1946 is an interesting and unusual chapter in the local history of the town. For those townspeople who engaged with the Indonesians hospitably and socially, it was a rewarding experience. For their local supporters in the union and communist movements it was political engagement in an anti-colonial revolution of international significance. For many other Casino locals it was an unhappy time as their town unfairly achieved a degree of national notoriety as the home of 'Little Belsen'. Perhaps the most unexpected outcome of all is that it was here, in this country town in northern NSW, that some of the first Indonesian blood was spilled for the Indonesian Revolution, perhaps the only blood spilt on foreign soil for that cause.

7

Mates and Merdeka

It took a few weeks for the Australian public to realise the significance of the unrest that was taking place in the NEI. However, with growing awareness that the conflict was somehow linked with reports about Indonesian rebels in Casino and with stories that began to emerge of black bans being placed on Dutch ships moored in Australian ports, it soon became very newsworthy. At this time too, the contacts and relationships between some individuals and groups of Australians and Indonesians began to take on a more political character. These Australians found themselves involved and allied with Asians in their struggle for independence against a European colonial power. Before the war, such an alliance and such mateship would have been unimaginable. The slogan and rallying cry of the Indonesian nationalist movement everywhere was *Merdeka* – freedom – a word popularized and frequently used by Soekarno to arouse his followers. It was a word that now became familiar to and frequently used by many of the Australians who supported the Indonesians.[1]

On the waterfront

On 21 September 1945, 85 Indonesian merchant sailors walked off the KPM ship *Bontekoe* in Brisbane, an act which became the catalyst for a four year waterside workers' ban against Dutch shipping interests in Australia. For the Dutch this shipping was urgently needed to transport home NEI administrators, military personnel and equipment, and desperately awaited relief supplies of food, clothing and medicine for the civilian population, former prisoners of war and civilian internees of the Japanese. Shortly after the walk off SARPELINDO called a meeting in the Brisbane Trades Hall of Indonesian crew members of Dutch ships in port. A resolution was taken to prevent the Dutch Government exiled in Australia going back to Indonesia and interfering with the Government of the Republic of Indonesia. In addition to this political agenda SARPELINDO also had an economic one: if demands for payment of deferred wages and improved pay and working conditions were not met its members would not go to sea in any circumstances.[2] SARPELINDO then approached the Waterside Workers Federation (WWF) and asked for its support, while Achmad Soemadi from the Indonesian Political Exiles Association contacted Mr E.V. Elliott, secretary of the Seamen's Union with a similar request for support in the struggle for Indonesian independence.[3]

As a result of these appeals the Trade Union machinery immediately swung into action, and set in train what one writer described as 'the most decisive act of international solidarity ever performed by Australian Trade Unions'.[4] On 24 September Mr E. Englart, secretary of the Brisbane Branch of the WWF informed Mr J. Healy, the Federal secretary, that the branch had passed a resolution recommending that members refrain from supplying labour to work Dutch vessels in the port pending guarantees satisfactory to the Indonesian peoples working in Australia; guarantees that the Dutch Government in Australia would not interfere with the Government established by the Indonesians themselves, and acceptance of the justified pay and conditions demands.'[5]

A copy of this resolution was sent to the Queensland TLC, which already had close ties with the Indonesian independence movement in Australia, particularly though its strong links with CENKIM. Accordingly on 24 September the TLC convened a meeting of its Disputes Committee to consider the matter. Representatives of the WWF and the Federated Storemen and Packers' Union also attended. After discussion, the TLC endorsed the WWF resolution and pledged full support to the Indonesian seamen. Resolutions were taken to meet with unions likely to be involved in repairing Dutch ships, to advise the Australian Council of Trade Unions (ACTU) and ask them to take up the matter with the Australian Government, and to produce leaflets explaining the dispute to the public. Later the same day the foreshadowed meeting with the relevant unions' representatives was held and as a result seven Dutch ships in Brisbane were declared 'black' for repairs by members of the Federated Shipwrights and Ship Constructers Union, Ship Painters and Dockers Union, Amal-

Mates and Merdeka

Indonesian seaman, who left a Dutch ship berthed in Melbourne after refusing to take the vessel to sea. Sympathisers with the Indonesian revolt against Dutch control in Java, the striking seamen claimed their ship carried materials "for the suppression of the newly-elected People's Government".
Photo; *Daily Telegraph* 27 September 1945.

gamated Society of Carpenters and Joiners, Electrical Trades Union, Boilermakers' Society, Plumbers and Gasfitters Union, Moulders Union and Federated Clerks Union.[6]

That evening, when attempts were made to use WWF members to load Dutch ships they refused and when they still refused the next day they were given an ultimatum by the Shipping Employers that unless they worked Dutch ships they would not be allowed to work on any ships. Determined not to comply, particularly after claiming that boxes labelled 'Comforts' contained phosphorus bombs and tommy guns, some 1,400 members were then locked out.[7]

On 25 September, the Disputes Committee held another meeting and representatives of involved unions all reported positive responses from their members. The President and Secretary of the Brisbane branch of SARPELINDO also attended and reported that the Indonesian seamen, who had walked off their ships without their personal possessions, had been taken to the Trades Hall where they spent the night. There was also discussion of their status within the strictures of the Immigration Act because they had left their ships. Anticipating this, the TLC had cabled Prime Minister Chifley and Immigration Minister Calwell asking them to extend the Indonesians' temporary residence, because any rigid application of the Immigration Act which led to their arrest could have serious

145

consequences such as a general strike.⁸ This, of course was a not too subtle, and ultimately unsuccessful, attempt at political blackmail. The meeting closed with a motion being passed to 'make use of every avenue for publicity including the press'.

If publicity was what they wanted publicity was what they got. When the dispute immediately hit the headlines across the country, the Indonesians' bid for independence was also publicised because the two issues were inextricably linked. For example the *Sydney Morning Herald* (29.9.1945) reported that the Federal Executive of the WWF recommended that its members declare 'black' any ship in which Indonesian seamen were on strike, and also any vessel carrying munitions or military supplies suspected to be for use against 'The Indonesian Democratic Government'. The *Herald* outlined the reasons for the Indonesians' declaration of independence and allegations of Dutch misrule, quoting information supplied by Jim Healy, WWF Federal Secretary. This was balanced by a statement from Commander Quispel of NIGIS who predictably accused Soekarno of being a quisling appointed as President of the Republic by the Japanese.

In Parliament, the issue of the bans was raised for the first time on 25 September when Mr Menzies, Leader of the Opposition, launched into a tirade against the 'Communist led' WWF, describing the waterside workers as 'those rogues who disfigure the life of Australia' and accusing them of intervening in foreign policy by refusing to load the ships of 'an allied power which has an honourable record in this war,' in support of 'the Quisling of Java'.⁹ Chifley retorted that if the Dutch authorities could not make their own subjects work, he could not imagine the subjects of another country would be likely to take action which might be regarded as scabbing'.¹⁰ Chifley, the former train driver and staunch unionist, knew full well the contempt felt for 'scabbing' – work carried out by individuals in contravention of union black bans. The WWF for its part quickly denied any intention to attempt to dictate foreign policy towards the NEI, maintaining it had as much right to express opinions about it as the Liberal Party did.¹¹

Government under fire

The shipping bans opened a Pandora's box of problems for the Government as it tried not to alienate the Dutch, or the unions from whom it traditionally gained so much of its political support. At the same time it was trying to maintain a neutral stance in its response to the developing Dutch/Indonesian crisis and all this under the eye of an increasingly critical Australian press, which lambasted the union/communist inspired bans and showed little sympathy for the Indonesian Republican cause. Mr Menzies and his Opposition, to whom anything involving Communists and left-wing unions was an anathema, also used the union involvement as ammunition to launch concerted attacks on the Government.

The Government at first appeared to play down the seriousness of the waterside dispute. For example when an Opposition Senator asked the Minister for Shipping how the Government was dealing with the bans the Minister pointed out that the trouble had started when Indonesians had walked off their ships, but following his discussions with Dutch authorities he was confident there would be no more trouble, provided the ships were not carrying arms or munitions.[12] However, pushing the line that the bans prevented food getting to the starving people in Java, the Opposition kept pressing the Prime Minister to clarify the Government's position. After further discussions with Dutch authorities, Chifley confirmed that the Government would ensure that genuine 'mercy' ships were loaded. But in what must have been an embarrassing disclosure for the Dutch, particularly when it was splashed across the newspapers, he also confirmed that four of the 'black' Dutch ships had been carrying arms and ammunition and that Dutch labour would have to be used for such cargo in the future.[13]

As far as the Republic was concerned, it was clear from the beginning what the sentiments of the Opposition were. Almost every speech its members made about the shipping bans was peppered with disparaging references to 'the Indonesian Quisling', 'Japan's Puppet Premier, 'the grave affront to a friendly power' or 'the so-called People's Government'. On the other hand the Labor Government maintained a neutral stance, publicly supporting neither the Dutch nor the Indonesians. Nevertheless the first speech in the Australian Parliament in sympathy with the aspirations of the Indonesians, was made by a Labor member, Senator Grant, in his spirited support for the principles of the Atlantic Charter as it applied to 'Asiatic races'. 'White imperialistic domination of the Asiatics is finished,' he said, 'whether the honorable senators opposite recognise the truth or not'.[14] Pointing out the irony of labelling the 'gentleman in Java' (Soekarno) as a Japanese quisling at the same time as Japanese were being used by the British to maintain order and land British forces in Java to 'suppress the natives,' he continued —

> The leader of the Opposition in the House of Representatives has said that the Government is offending our neighbours. Who are our neighbours? Are they the few Dutch imperialist exploiters who control rubber interests in Java and who have bled 75,000,000 natives for the last 350 years paying them an average wage of 2d a day? Seventy five percent of the natives of Indonesia cannot read or write. The Dutch were unable to defend their own possessions. Now they want to return to exploit the natives again as they did in the past.[15]

These were strong sentiments indeed from a member of a Government that maintained it was not taking sides in the dispute.

Running the gauntlet

In Brisbane, among the Dutch ships lying idle was the KPM vessel, *Van Heutz,* the first ship affected by the black ban. Following the refusal of the Brisbane wharf labourers to load this ship, whose cargo included troops, arms and ammunition, the Dutch brought 400 of their troops from Wacol to do the job. When the ship was finally loaded, the next problem was finding a crew to man her. Successive Indonesian crews walked off, until finally the Dutch brought some on board as virtual prisoners.[16] With an unwilling crew and a depleted cargo *Van Heutz* finally limped down the Brisbane River and out to sea en route for Java, with tugs refusing to tow her and short of fuel because coalers would not supply her. She was given a noisy farewell by an accompanying launch full of Indonesians and Australians shouting slogans. When after an unusually long voyage she reached Bowen, the local branch of the WWF imposed a black ban on her and as a result she was unable to take on coal and had to wait until a Dutch ship already at sea arrived to fuel her.[17]

In Melbourne the *Karsik*, which had been loaded before the bans were applied, was unable to sail because its Indonesian crew had walked off, claiming that guns and ammunition had been loaded on the ship in 'innocent looking boxes'. The Netherlands Vice-Consul called this allegation 'bare faced lies' and the Dutch recruited a crew of Indian lascars. When they arrived some 200 Indonesian seamen and Australian wharf labourers demonstrated on the wharf and tried to persuade them to leave the ship, but to no avail, as they were being paid by the British and feared reprisals if they joined the strikers.[18] The *Karsik*, (which was actually carrying crates of Dutch *guilders* needed to replace currency issued by the Republic) still had difficulties at the hands of Australian unionists even after she managed to get her replacement crew. As happened in Brisbane with the *Van Heutz*, in Melbourne too tug crews refused to tow *Karsik* out of port, coalers refused to replenish her supply of fuel, and she had to make her way out of port under her own steam. Some time later when she steamed into Bowen with seriously diminished coal stocks, she was also denied coal and forced to languish in port for some time until eventually being refuelled by a Dutch ship.[19]

By the end of September shipping bans were in effect in Brisbane, Melbourne and Sydney, and according to *Tribune* (28.9.1945), the NSW and Queensland TLCs had endorsed the actions of the 15 unions that, in this initial phase of the boycotts, were involved in what they saw as holding up the flow of arms and troops for suppression of the Indonesian Republican Government. The Australian unionists' actions attracted international publicity and union support. Indeed, as early as 24 September, the *New York Times* had reported that longshoremen at ports on the west coast of the United States, under their Australian-born Union President Harry Bridges, refused to load four Dutch ships with material intended for use against Indonesian nationalists. The Australians' actions were also endorsed, and in some cases mirrored, by trade unions in New Zealand, Holland, Britain, India, Canada, Egypt, Burma, Ceylon, Singapore and some ports in China. In addition, strong local support was also given by members of the Indian Seamen's Union, the Chinese Seamen's Union and the Malayan Merchant Navy Association, all established in Australia at the time.[20]

Demonstrations of support for the bans and the Republic

On 28 September, the first pro-Indonesia street demonstration was held in Sydney, when between 300-500 protesters, including some 50 Indonesians, all chanting '*Merdeka,*' attempted to march down York Street at lunch time to the office of the Dutch shipping company KPM. When police halted the procession and seized anti-Dutch banners, the marchers retreated to Wynyard Park for a meeting in support of Indonesian freedom. Speakers included Mr Stan Moran from the Sydney Branch of the WWF, an AIF private 'just back from Borneo,' and an Indonesian.[21] This incident was sensationalised on the same day by the afternoon *Sun* newspaper with its headline, 'Police Clash in City With Indies Mob,' accompanied by a photograph of jostling policemen 'swooping on the crowd'.

The story even made the *New York Times*, which reported that police had 'broken up an Indonesian independence meeting and battled striking Indonesian seamen,' who were assisted in their meeting by Australian Communists.[22]

On 29 September, the NSW TLC organised a public meeting which was attended by 1,000 people in the Sydney Domain, in those days a popular Sunday venue for soap-box orators. The rain falling at the time did not dampen the enthusiasm of the audience who cheered Indonesian seamen who addressed them. One of the speakers was ex-Digulist Soeparmin, who proclaimed, 'I would rather be dead than back in Tanah Merah' while another Indonesian, Jim Lumanauw, declared that the Indonesians would no longer be exploited by the Dutch.[23] The meeting passed a resolution declaring support for the Indonesian independence movement and pledging to do everything possible to prevent Dutch war materials and forces leaving Australia.

The next public appearance of striking Indonesians in Sydney was in the Six Hour Day March on 1 October. Three hundred seamen took part, supported by groups of Chinese, Indian and Greek seamen. The *Daily Mirror* described the banner-bearing Indonesians as 'a determined collection of objectors to the rule they are so tenaciously opposing,' who were warmly cheered by the onlookers along the route.[24] The Indonesians' participation in the march was duly reported to the Commonwealth Investigation Branch in Canberra together with the identities of citizens writing letters to the

Indonesian seaman speaking at a pro-Indonesian demonstration in Wynyard Square during the lunch hour yesterday before police broke up the 500 demonstrators and took away many of their banners.
Photo: Daily Telegraph 29 September 1945.

Daily Telegraph expressing views favourable to the Indonesians, and information about a meeting of 330 similarly disposed employees at Garden Island.[25]

In Melbourne on the same day, a public meeting called by the CPA was held in the Savoy Theatre. With the theme 'Hands off Indonesia' this meeting also attracted an audience of 1,000 people. Unionists and CPA members addressed the crowd, as did Indonesians, including ex-Digulists. After the meeting everyone marched with banners and the Australian and Indonesian flags along Bourke Street and Swanston Street to St Pauls Cathedral, outside which there were more speeches and the singing of *Indonesia Raya*.[26] The day after this meeting, Dutch soldiers, accompanied by Australian police, manhandled and used armed force to arrest three Indonesians – two corporals in the NEI army and one employee of NIGIS – at *Roemah Indonesia* in Bourke Street.[27] No explanation was given for the arrests, but as one of the men had been a speaker at the meeting it is likely that the Dutch were cracking down on anyone they perceived as being disloyal to them. Alerted to the manner of these arrests, the ever-vigilant Australian Council for Civil Liberties protested to the Commonwealth Government that 'armed force had been used by forces of a foreign power on Australian territory'.[28]

Even in far away Western Australia public meetings in support of the Indonesian nationalist movement were 'largely attended'. One held in Fremantle was addressed by the Secretary of the local Communist Party whilst the main speaker at another meeting in Perth was a 'prominent unionist speaking in a personal capacity.'[29]

The shipping bans and growing momentum of expressions of Australian solidarity were reported in the Republican press in Indonesia under such headlines as 'Indonesians in Australia fight for Indonesia's Independence: Australian workers and Communists help them'.[30] Such reportage played a part in forming the impression among Indonesian Republicans that there was wide-spread Australian support for their aspirations and their struggle. The nationalists in Australia would only have had to read the Australian newspapers to know that such was not the case.

Press opposition to the bans and the Republic

Apart from the Federal Opposition in Parliament, from early October the main indictments of the boycott and the Republic came from the press, with the notable exception of *Tribune* and other Communist organs. The following fragments (from October 1945) capture the tone of some of the metropolitan dailies and magazines, particularly after the demonstrations mentioned above. One of the first off the mark was the Hobart *Mercury* with its simplistic and misleading editorial of 2 October —

> Further information on the nature of the nationalist movement in Indonesia shows that the action in support of it by workers of the Australian waterfront has been entirely misplaced, no matter how well meant. The Indonesian independence movement has been revealed as 'a malicious Japanese legacy intended to be a nuisance to the Dutch'.

Denigrating the pro-Indonesia meeting at the Sydney Domain, The *Bulletin* (3.10.1945) produced one of its typically racist car-

Mates and Merdeka

"Better to be in Hell than Colonised Again" and "Remember the Atlantic Charter" were two of the slogans carried by the many Indonesians who marched in Monday's Six-hour Day procession.
Photo: *Tribune* 5 October 1945.

toons, entitled 'Logical Consequence.' This depicted a loin-cloth clad Aboriginal family standing on the wharf near a Dutch ship while grinning idle wharf labourers and crew looked on. The caption, scurrilous even by *Bulletin* standards, had the Aboriginal man with outstretched arms pleading with the wharfies, 'Me head Arunta P'visional 'Public. Gibbit bacca, gibbit Gubment, gibbit Australia'. The *Sydney Morning Herald* and the *Daily Telegraph* (3.10.1945) both reported that a Cabinet sub-committee had found that the strike by Indonesian seamen was actually instigated by Communists as part of a plot to undermine the White Australia Policy, a finding apparently based on the rather flimsy evidence that some of the phraseology found in Communist produced pro-Republic pamphlets was similar to that found in Communist statements opposing the White Australia Policy. The *Advertiser* (12.10.1945) told its readers, 'Dr Soekarno's men have imposed a reign of terror and are resorting to thuggery in the good old Nazi style – join the movement or be beaten up'. The *Courier Mail* (15.10.1945) chided those Australians who had taken talk of Indonesian democracy at face value and supported a dispute of which they had no real knowledge. *The Southern*

Cross, (19.10.1945) organ of the Roman Catholic church in Adelaide, attributed not only the bans but the whole Indonesian independence movement to the Communists in this amazing piece of sophistry entitled 'Soekarno and the Suckers' —

> From the first the Indonesian trouble looked surprisingly like a Red racket, because it was the Communist element in Australia who were most vocal in support of Soekarno and his men. Two things now appear clear enough. First, Soekarno was a quisling of impressive malodourousness. Second, however strong are the claims of Java for independence, a Dutch withdrawal at this stage would be a betrayal of the Javanese to Red anarchy and a gross dereliction of duty.

How a so-called (Fascist) quisling could at the same time be leader of an alleged Communist independence movement was left to readers to figure out. In fact, the public was ill-served by the mainstream press of the day, most of which failed to present any kind of balanced, analytical reporting of the independence struggle and blithely attributed it to either Fascist or Communist influence.

The striking Indonesian seamen

From the time the first Indonesians walked off their ships, one of the problems that vexed the Commonwealth government was how to get them out of the country. In an effort to find a solution Dr John Burton, Acting-Secretary of the Department of External Affairs and Mr J. Kevin another senior officer, held discussions in Canberra in September with Netherlands Counsellor, Mr Mountijn. From the Australians' point of view at this stage there were two possibilities: they could use Australian law to force the Indonesians back to their ships, provided the Dutch would guarantee that no reprisals would be taken against them when they reached the NEI, or they could remove the Indonesians to some off-shore territory under Australian jurisdiction, such as Nauru.[31] Kevin's memo about these proceedings provide one of the few records of Dutch reaction to the seamen's actions. Mountijn said he 'regarded the seamen as irresponsible natives who should never have been allowed contact with whites'. Angrily asserting that they were still under Dutch law and therefore could be punished, he insisted that the Commonwealth should fully co-operate with this even if it meant forcing them back to punishment in the NEI.[32] After it was pointed out that the seamen were now under Australian, not Dutch, jurisdiction, Mountijn informed Calwell that in that case Dutch authorities would agree with any moves to deport the seamen to Australian-controlled territory.[33]

Minister for External Affairs Evatt was in Washington at the time, but was kept informed of developments. In a cable on 28 September Burton explained the uncompromising attitude of the Dutch: unless the Government deported the seamen to the NEI, the Dutch would wash their hands of them, leaving them as the total responsibility of Australia. Chifley was adamant that they had to leave the country, but Burton's concern was that sending them back to likely punishment in the NEI would cause a widening of the waterfront dispute. The Dutch would give no assurance that the seamen would not be punished so Burton's solution was to send them to some Australian territory such as Nauru, and hold them there until the NEI situation was clear.[34]

Evatt was opposed to the use of deportation (to the NEI) as a weapon, particularly with the likelihood of the Dutch inflicting 'drastic punishment' on the seamen, not for industrial but for political reasons. His desire was that because the Immigration laws probably did not cover deportation to territories like Nauru, and because the whole problem had an industrial, political and international character, it should be 'settled by agreement'.[35] This was easy for a minister not on the spot to say, but not so easy for those faced with the dilemma of containing the 300-400 Indonesian seamen soon on the loose in Melbourne, Brisbane and Sydney as well as repatriating them in some way acceptable to the seamen themselves and their union supporters, but without further antagonising the Dutch.

From merchant sailor to prohibited immigrant

On 1 October, the Commonwealth Peace officer on duty at Port Melbourne reported that Indonesian seamen on the Dutch vessel *Merak* stopped work that day and walked off the ship with their luggage. After waiting around the pier for a while they were taken by truck and taxi to *Roemah Indonesia* in Bourke Street They were refused entry by the manager, who told them that because they refused to work for the Dutch Government, it no longer recognised them and they should ask the Australian Government for assistance. As the door was guarded by uniformed police, the men had no alternative but to leave, even though Indonesians already staying there offered to make room for them. Finally, trade union officials took them to Unity Hall, the headquarters of the Australian Railways Union, to be given a meal and found quarters for the night in the city. Showing that they meant business, the Dutch told the *Karsik* crewmen already at the hostel that they would have to leave the next day.[36]

Melbourne at this time was a nest of Indonesian rebels. More than 50 soldiers and navy personnel stationed there had mutinied, been arrested and taken to Casino for court martial, and nearly 60 Indonesian civilians working for Dutch establishments such as NIGIS had resigned saying they would no longer do anything to assist the Dutch Government. A number of these were ex-SIBAR men who had only been prepared to co-operate with the Dutch until the war against fascism was won. Now into this rebellious mix stepped the 62 striking seamen from the *Merak*, who soon found themselves occupying headlines in the daily press when they were arrested on 2 October and charged with desertion. Reports of how the arrests took place are rather confused, but one paints a dramatic scenario about the apprehension of 33 of the seamen who were quartered at a hostel called Red Shield House. According to this report 'a strong posse of police' with Dutch officials present, made a surprise raid in the early hours of the morning, barged into the rooms where the Indonesians were sleeping and told them to get dressed. When they refused to do so, three or four of the leaders were 'dragged down the narrow staircase' and shoved in a prison van, whereupon the others followed quietly.[37] The remainder were rounded up from another hostel and all were taken to the City Court, charged with desertion and fined 3 pounds each.[38] As soon as they were released, they were charged again, this time with vagrancy, but when the police tendered no evidence, this charge was dismissed.

These proceedings were all just a prelude to the main game as became evident when the seamen were then detained as suspected prohibited immigrants, pending their taking the iniquitous dictation test the Commonwealth used to rid itself of undesirable aliens under the 'White Australia Policy'. A rather poignant relic of this bureaucratic farce – farce because none of these men were seeking to become immigrants – remains in the archives in the form of reports from the Commonwealth Investigation Branch officers who assisted in administering the tests, with copies of the tests themselves. With the aid of an interpreter each Indonesian was identified by name and nationality, asked whether he had received permission to stay in Australia – the answer of course was 'no' – and informed that he would be given a dictation test in English. The selected passage began, 'We have absolute evidence that the ice-caps around our poles once extended further than now ...' ensuring that largely poorly educated seamen from the tropics would stand no chance of passing. Inevitably all failed the test, were declared to be prohibited immigrants, and charged accordingly. That evening the Council for Civil Liberties sent a telegram to the Minister for Immigration —

> Council for Civil Liberties lawyers will defend in Melbourne City Court tomorrow Indonesian seamen who are charged as prohibited immigrants. Men are anxious return to East Indies in any but Dutch vessel. We respectfully suggest commotions would be allayed and courts relieved of embarrassment if you could announce return in such conditions as would be acceptable to Government. We are confident you would agree it is absurd to imprison as prohibited immigrants men who do not wish to immigrate.[39]

The Indonesian KIM in Melbourne also contacted the Minister to assure him that all the Indonesians involved were fully agreeable to leave Australia voluntarily, if they were sent back to Republican controlled parts of Indonesia. They requested that striking civilians and members of the NEI military depart at the same time. In response, Calwell made it clear that any offer of repatriation he made would only apply to seamen and civilians, because the Australian Government would not interfere in matters of discipline of the armed forces, which were the responsibility of the Dutch.[40]

When the matter came before the magistrate the next morning the defence counsel, Mr Dethridge, successfully obtained an adjournment, so as to give the Commonwealth Government the opportunity to repatriate the Indonesians in non-Dutch vessels. The men were then released on bail of £50 each, raised by trade union and other friends.[41] Following a conference with immigration authorities, the 33 striking crew members of the *Karsik* had voluntarily submitted to arrest on the same charge and appeared in court at the same time.[42] The seamen all agreed to leave Australia voluntarily and the Minister for Immigration offered through the Commonwealth to provide facilities for them prior to their repatriation to an area not controlled by the Dutch.[43] Accordingly an empty internment camp at Tatura, a rural town about 150 kms north of Melbourne near Shepparton, was made available to house them all while they waited for a ship to take them back to their own country. All expenses of their upkeep were paid by the Commonwealth and they were free within the confines of the camp. Calwell made it clear to Brian Fitzpatrick of the Council for Civil Liberties that the Indonesians were not being interned and that they would not be deported: they were voluntarily complying with the arrangements being made for them.[44] The number of 'guests' at Tatura swelled when Dutch authorities forced 65 Indonesians no longer in Dutch employ, who were staying at *Roemah Indonesia*, to move out.[45]

In Brisbane the striking seamen were camped in the ballroom of the Trades Hall, temporarily subsisting on meals provided by local Chinese restaurants.[46] Brigadier Simpson, D-G of Security, found himself yet again embroiled in Indonesian affairs when he received a phone call on 3 October, informing him that these seamen, by now numbering about 200, had that morning left the Trades Hall and marched in a body to Camp Colombia at Wacol, where there were already 200 striking Indonesian civilian employees who were not receiving any pay because of their refusal to accept orders from Dutch military authorities.[47] On arrival the seamen insisted on food and accommodation, which were reluctantly provided by the Dutch officer in charge. Trouble had already erupted in the camp the previous day between the civilian strikers and loyal to the Dutch Indonesians domiciled there. Not wanting an influx of more troublemakers, the Australian Army CO for Queensland asked Simpson's help in getting the seamen interned. Simpson, who had probably had enough of coping with problems of interned Indonesians, informed the Acting Attorney-General that he was not in favour of interning them, but felt they should be dealt with under the Immigration Act.[48]

On 5 October a meeting of the Queensland TLC was informed that that morning 204 seamen at Wacol had been arrested by Australian civil and military police, under the Prohibited Immigration Act.[49] If the facts reported by the *Courier Mail* (6.10.1945) were accurate the arrest procedure seems to have been mounted like a major military operation. It appears that 100 civilian police and 75 military police loaded 204 unresisting Indonesians onto 30 trucks and took them to Gaythorne internment camp which, under a hastily conceived Government Gazette, was designated as a prison under the State Prisons Act. Once there they were guarded by civilian police until taking and failing the dictation test the next day.

On 8 October, 51 of the seamen were taken to the Brisbane Summons Court charged with being prohibited immigrants. Their defence counsel was Mr Max Julius, an alleged communist and active supporter of the Indonesian Republican cause. After some legal manoeuvering during which Mr Julius threatened to drag out proceedings, plead not guilty and defend each of the 204 Indonesians individually one after the other if the adjournment he sought was not granted, the magistrate capitulated despite the objections of the Crown. Like his counterpart in Melbourne, Mr Julius was playing for time awaiting the outcome of the Commonwealth's efforts to find a ship and repatriate the Indonesians.[50]

When the case returned to court on 11 October, Mr Julius tried to gain another adjournment, explaining that a ship was being sought and suggesting that charges be withdrawn and the Indonesians go voluntarily to camps while waiting for a vessel. The Crown prosecutor opposed the adjournment and this time the magistrate refused to grant it whereupon Mr Julius formally pleaded guilty as each man's name was called, and a sentence of 6 months' prison was imposed on each. The prosecutor made it clear that the intention was to confine the Indonesians, (at Gaythorne) but not to treat them as prisoners.[51]

Thus, in a matter of only three weeks, some 300-400 ordinary Indonesian merchant seamen had achieved extraordinary outcomes. They had defied their colonial masters and walked off their ships, thereby prompting industrial action by Australian unionists which held up virtually all Dutch shipping in Australian ports. As a result of this, Australian and international attention had been drawn to

Indonesian seamen leaving the Police Court yesterday morning after one of their number had been charged with being a prohibited immigrant. Men were transported to and from the Court by Australian Army vehicles, under civil and military police escort.
Photo: Courier Mail, 9 October 1945.

the Indonesian struggle for independence. They had been arrested, tried and convicted by Australian courts as prohibited immigrants, and were now being fed and accommodated at the expense of the Commonwealth of Australia while waiting to be repatriated to their homeland under arrangements agreeable to them.

8

The First Repatriation

The Australian Government's rationale in dealing with the repatriation of striking Indonesians was firstly, the seamen had to leave Australia in compliance with immigration laws: White Australia would not tolerate their presence any longer than necessary. Secondly, and to its credit, recognizing that the great majority had acted from political motives and were not criminals, the Government was not disposed to return them forcibly on a Dutch ship to Dutch-controlled territory. Getting them home safely meant venturing into hitherto untried logistical and diplomatic territory, and was a huge challenge to the Government's resolve.

Esperance Bay

The first task was locating a suitable non-Dutch ship so Chifley and Calwell enquired whether any Army vessels were available and found that two British transports, *Esperance Bay* and *Largs Bay*, carrying liberated Australian pows from Changi, would shortly be arriving in Sydney.[1] The Government quickly lodged an application with the British Ministry in Australia for use of one or both of these ships to take civilians, including the seamen, to ports in Indonesia. Chifley asked the Australian High Commissioner to the UK to press British authorities for their speedy agreement in order to 'remove possible causes of international friction'.[2] On the same day External Affairs informed Evatt that the situation was being handled smoothly, and that Australian authorities expected no repercussions from the Dutch even though they wanted more drastic action than the Government was prepared to concede.[3]

On 10 October 1945, when Lord Louis Mountbatten's Southeast Asia Command (SEAC) headquarters approved a request to disembark Indonesian merchant seamen in Jakarta,[4] the way was clear for the repatriation to proceed and the *Esperance Bay* was allocated for the job. A request was made to the Department of the Navy to demobilise Lieutenant Kenneth Plumb of the Security Service Intelligence Corps, who was Australian Liaison Officer with NEFIS in Brisbane and therefore presumably knowledgeable about Indonesian and Dutch matters, to accompany the Indonesians. To allay any unease or tension the passengers might feel about a Security Service officer accompanying them it was necessary for Plumb to come as a civilian officer of the Department of External Affairs.[5] No interpreter was supplied, possibly because there were no Indonesian speaking officers in the Department. Instead, Plumb would have to rely on Indonesians who spoke English. As for the matter of security during the voyage, it was decided that there would be no armed guard on board, only a contingent of 11 (eventually increased to 40) D.E.M.S. (Defensively Equipped Merchant Ships) ratings, an arrangement with which the ship's captain was apparently satisfied.[6]

On 12 October Chifley informed Mountbatten of the arrangements and the imminent departure of the *Esperance Bay*, stressing his government's attitude that the Dutch and Indonesians had to work out their own problems, but that it would not forcibly return the Indonesians, all of whom were in sympathy with Soekarno's movement, to Dutch territory. Chifley requested Mountbatten's assistance in ensuring that the Indonesians were disembarked 'without incident and without risk of punishment by the Dutch'.[7] At the time Mountbatten was facing increasing difficulties in handling the situation in Java. He was facing criticism because he had only sent a force of 3,000 British troops to disarm the 50,000 Japanese at large on the islands and at the same time rumours were circulating of impending bloodshed and of thousands of armed Indonesian rebels standing ready to drive off any Dutch troops who tried to enter Java .Chifley's request could not have come at a worse time for him.

The Sydney contingent

The proposed route of the *Esperance Bay* was Sydney-Brisbane-Darwin-NEI, departing Sydney on 13 October. An account written by Mr C. Marks, Boarding Officer with the NSW Customs and Excise Office, about arrangements for collecting the complement of 568 passengers boarding in Sydney, provides us with a breakdown of

The First Repatriation

its composition. First there were 185 Indonesians from Melbourne, including the crews from *Merak* and *Karsik*, who were arriving by train from Albury to be taken by trucks to the No 9 wharf, Pyrmont where the ship was berthed. Then there were two groups of Indonesians residing at KPM hostels in Sydney – 163 at The Lido (North Sydney) and 32 at the Belvedere (Darlinghurst). Next were 72 crew members of the Dutch ships *Swartenhondt* and *Van Swoll*, both berthed at Blues Point, and 47 crew members of *Patrus*. All of these were to be taken to the ship by military transport. The final contingent comprised 69 from the *Van der Lijn, Japara* and *Pahud*, which were anchored 'in the stream,' so that the crews were being moved to the *Esperance Bay* by launches.[8] Presumably all these crewmen were striking or threatening to, but there is no record of court proceedings against them as there were against the strikers in Melbourne and Brisbane.

On the evening of 12 October, the AIA held an information and culture night in the Sydney Town Hall to publicise the Association and to farewell the repatriates.[9] After some cultural performances and speeches, the Vice-President, Mr Campbell, told the audience that the *Esperance Bay* would leave the following day and demonstrated his complete confidence in the good intentions of the Australian Government when he told the Indonesians, 'I will give my guarantee you will reach your homes without Dutch interference'.[10] He was not to know that things would not turn out quite the way he expected.

Morning departure

The departure of *Esperance Bay* from Pyrmont on 13 October, as described by the *Sunday Telegraph*, must have presented a colourful spectacle. All the ingredients were there to make the scene memorable: excited passengers going on board loaded with all sorts of goods to take home, and trade union officials, well-wishers (including Molly Warner), Dutch officials and sobbing Australian sweethearts gathered on the wharf to see them off. High drama was added to the proceedings when the Dutch consul, Mr J.D. Pennick and other officials were booed loudly by seamen shouting, 'Down With the Dutch!' Another Dutch official, Captain de Bruyn, also aroused the wrath of the crowd when he called from the gangway and tried to persuade

Spokesman for departing Indonesians, Jim Lumanauw (centre) of Sourabaya, and vice-president of the Australia-Indonesia Association, Mr C. H. Campbell (right) argue with the Dutch officer, Captain De Bruyn, who tried to persuade men to leave the Esperance Bay and return to work.
Photo: Daily Telegraph, 14 October 1945.

some of the men to leave the ship, claiming that they had boarded under duress. This allegation was hotly denied by the Indonesian spokesmen, Mangowal and Lumanauw, and by Mr Campbell from the AIA.[11]

In fact this became another of the growing number of contentious issues between NEI and Australian authorities in the post-war period. The Netherlands Minister, Baron van Aerssen later complained to the Prime Minister that despite NEI officials supplying immigration officers with lists of names of Indonesians who wanted to join the *Esperance Bay*, the KPM hostel in North Sydney, the Lido, was emptied indiscriminately without any attempt to check the names. Similarly, the captain of *Swartenhold* complained that five of his best crew members, who were not on strike, were taken against their wishes. Van Aerssen summed up his annoyance as follows —

> All customary requirements prior to boarding the vessels for overseas ports such as embarkation permits, taxation clearances, export licences and baggage clearances were completely ignored ... These facts in my opinion indicate a lack of control

The First Repatriation

on the side of the Australian authorities. The Netherlands authorities, who in conformity with arrangements made, supplied the Immigration and Passport Officers with a complete list of the Indonesians who were to embark on the *Esperance Bay* must dismiss all responsibility for any difficulty arising from the above mentioned facts.[12]

Captain Thomas Stapleton was the senior British medical officer on board and his account of the repatriation also suggests that the boarding of the passengers was quite chaotic with no control over it and no inspection (by customs or anybody else) of the luggage. 'In fact nobody seemed certain how many people were on board,' he later wrote.[13]

None of this worried the Indonesians' supporters, and as a grand gesture of solidarity, Mr E.V. Elliott, Federal Secretary of the Seamen's Union, presented the repatriates with a large Republican flag to be given to Soekarno, on behalf of the trade union movement in Australia. During his speech Elliott said that the whole Australian trade union movement was behind the independence struggle of its Indonesian brothers, and then everyone joined in three cheers for the Indonesian Republic.

Politics were not on the minds of the sweethearts left behind. Alice Stevens of Campbell Street, had an Indonesian fiancé, presumably a non-striker, who had already left Australia. Alice had given a farewell dance for some of the departees and sobbed loudly as she farewelled friends. Mrs Doreen Coughlan, soda fountain attendant at the Trocadero, 'wanted nothing more' than to follow her boyfriend, Tajib, to Surabaya and marry him, as soon as she obtained her divorce, while Ilene Hyde, waitress of College Street, wept as she farewelled her fiance Jim Moespadjab of Java.[14]

Apart from these matters of the heart there were also some unresolved financial issues about deferred pay owed to the Indonesians by their erstwhile Dutch employers. Learning of this Molly Warner came to the rescue and offered to approach the KPM authorities in the name of the AIA, and try to retrieve the money owed to former seamen. To do this she needed power of attorney authorising the AIA to act on their behalf. Some of the Indonesians began preparing makeshift forms with personal details of each claimant, but there was no time to complete the job before the ship sailed, so Molly agreed to take the train to Brisbane that night to collect the forms when the ship called there.[15]

At last all the boarding procedures were complete. As the *Esperance Bay* pulled away from the wharf for what was to be a controversial voyage, Indonesians on board and on land joined in singing 'a halting version' of Waltzing Matilda, and the Republican anthem *Indonesia Raya*, while the Republican flag was waved from the deck.[16]

Heading north

While the *Esperance Bay* steamed north to Brisbane to pick up more passengers, Australian authorities continued to grapple with the next major problem: exactly where to land them when the ship reached the NEI. Cyphers from the Department of External Affairs to SEAC requested urgent advice about suitable ports in Java and Sumatra, stressing that untoward incidents and any risk of Dutch punishment had to be avoided at all cost.[17] There must have been great consternation when, on 14 October, a blunt cable from SEAC arrived stating —

> ... owing to the extreme delicacy of the situation now in Java and Sumatra, both from the point of view of food supplies and the political situation it is impossible to permit any disembarkation of repatriated Indonesians in these islands until further notice.[18]

Stunned by this, Chifley immediately cabled Mounbatten informing him firmly that the repatriation had started and must proceed. He reiterated that all the arrangements had been made with the agreement of Dutch authorities (even though they would have preferred forceable expulsion on Dutch ships) and that the Indonesians could not possibly remain in Australia indefinitely. He dismissed the matter of food shortages by pointing out that the Indonesians would be dispersed at ports in Java, Sumatra and Dutch Timor so would not cause undue strain on supplies. Finally, he emphasized that failure to land the Indonesians under the terms agreed to would be regarded as a breach of faith which could lead to further industrial trouble in Australia.[19]

The First Repatriation

Chifley's persuasive arguments appeared to have won the day when he received a cable from Mountbatten saying that in view of the desire to repatriate all the Indonesians from Australia, the Indonesians could now land in Sumatra, and no arrests or punitive action from the Dutch would be allowed.[20] There the matter rested as the *Esperance Bay* steamed into Brisbane, berthing at 9.30 am on 15 October. En route from Sydney, the Indonesians had set up a Committee of Management (comprising Soeparmin, Soedijat and Senan) which, at Plumb's request, had compiled a list of the passengers who embarked in Sydney, no other list having been prepared by any authorities.

Brisbane embarkation

Compared to Sydney, the embarkation in Brisbane was a low key and more orderly affair. Prior to the *Esperance Bay*'s arrival, the 600 or so Indonesians at Gaythorne were transferred to a staging camp at Lytton, ready for easy access to the ship's berth 2 miles away. Before they would agree to leave Gaythorne, the Indonesians tried yet again to claim the deferred pay – the 3s 3d per day balance from the 6s 6d per day – that had been promised to them. When Customs officers tried to verify this claim Australian Army authorities confirmed that this promise had indeed been made, but a senior Dutch official denied that any such arrangement existed. On being informed of this the Indonesians almost rebelled again as they debated whether they would co-operate with the transfer to Lytton or not. But eventually, to the relief of the authorities, they agreed to go voluntarily and were joined there by a further 91 who had been living in hostels in Brisbane. In the meantime, the first group of 153 strikers released from Casino were brought by train to Clapham Junction, Brisbane, from where they were transported, 'complete with a colossal amount of luggage,' straight to the ship. The final number to board in Brisbane was reported as 884, bringing the total complement of Indonesian passengers to 1,416.[21]

All preparations were scrutinised by the Security Service, with the Brisbane officer-in-charge assuring the ship's captain that Commonwealth authorities intended to prevent open access to the wharf, as there had been in Sydney. 'The master was somewhat resentful of the conduct of affairs (in Sydney) and was grateful of guarantees

Indonesians who will be shipped back to their home islands to-day in the Esperance Bay waited philosophically yesterday at Fort Lytton. They gave their word to military police that thay would not stray from the area.
Photo: Courier Mail, 15 October 1945.

that there would be no repetition in Brisbane,' wrote this officer to the Director-General.[22] It was during this discussion that the captain revealed that many of the Indonesians who boarded in Sydney had been seen to possess knives and more alarmingly, one allegedly had a pistol. This must have prompted the captain to rethink his security arrangements, as he now requested a Naval escort, preferably a cruiser or destroyer, to accompany the *Esperance Bay* beyond Darwin.[23] The Captain's fears were compounded by his awareness that so many of his passengers were experienced seamen and would be capable of taking over the ship if they were not landed at ports acceptable to them.[24]

It was also discovered prior to departure that some of the Indonesians had large sums of money in their possession. The Committee of Management wished a Government representative to take this money into safe custody, as it would have been useless when they arrived home. In consultation between the Committee, a Brisbane TLC official and AIA members Molly Warner and Anne Warnerford, who had come up from Sydney, the Indonesians agreed that the money would be deposited in the current Victory Loan. An amount later ascertained by officials to total almost £35,000 was

The First Repatriation

collected in a sealed bag and deposited with the Commonwealth Registry of Inscribed Stock, subscribed in the names of Guy Anderson, Molly Warner, Anne Warnerford, all of the AIA, and Michael Healy of the Brisbane TLC. The Indonesians agreed as well that the deferred pay Molly and her friends were trying to obtain on their behalf from the Dutch would also be deposited in the Victory Loan.[25]

Worries about security

When the *Esperance Bay* finally got under way on the afternoon of 16 October, *en route* for Darwin, there were still two important matters unresolved. One of these was the captain's increasing concern about security arrangements. On 18 October the Secretary of the Department of the Navy cabled his own Minister and the Department of External Affairs informing them that there was no cruiser available to meet the captain's request for an escort. He proposed instead embarking a party of two to three hundred armed soldiers at Darwin to act as an escort and with authority to use force only if 'moral persuasion' failed in the event of any attempt to take over the ship.[26] External Affairs quickly moved to squash this suggestion, pointing out that while in Brisbane the captain, together with Plumb and the Security Service were not in favour of armed guards, whose presence could be provocative in light of the assurance given to the Indonesians that they would be landed with no punitive action. Even the DEMS ratings were unarmed except for blackjacks. External Affairs pointed out that the journey proceeding without incident depended on the confidence the Indonesians felt in the Government and in Plumb's handling of them. To satisfy the captain's wish for a naval escort, the destroyer HMAS *Arunta* was assigned to escort *Esperance Bay* from Darwin.[27] Plumb himself had no concerns about security and informed his masters that the Indonesians were co-operating fully with the captain and himself through their own management committee and sub-committee.[28]

Destination unknown

The second unresolved issue as the *Esperance Bay* steamed towards Darwin related to the ongoing uncertainty about where disembarkation would take place. As we have seen Mountbatten had reluctantly agreed that Sumatra was acceptable to SEAC, and had ignored reference to Java, while the Australian authorities seemed to have the mistaken impression that some of the Indonesians wished to go to Dutch Timor, then under Australian Forces command. In fact, as Plumb explained in his message about security matters, the management committee had told him that most passengers wished to disembark in Java – though not in Jakarta – and the remainder in Sumatra. No one had any desire or reason to disembark in Timor.

Then on 21 October, Mountbatten dropped a bombshell. He cabled Chifley to inform him that due to the 'very grave' situation in Java and Sumatra and what appeared to be the imminent outbreak of civil war, he could not allow the Indonesians to land there after all, so they should be taken to Timor. He explained that the British Commander in the NEI, General Christison, had been approached by Dutch representatives (including Dr van Mook) demanding that the Indonesians be taken to Timor, but under no circumstances to Java or Sumatra, where 'their arrival might tip the scales in favour of the Extremists'.[29] Mountbatten then claimed that when he agreed previously to the Sumatra landing, he had not realised that the Indonesians included 'large numbers of political prisoners exiled to New Guinea ... and who are extremists'.[30] Here was another example of wily Dutch subterfuge. The real 'extremists' from Digul had, at Dutch insistence, been isolated and interned in Cowra and Liverpool and eventually returned to the Dutch New Guinea long before the first repatriation. It is true that the passengers who embarked in Brisbane did include former Digulists, some of whom had been among the strikers in Casino, but most of the passengers were the seamen who had gone on strike. Van Mook had obviously used the well tried ploy of applying the term 'extremist' to any Indonesian who opposed the Dutch in any way, and Mountbatten had believed him.

Chifley was not swayed by Mountbatten's arguments, pointing out that although he appreciated General Christison's difficulties, it would be impossible to disembark all of the passengers in Timor because of the limited resources there. But his main concern was his Government's pledge to do everything in its power to return the Indonesians to Republican territory.

Unable to solve this impasse with Chifley, Mountbatten appealed to the British Cabinet Office in a cable dispatched on 23 October, by which time the *Esperance Bay* had arrived in Darwin. Mountbatten made it clear that he accepted Van Mook's claim that the majority of the Indonesians were 'undesirable characters' who should not be landed in Java or Sumatra, and that he supported Christison's view that they should be landed at Dutch Timor or nearby small islands. The problem was exacerbated by the fact that at the time SEAC was not yet permitting any Dutch forces to land in the NEI, so allowing the Indonesians to do so would certainly antagonise the Dutch and 'greatly embarrass' Christison. On the other hand, he did acknowledge that not allowing the Indonesians to land in Java and Sumatra would embarrass the Australian Government, which would be open to charges of breaking its pledge.[31]

As a courtesy, a copy of this message was also sent to Chifley, who immediately cabled his British counterpart, Prime Minister Attlee, to press his side of the argument. Suggesting that Mountbatten was paying too much heed to Dutch authorities in Jakarta, he pointed out that NEI authorities in Australia had finally agreed to the voluntary repatriation in the *Esperance Bay*, even demobilising many (from Casino) so that they could take part. Regarding Van Mook's assessment that the majority of passengers were 'undesirable characters' Chifley commented wryly —

> ... in our experience the Dutch are perhaps apt, particularly under present circumstances, to regard as 'undesirable' any Indonesian politically out of sympathy with them, irrespective of whether he is an extremist in our sense or not.[32]

Chifley also dismissed the suggestion that the arrival of 1,400 Indonesians, particularly if they were dispersed in different areas, could 'tip the scales' in favour of the rebel element. Finally, he demonstrated his determination not to break faith with the Indonesians when he said that it was quite impossible to divert them as Mountbatten had suggested and he would not tolerate the Australian Government's arrangements being vetoed by Dutch officials in Java. He proposed that as British forces had meantime landed in Surabaya, the Indonesians be disembarked there under British surveillance.[33] Although his Government was still maintaining a neutral attitude in the Dutch/Indonesian dispute, Chifley appeared to be siding with the Indonesians in his determination to honour his pledge to them, even if it meant opposing Mountbatten, Supreme Commander of SEAC, and the British Government, and antagonising the Governor-General of the NEI into the bargain.

Attlee's response brought Chifley no comfort. Although expressing sympathy with 'the difficult position' which had arisen, Attlee agreed with Mountbatten's view and insisted that his Government could not be party to any action which might aggravate the delicate position in Java and Sumatra, embarrass Christison and 'precipitate a crisis'.[34] Referring to his own difficulties in handling the Dutch over the NEI problem, he reiterated that the Indonesians should not be allowed to land in Java or Sumatra. He suggested that landing them in Dutch Timor or elsewhere in the NEI could be regarded as fulfilling the pledge to repatriate them to the NEI and that if challenged by the Indonesians, Australia could save face by attributing responsibility for the decision to the Allied Military Commander.[35]

Chifley must have been exasperated and frustrated by this response. Indeed his feelings were thinly veiled in his immediate reply to Attlee when he said in part —

> I do not wish to recapitulate the facts stated in my previous telegram and I note that you have not commented on them but have based your refusal on the grounds that it would embarrass you in handling difficult situation with the Dutch.[36]

By now, Chifley realised that he was getting nowhere and would have to compromise if he wanted to get any of the Indonesians home safely. He therefore reluctantly undertook to land in Timor, as a temporary measure, those Indonesians regarded by the Dutch (in agreement with the Australians) as 'extremists or dangerous,' anticipating that there would be no more than 100 in this category. 'I am not sure whether I can do this without serious trouble,' he wrote, 'but I shall endeavour to do so ...' However he was adamant that the remainder must be returned to their homeland (i.e. Java and Sumatra) and went on, 'In their own interests the Dutch would be well advised to accept this solution as any alternative will result in increased antagonism towards them in this country'.[37]

Tensions at Kupang

Escorted by HMAS *Arunta*, *Esperance Bay* sailed from Darwin for Kupang, Dutch Timor, on 25 October. The Australian Timor Force Commander in Kupang, Brigadier Dyke, had been instructed to make arrangements for the disembarkation of between 50 and 200 Indonesians – because no one was sure what the agreed number of extremists would be – and to ensure that those disembarked should not be penalised by the Dutch, treated as prisoners or discriminated against.[38] Of course at this stage the Indonesians themselves had not been told of these plans and indeed Plumb himself only knew that he had to proceed to Kupang and await further orders. Brigadier Dyke was not thrilled at the prospect of receiving any Indonesians, let alone 'extremists,' as there were food and accommodation shortages, and already troubles with a number of Indonesian servicemen who had rebelled against the Dutch and been confined by them on nearby Semau Island. He cabled Landforces in Melbourne to this effect, asking that the Indonesians not be landed in Kupang.[39]

Apparently this request was ignored, as when the *Esperance Bay* dropped anchor off Kupang on 27 October, Dyke went on board to discuss with Plumb the logistics of landing between 50-200 Indonesians, while they both waited for final orders from Canberra.[40] When those orders did arrive later that same night, they included a list of 44 alleged extremists who were to be landed before the ship proceeded to Surabaya. The events that followed must have been a nightmare for Plumb, exacerbated for him by an important omission in the planning of this first repatriation.

The oversight of not providing Plumb with an interpreter meant that in all his negotiations he had to depend on Indonesians with a good command of English. In so doing he was placed in the situation of having to give away information which he might normally have wanted to keep to himself. This proved to be the case on 28 October when he called for assistance in identifying the 44 people on the list, and was forced to inform his interpreters that these people were to be disembarked at Kupang. With the help of the Management Committee and sub-committee, in particular spokesman Vic Paath,[41] it was discovered that some people on the list were not even on board, some had never had any political involvement, and in some cases three people all had the same name.[42] One of the influential members of the sub-committee was Jim Lumanauw, (labelled by Plumb as a troublemaker), who wrote a report of the repatriation to Molly Warner. His account of Plumb's dilemma is as follows —

> Now he (Mr Plumb) was faced with a very knotty problem because it appeared several people had the same name. We were asked to co-operate and pick out the 'right persons' in order that the innocent people would not be victimised. It was naturally impossible for us to pick out the 'right persons' so Mr Plumb decided that the persons having identical names could stay on board till he received some more information about them. The original list of 44 was reduced to 20 the reason being the identical names and the persons whose names were called out but had never boarded the ship.[43]

It had been decided that the designated persons would be landed on 29 October, and at 11.00 hours they were told to assemble with their baggage. At the same time, 50 armed AMF personnel came on board in case of trouble. One man Salindeho, who was ill, was disembarked straight away, so that he could be admitted to the camp hospital at Kupang as soon as possible, while the remainder were given lunch on board prior to landing. To this point Plumb later described their attitude as 'reasonable and co-operative' with no serious objection to the disembarkation being voiced,[44] but this was soon to change as the next dramatic events unfolded. Jim Lumanauw gives a graphic account of the escalating tensions as the Indonesian sub-committee called an emergency meeting attended by almost all the passengers. This meeting passed a unanimous motion that if 19 men now had to go ashore everyone would go ashore. When Plumb was notified of this development he called a conference with the Indonesian committees. Lumanauw describes a 'heated debate' between Plumb and Vic Paath, who pointed out that the Australian Government had guaranteed 'ALL INDONESIANS' safe passage. Lumanauw told Plumb in plain words that the Indonesians did not want to be treated like cattle and that their decision was final- that is if 19 disembark they all disembark.[45] Plumb tried to explain that the decision had been taken at the behest of Mountbatten, and that as he was in charge of occupied areas his word was law.[46] While this debate was going on,

The First Repatriation

another 50 armed troops were boarded and 50 naval ratings stood by in reserve.

Brigadier Dyke clearly saw the situation as serious, reporting that evening to his superiors, 'It also became obvious that many of the passengers were armed,' and, 'Plumb explained again and again that their dissatisfaction was illogical and contrary to their own interests ... they remained adamant and demanded the ship either proceed to Sourabaya or return to Darwin ... direct threat to achieve their object if necessary by violence made to Plumb'.[47] Strangely Dyke did not clarify just how 'it became obvious' that many were armed, (in his later report Plumb stated that it was not known to what extent the passengers were armed) but he was not prepared to take any chances. He and Plumb made the decision that the ship would proceed to Surabaya with all passengers on board and informed the Indonesians. Dyke justified the decision saying —

> I did not authorise removal of 19 persons by force because it certainly would have caused a most serious outbreak of violence resulting inevitably in loss of life. I was not prepared to sacrifice lives of Australian soldiers.[48]

This may have been over-reaction on Dyke's part. The whole premise that the Indonesians were armed seems to have been based on one weapon being spotted in someone's possession when the Indonesians were embarking in Sydney. Neither in his nor in Plumb's reports is there any concrete evidence that these weapons existed, merely speculation. The allegation that so many of the passengers were allegedly carrying knives could be explained by the fact that many of them had been seamen for whom knives are tools of trade.

All the players in this drama, for their various reasons, must have been relieved when the *Esperance Bay*, accompanied by *Arunta*, sailed from Kupang at 7pm on the evening of 29 October, bound for Surabaya. The armed guard of 100 soldiers and 50 ratings from *Arunta* remained on board. Two days later, as the ship approached Surabaya, orders were received from SEAC that because of the serious fighting which had broken out there between the British and Republican troops, *Esperance Bay* could not berth and had to proceed to Jakarta. The Indonesians were informed of this development but they were not informed of the rest of the orders which were; on arrival, the ship was to anchor well off shore at Tanjung Priok, the Australian guard was to be reinforced, all Indonesians were to be disarmed, leaders and extremists were to be shipped back to Kupang and remaining Indonesians were to be landed.[49]

If Plumb thought carrying out these orders was a formidable task, he made no mention of it in his matter-of-fact report of what happened after *Esperance Bay* anchored as ordered off Tanjung Priok on 2 November. He said that after consultation with a British Field Security Officer who came on board, it was decided to start disembarking the passengers the next morning, with the exception of the 19 listed for Kupang plus Lumanauw, whom Plumb seems to have added to the list on his own initiative. 'When it became known that these 20 persons were not to be disembarked at Batavia,' he wrote, not mentioning how 'it became known,' 'a strong delegation declared that no Indonesians would leave the ship unless our decision was rescinded'.[50] When further discussion proved futile Plumb ordered the confinement of the 19, plus Lumanauw, while the remaining Indonesians were removed from the ship 'under duress,' and passed into the care of Republican authorities. The 'extremists' were transferred to *Arunta* for the voyage back to Kupang.[51] No mention was made of any attempt by Plumb to disarm the Indonesians as ordered, perhaps because there were no weapons after all or perhaps it was just too hard a task to attempt in the circumstances.

Jim Lumanauw, the target of Plumb's displeasure, gave a more dramatic version of what happened when the Indonesians realised that some were not being allowed to disembark. According to him the landings (passengers ferried ashore in Japanese submarine chasers) had already started when suspicions were aroused because Soehidjat, a member of the Management Committee whose name was on the list, was stopped as he joined the next group preparing to disembark. Plumb said that he wanted the Committee to go last of all because he needed some information from them. When another man whose name was on the list was stopped, it was no longer possible for Plumb to disguise his intentions. 'Now everything was clear,' wrote Lumanauw, 'the 19 men could not land in Batavia'.[52] Plumb was again told that all Indonesians should be landed or none would, whereupon he said he was following Mr Chifley's orders and could

The First Repatriation

do nothing about the situation. (Lumanauw wryly noted that earlier Plumb had claimed to be following Mountbatten's orders) Then, according to Lumanauw, under the pretext of inviting the leaders for further discussions, Plumb had them arrested and held in the orderly room by armed soldiers. As the landings continued at gunpoint, the remainder of the Kupang contingent were separated and joined them. 'Our resistance was broken by force,' said Lumanauw, 'and we were removed to the ship's jail,' a place that was, 'filthy and full of mosquitoes'. The next morning they were all transferred by barge to HMAS *Arunta*, where, despite poor accommodation, 'the captain did everything possible to make us as comfortable as possible and he and the rest of the crew were very sympathetic to us'.[53]

Thomas Stapleton's story

Through his duties in the sick bay, where he alleges many of the passengers were ill with what they called 'woman sick (VD), Stapleton spent a lot of time with the Indonesians and got to know them well. He claimed that he knew a lot of what was going on aboard ship because, being a teetotaler, he swapped his beer ration with Plumb, whom he neither liked nor respected, in exchange for the gist of all his coded telegrams. His version of the above events is very dramatic indeed with the claim, 'I am probably the only person who knows the full story as I had the confidence of the ships' officers, the representatives of the Department of External Affairs and the Indonesians'.[54] The gist of Stapleton's story was that Plumb decided the Kupang party would be separated from the others by force and arrested, and Indian troops would be put on the ship to effect this. The troops would come on board early the next morning (presumably so they would not be seen) and take up positions at the head of the gangways. Then the names of the required men (who were confined in the orderly room) would be called over the ship's loudspeaker at half hourly intervals and asked to come on deck. If they had not complied by 10am the Indian troops were to seize them by force, even if this meant shooting. Stapleton claimed that the evening before this plan was to take effect he went down below and brought Lumanauw and Soedijat up on deck and told them everything. 'It was an emotional scene- at the end of an hour all three had tears pouring down our faces,' said Stapleton. Apparently discretion prevailed and the Indonesians undertook that half a minute before the deadline for force to be implemented, they would come up the gangway. And that is what happened – they came up one by one and were arrested.[55]

Whichever of these accounts we choose to believe, the end result was the same – Dutch interference influenced Mountbatten and prevented the Australian Government from repatriating all of the Indonesians in accordance with its undertaking to them, and 27 (including the wife and children of one 'extremist', Ilias Jacoub) found themselves taken back, against their will, to Timor. The men were kept on Semau Island, off-shore from Kupang, with all their essential needs catered for by the Australian Timor Force while Ilias Jacoub and his family stayed in the town. The Acting-Secretary of the Department of External Affairs wrote in a memo to the Department of the Army, that they had been placed on Semau Island necessarily, but nevertheless in breach of an assurance unable to be fulfilled on account of political and other conditions.[56] It was awareness of this breach that made the Australian authorities determined that the Indonesians would be well looked after and their sojourn in Timor would be as brief as possible before ultimately they too would be repatriated to Republican Java.

The Indonesian Republican authorities were also aware of the broken pledge, as became clear when a message was received by W. Mac Mahon Ball, Australian Political Representative to the NEI, from Subardjo, self-styled Foreign Minister of the Indonesian Republic, expressing gratitude for the repatriation itself, but indignation at the detention of the 27, with a request for an explanation for this 'inhumane illegal action'.[57] Ball's instructions from Canberra were to explain personally and informally that the only way to ensure the landing of the majority had been to return the 27 to Kupang where they would be under Australian control and returned to Java as soon as possible.[58]

When, in January 1946, plans were underway to withdraw Timforce, and hand Timor over to Dutch authority again, the fate of the 'extremists' was of paramount importance to the Australians. When SEAC suggested that the Indonesians be simply handed over

The First Repatriation

to the Dutch, the idea was firmly rejected by External Affairs, and by Mr Calwell, who declared, 'I would bring these people back to Darwin rather than follow the expedient course ... of surrendering them back to the Dutch'.[59] Eventually, in May, they were transferred to Labuan, a small island that was part of then British North Borneo. After a brief stay there and then in Singapore they finally arrived in Jakarta, despite all the efforts of the Dutch to prevent this, and were handed over safely to Republican authorities on 23 July 1946, a little over eight months after the other *Esperance Bay* repatriates.[60]

The Australian press had a field day with the *Esperance Bay* affair. A prime example of the hyperbole which marked much of the reporting was Ronald Monson's extraordinary claim in the *Daily Telegraph* (5.11.1945) that, 'Fourteen hundred Indonesians being repatriated from Australia in the liner *Esperance Bay* produced hidden arms and dominated the ship'. The *Sun* (5.11.1945) reported 'risk of murder' and the possibility of 'terrific bloodshed,' had the Indonesians attempted to take the ship. On 6 November the *Sydney Morning Herald* reported claims by the leader of the Australian Country Party, Mr Fadden, that 'big stocks of arms' were taken on board by the Indonesians, claims dismissed as 'mischievous, misguided and ill-informed' by the Acting-Minister for External affairs, Mr Makin. The debate continued over the next few days, with Government spokesmen playing down all suggestions of mutiny or danger to any of the ship's personnel and praising the success of the operation, while Mr Fadden continued to claim the opposite and demand an investigation into the affair. By 9 November reports were circulating from the London *Daily Mail* correspondent in Jakarta claiming that ship's officers from the *Esperance Bay* described a 'nightmare voyage,' and denying Australian claims that the Indonesians had been 'co-operative.' (*Sun*, 9.11.1945). The *Tribune* (9 November) took another tack and reported the 'victimisation' of the detained Indonesians, for which it blamed Mountbatten, and praised the 'courageous diplomatic action' of the Australian Government in repatriating the Indonesians and attempting to safeguard them against Dutch reprisals.

This praise was merited, despite the piecemeal way the repatriation was implemented. Mistakes were made, probably due to the speed with which the operation was put together because the

*Indonesians from Esperance Bay on their return home.
Photo: Album Perjuangan Kemerdekaan 1945-50.*

Government wanted to move all of the Indonesians out of Australia as quickly as possible. Sending the *Esperance Bay* on its way before a firm decision about an acceptable disembarkation point had been negotiated compounded Mr Plumb's difficulties, as did the lack of an interpreter. Failure to search the baggage of the passengers provided ammunition for those wishing to discredit the Indonesians and the Government with the accusations about hidden weapons. But the fact remains that the Australian Government did show great moral courage in standing up to Mountbatten and the British Prime Minister in order to keep its pledge and safely land almost all of the 1,400 Indonesians in Republican territory. Even when a compromise was unavoidable, the people detained at Kupang were not abandoned to the Dutch.

In its bulletin *Civil Liberty* (December 1945), the Australian Council for Civil Liberties praised the 'generosity and promptness' of the Commonwealth Government in repatriating the Republicans despite 'a difficult and delicate situation' and spoke of its own role as liaison organization between the seamen and Mr Calwell who modestly commented —

> I think it is a case of honours shared rather than applause being offered to one who for the time being was vested with Ministerial authority and responsibility ... All the officers of my department in all ports affected, and in the national capital, were strongly imbued with the desire to do the right thing by Australia, the Indonesians and our Dutch ally.

However, any sigh of relief Australian authorities may have breathed in expectation that the departure of 1,400 rebels would mark the end of their troubles with the Indonesians and the Dutch, proved to be premature. There were still plenty of difficulties to come.

9

Turbulent Times

The departure of 1,400 Indonesians on the *Esperance Bay* may have greatly reduced their numbers in Australia, but this was not the end of the story. Those remaining, and their growing numbers of supporters, continued to challenge Dutch authority with ongoing pro-Republic propaganda and acts of defiance and rebellion. At the same time the Australian Government found itself increasingly out of step with the Dutch, particularly concerning their methods of dealing with their troublesome 'subjects,' and their expectations of the help of Australian authorities in doing so. All this continued to provide the press with opportunities for more of the sensationalist reporting which had become the norm when dealing with Indonesian affairs.

Bashings in Bundaberg

A prime example of press exaggeration occurred when late in October 1945, in the north Queensland town of Bundaberg, allegations began circulating that Indonesian members of the NEI forces at the Dutch base at Bundaberg aerodrome had refused duty and had been either 'shot at,' 'bashed,' 'wounded,' bludgeoned,' or just 'manhandled,' while being placed onto a plane for removal – depending on which Sydney newspaper was reporting. At the same time it was claimed that RAAF men at the aerodrome had themselves gone on strike in protest at this treatment and refused to work for the Dutch.[1]

The local paper, the *Bundaberg News Mail* (27.10.45) presented a more tempered account of events. The Dutch Commanding Officer, Colonel van Haselen said that 10 of the Javanese had come to him a few days previously announcing that they did not want to work any more, and wished to leave the camp and go back to Java. Because they were under military law the CO undertook to send a cable to

Jakarta to ask if they could be released. When no reply was forthcoming the Indonesians went on strike and were arrested. 'During the arrests,' said the CO, 'a struggle ensued and some men were injured,' but he denied bashings and shootings. The prisoners, including the wounded, were put on a plane and sent to Victory Camp at Casino.

Perhaps the most imaginative version of events was that of Mr James Harris of the Bundaberg branch of the CPA. 'Australian RAAF men stopped working when they saw the brutality of the Dutch,' he said. 'The Dutch kicked and beat with batons the small gallant lovers of their country, bundling them into a plane where further brutality can be carried out'.[2]

Fairly predictable claims and counter claims about what really happened were reported over the next couple of days. An RAAF inquiry found that the RAAF men had not gone on strike, but they did resent the 'high handed attitude' of the Dutch toward the Indonesians. As for the violence itself, the only admission made by the Dutch CO was that when the Indonesians struggled and refused to enter the plane, they were dragged on board and contrary to his orders, one was hit behind the knees with a baton.[3]

Unsurprisingly the whole incident was soon being blamed on the Communists, firstly because they had allegedly influenced the Indonesians to strike in the first place, and secondly because they had exaggerated the whole story of the 'bashings' in the interests of anti-Dutch propaganda. The Mackay *Daily Mercury* (29.10.1945) noted that even the Javanese admitted that reports claiming they had been 'bludgeoned and bashed on a plane,' were grossly exaggerated. The *Bundaberg News Mail* (30.10.1945) made similar allegations of exaggeration by the Communists, but strangely none against the Sydney press which had published the embellished story in the first place. In its editorial, the *News Mail* concluded that the 'rebellion' had only been a small affair and that the 'more intelligent' Indonesians, who 'wisely listened to their commander' went about their business normally.[4] Whatever the truth of the matter, Bundaberg had become another Australian 'hot spot' where Dutch authority was challenged by Indonesian servicemen, and some of the local community, particularly members of the CPA, supported their cause.

Solidarity on the waterfront

With so many Indonesian seamen now repatriated, and most of those still remaining in the major ports on strike, the Dutch had to do something to obtain crews for their ships. Their solution was to employ Indian lascars, brought into Australia and transferred from British to Dutch control for this purpose.[5] But what the Dutch did not foresee was that the Indians, also subjects of a European colonial power, would throw in their lot with the Indonesians attempting to rid themselves of colonial rule. On 30 October *Tribune* claimed that Indian seamen had brought about a complete boycott of Dutch ships in Sydney, when 40 of them walked off the Dutch ship *Pahud*, in support of Indonesian independence. Through their newly established Indian Seamen's Union, they also demanded equitable pay and working conditions for themselves. Rupert Lockwood gives a stirring account of the hardships suffered by the penniless Indians who walked off their ships, and of daring escapes some made in launches from ships actually under way. There was even a full-scale mutiny when the Indian stokers and engine room crew cut off the steam of one ship, *Patras*, which had left Sydney and was actually in the Tasman Sea en route for Jakarta when this happened. (When she was leaving Sydney Harbour, *Patras* had been pursued by a launchful of unionists, Australian and Indian, who tried to persuade the Indian crew to mutiny) As the ship wallowed in the swell, the Indians agreed to raise steam again, but only enough to turn about and return back to Sydney. On arrival they immediately walked off the ship and joined the other strikers.[6]

Showing defiance and going on strike was one thing, but with their employers, not unreasonably from their point of view, now refusing to pay them, the striking Indonesians and Indians found themselves in a desperate financial situation. They were in part rescued from this by Australian supporters, among whom were two staunch members of the CPA, Phyllis Johnson and her husband John.

Phyllis and Johnno Johnson's story

The Johnsons werte proud members of the Communist party who worked as volunteers helping coloured seamen who were housed at the Mission for Seamen in George Street, Sydney. Here they came into contact with striking Indian seamen and met Clarrie

Campbell, their union's treasurer.[7] One of the prominent Indian activists and supporters of the Indonesians was Danny Singh and it was he who alerted the Johnsons to the fact that there was an Indian crewed Dutch ship which was carrying war materials. Phyllis' graphic account of the incident goes like this —

Danny Singh came in (to the Mission) and said 'There's a ship at Ball's Point and the Indian seamen are very concerned about this ship which was loading war materials to go to Indonesia to maintain Dutch rule'. It was a dreadful night, it was raining and blowing and we went over to Ball's Point. Because it was an 'Indian' (crewed) ship I sat on the wharf drenched with rain and John went on the ship. Then up they came with their prayer mats. I found a phone in the middle of the night and rang my sister-in-law's brother, a carrier and he came and picked up the seamen and took them to a coloured seamen's establishment in Harris Street.

This marked the beginning of the Johnsons' wholehearted embrace of the cause of Indonesian independence (and later Indian independence from the British) and threw themselves into the fray.[8] They both became passionate soap-box orators at the Domain, and participated in any pro-Indonesian demonstrations that took place around town. Phyllis used to make her way along the wharves where Dutch ships were tied up trying to incite crews to strike by shouting through a megaphone, '*Merdeka*! Indonesia calling! Walk off the ship! Support Indonesian Independence!' She was so successful that the Mission for Seamen was soon overcrowded with Indian, Papuan and Chinese seamen all striking in support of the Indonesians. Lack of adequate shelter and food became an increasingly serious problem, which led 60 striking Indonesian seamen to try to gain entry to the Belvedere Hostel in Darlinghurst. Three lorries loaded with the 60 Indonesians, their cabin trunks, and two Australian trade union representatives, pulled up at the hostel on the evening of 27 October. The Australians asked for accommodation for the Indonesians but

Without other accommodation available, the striking Indonesian crew of the Dutch "hospital" ship Tasman, took up quarters at the Dutch company's hostel, The Lido, North Sydney. The ship was suspected of carrying munitions and the crew refused to sail.
Photo: Tribune, 2 November 1945.

the Dutch person in charge refused on the grounds that the hostel was already filled to capacity. A request for the Indonesians to occupy the verandah was also refused. The police were called and the Indonesians were persuaded to leave, disappearing into the night in the lorries that had brought them. As a precaution, the iron gates of the hostel were tied shut and a police guard stayed on duty overnight, but there were no further incidents at the Belvedere.[9]

However this refusal led to the next 'raid' on Dutch territory, and this time the Johnsons were in the thick of it. At intervals during the last few days in October, trucks carrying small parties of striking Indonesian and Indian seamen and their belongings, together with some Australian supporters, had started arriving at the Lido, the KPM hostel in Walker Street, North Sydney where it was assumed that there was now plenty of vacant space following the departure of the first repatriates. It was here therefore that the men refused entry to the Belvedere headed. As was the norm with Indonesian-related events at this time, the details of what happened next vary. Phyllis Johnson's version was that the Dutch in the hostel, some of whom were armed, were 'kicked out.' There were various stand-offs between hastily summoned Dutch reinforcements and Australian unionists, while the Dutch manager called in the North Sydney police to evict the intruders.[10] But because it turned out that someone in the Lido had actually given the 'invaders' a key, the police said that as no forcible entry had taken place, they had no power of eviction.[11] However it happened, the upshot was that over 200 Indonesians and Indians installed themselves and took over the Lido.

Now that they had a roof over their heads, the next problem was feeding the strikers, and here the Johnsons played a leading role. Phyllis became a skilled fund-raiser as she set off each day by tram, bus or train, with some of the 'coloured' seamen, and targeted places such as the Chullora Railway Worshops, and factories all over Sydney to ask for donations. She often received 'dirty looks' and racist comments from members of the public on these excursions. She used to address the workers during their breaks to explain why the seamen were on strike, and described as 'magnificent,' their response to what she called 'a tremendously important working class struggle.' Johnno Johnson turned his hand to becoming the providore, learning how to cater for the dietary laws of his 'clients' according to their respective religions and to ensure that meat and poultry were slaughtered correctly to comply with Muslim rites. A team of Australian helpers, including the ever-present and loyal Laura Gapp who worked in the kitchen, became accustomed to the hot curries beloved by their Indonesian and Indian friends. The Johnsons and others continued to provide this vital help right up to the time the Indonesians were all eventually repatriated.

Strange goings-on in North Sydney

Whilst this camaraderie was played out inside the Lido, some unfavourable stories about arcane practices at the hostel appeared in the press. On 17 November a bizarre report appeared in the *Daily Telegraph* about the Indonesians' neighbours in Alfred Street, North Sydney complaining that women and children had been frightened by Indonesians appearing in the street dressed as 'ghosts'. No explanation of this phenomenon was forthcoming. But that was not all. Other complaints were that they had —

> Killed roosters by scraping their throats in accordance with Indonesian religious rites; played weird Eastern music 'like banging on a tin can' (still the way some Westerners describe *gamelan* music) until the early hours of the morning; left large garbage cans which gave off an offensive odour at the back of the premises.

Such stories did not endear the seamen to the good citizens of North Sydney. Subsequently, the *Sydney Morning Herald* (20.11.45) reported that the Chief Inspector of North Sydney Council declared the Lido a 'menace to health,' and accordingly the lessees, KPM, had been handed a notice to vacate the building. This they were naturally unable to do because the strikers would not leave. However, at a Council meeting to discuss the problem, the Mayor of North Sydney described the presence of the Indonesians and Indians at the Lido as 'almost a political matter and one bristling with difficulties'.[12] This was an astute observation that went beyond the health problem to the heart of the matter. It may be the reason the council relented, because instead of vacating, KPM was ordered to supply sufficient garbage bins and adequate sanitation facilities, 'for the preservation of public health and decency'. KPM must have complied because the Indonesians stayed at the Lido until they were repatriated.

Mutual irritation

The Lido and Belvedere incidents, and an apparently similar situation in Brisbane where striking Indonesians who also had nowhere else to go 'invaded' Camp Columbia, became the triggers for another round of bickering between Australian and NEI officials at the highest levels. On 29 October, the Netherlands Minister, Baron van Aerssen made 'strenuous representations' for Commonwealth action against the Indonesians, whom he accused of breaking into hostels in Sydney and Brisbane, and menacing Dutch property and personnel. He wanted Australian Military Authorities to evict the trespassers by force.[13] But the relevant Australian authorities found that the Brisbane and Sydney police had received no reports of threats or violence which would bear out the Baron's allegations, and in any case they were averse to calling out the military in a civil matter in peacetime.[14] The Baron would not have been pleased when the Acting Minister for External Affairs notified him that there were no grounds for taking the steps he requested, and concluded —

> It concerns me that you are apparently receiving reports of doubtful accuracy or reports which are inadequate. Such create much unnecessary work in Netherlands and Australian quarters and sometimes irritation which we would both wish to avoid. They can only make more difficult our day to day relations which we would both desire to be marked by harmony.[15]

Neither side backed down from their stances on this particular issue as the verbal scrapping continued for the next couple of months. Nor was there any sign of softening in the attitude of the Dutch towards the Indonesians who disobeyed them, or any concern for their welfare. The Dutch washed their hands of them and left it to Australian Government to either look after the strikers or deport them. An undated confidential Australian Government report from the Department of External Affairs about Australian-Dutch relations 1945-1946, listed this matter of 'Indonesians in Dutch Establishments' as one of the causes (among many) of the deterioration in those relations and asserted —

> ... the Netherlands Minister was informed, *inter alia*, that in Australia it is not customary to call out the military in aid of civil power where the latter provides all reasonable remedies. In the issues under discussion there existed such remedies as ejectment proceedings, but these the Dutch Authorities appeared unwilling to take, apparently feeling that the circumstances called for a show of military force against the Indonesians. It has invariably been impossible to bring Dutch officials round to realise that Australian administration acts must conform with Australian law. In the present and other contexts they have sought military action which could only have been improperly undertaken.[16]

In fact, following the Indonesian declaration of independence on 17 August the actions of the Indonesians were like a series of spot fires breaking out and spreading from a major conflagration. As the Dutch struggled to control or extinguish these fires their methods often came into conflict with Australian practice, leading to an ever-widening rift between the two authorities. The fanning of the flames by the sensationalist reporting of the Australian press did not help matters.

The Stirling Castle incident

In November another demonstration put Indonesians and their Australian supporters back in the spotlight. On 4 November, 1,600 Dutch troops arrived in Sydney aboard the British ship, *Stirling Castle*. They had boarded in Liverpool, England, and were heading for Java presumably to be used against the Indonesian rebels. The *Sydney Morning Herald* (5.11.1945) leaked the fact that these troops had originally been destined for training in Brisbane but now were not allowed to land because the Commonwealth Government had rejected proposals to train Dutch troops in Australia.[17]

Having been alerted to the presence of these troops, a party of Indonesians from the Indonesian Independence Committee in Sydney acquired a launch and some loudhailers and that same afternoon approached the *Stirling Castle* and the nearby Dutch hospital ship, *Tjitjalengka*. A spokesman, Raymond Moningka, shouted in Dutch to the soldiers and sailors, 'You are going to Java to fight against people who have not had right treatment, according to the promise of Queen Wilhelmina in December 1942'.[18] The response of his audience was to drown him and other speakers out by loudly singing patriotic songs and the Dutch national anthem, and pelting the launch with bottles and tins.[19]

Undeterred, or perhaps provoked by this, two days later Australian activists staged a major pro-Republic demonstration at No. 8 Woolloomooloo Wharf, where *Stirling Castle* was berthed. The course the demonstration took can be gauged by the headlines: 'Dutch Troops Hose Crowd on Wharf ... Women Get Wet, Scream, Swear' (*Daily Mirror* 7.11.1945); 'Dutch and Reds in Wharf Riot' (*Sun* 7.11.1945); 'Bottles Thrown in Wharf Riot' *(Daily Telegraph* 8.11.1945); 'Communists Hosed by Dutch troops' (*Adelaide Advertiser* 8.11.1945) 'Mob

Riot in Sydney- Waterside Workers Attack Dutch Troops' (*The Age* 8.11.1945); 'Hostile Crowd Hosed and Pelted by Dutch Troops (*Sydney Morning Herald* 8.11.1945).

The demonstrators obviously came off second best. According to the police version of events a group of people gathered at the entrance to No. 8 wharf forced their way past the guard and gained admittance. They then opened the gates and let 200-250 demonstrators through. The leaders started calling to the troops on board *Stirling Castle* not to fight the Indonesians, and using 'abusive and insulting' language to the Dutch Provosts, with one woman allegedly throwing a piece of wood at one of them and knocking off his hat. The troops retaliated as they had the previous day by throwing missiles at the crowd and this time Wallace Dawson, 'a known Communist' was hit by a bottle, and Daisy Young of Bondi, another 'known Communist' was struck by a plate.[20] The climax came when the troops turned the ship's hoses on the demonstrators who, as Phyllis Johnson recalled, 'were soaked to the skin'. 'Young women screamed as the water soaked their flimsy dresses and men with dripping faces shook their fists angrily,' said the *Daily Telegraph* (8.11.1945). Contrary to newspaper reports, the police did not mention any brawls nor did they claim that the incident, which they strongly suspected was organised by the Communists, had turned into a 'riot.' In fact they noted that by the time a squad of police arrived the disturbance had cooled down and 'no names were taken.'

The *'Stirling Castle* Incident' was also mentioned in the Commonwealth Government's report on the deterioration of Australian-Dutch Relations which insisted that it was Dutch Army Headquarters which had not allowed the Dutch troops to land in Sydney. However, statements attributed to Dutch officials had twisted the truth and made it appear that the order came from Australian authorities. The document commented —

> The Stirling Castle incident has been thrown out of proper perspective partly by Dutch press statements made at the time and partly by the activities of unstable elements who visited the Sydney wharves when the ship was alongside and there staged demonstrations against the troops in a manner which came close to hooliganism.[21]

Red faces and Radio Australia

As if the Government was not having enough problems with the press, the Opposition, the shipping bans and the Dutch in its handling of Indonesian matters in these turbulent final months of 1945, in November one of its own organs, Radio Australia, was responsible for causing it considerable embarrassment. During the war years, the Radio Australia shortwave service had been used as a medium of propaganda by NIGIS in its Dutch and Indonesian language broadcasts to Java. Theoretically the broadcasts were under the authority of the Department of External Affairs, but in fact NIGIS had control of the programs, basically because none of the Australian staff spoke Dutch or Indonesian.[22] The content of the broadcasts was devoted largely to promoting the then consensus between the Australian and NEI governments that the Dutch would resume control of their colony when the Japanese were defeated, because they were the rightful rulers. By the time the war ended control of the shortwave service was back in the hands of the Department of Information under the authority of the Department of External Affairs and as such was a medium to reflect government policy. But by now on the matter of Indonesia's bid for independence, not all ministers in the government were united about what that policy should be. Chifley, maintaining the Government's official policy of neutrality, was trying to keep the peace between Mr Calwell, who was in favour of the reinstatement of Dutch rule, and Dr Evatt who was trying to mediate between the Indonesians and the Dutch and gain Dutch support for his bid to gain presidency of the General Assembly of the United Nations.

The acting controller of Radio Australia at the time of the embarrassing incident was Geoffrey Sawer, a lecturer seconded from the Law School at the University of Melbourne. He claimed that late in 1945 Evatt told him in confidence that the Americans were supplying weapons to the Dutch (after removing American markings), and so should be criticised for this, but without offending General MacArthur. The best way to do this, said Evatt, would be for Australia to propose that the great powers agree on some policy about Indonesia which provided for the rapid development of self-government for the Indonesians. Accordingly Sawer and another writer, Michael Keon, prepared some scripts along the lines suggested, although no mention was made about the Americans supplying arms to the Dutch.

Three broadcasts (one to America and two to Asia) had been made before they came to the attention of the Government. The first, by Geoffrey Sawer on 5 November, gave an account of the *Esperance Bay* repatriation and justified the Government's actions in keeping the repatriates out of Dutch hands saying,' ... Australia cannot be blind to the fact that 40 (sic) million Indonesians in our near north may well, in the long run, be more important to our security ... than the few thousand Dutch who have hitherto controlled that area'.[23] But even more provocative was the this —

> Moreover, a Labor Government in Australia is necessarily influenced by conceptions of emancipation and advance to self-government of subject people ... there is a certain element of hypocrisy in the policy towards Indonesia which has hitherto been followed by all the great powers ... The US has attempted like Pontius Pilate to wash its hands of the matter ...[24]

A further comment that the United States was in practice underwriting the policy pursued by Lord Louis Mountbatten prompted a protest message some days later from Mountbatten himself.[25] The extremely embarrassed Prime Minister immediately apologized to Mountbatten and repudiated the broadcasts asserting that they did not represent Australian Government policy.

Sawer was summoned to Canberra for a meeting with Chifley, Evatt and Calwell. When he told Chifley that Evatt had led him to believe there was an Australian view about Indonesia and that it was up to the short-wave service to convey it, Evatt remained silent and gave no sign that he had had a hand in instigating the offending broadcasts. Chifley accused Sawer of trying to construct a policy which did not exist. The meeting concluded with both men agreeing amiably that Sawer should return to Melbourne University at end of the year and Sawer was instructed not to mention Indonesia and the Dutch again in any of his broadcasts.[26] The *Argus* (17.11.1945) satirised this incident with a cartoon depicting Chifley asking Calwell, 'By the way Arthur, what is our policy on Indonesia?' Clutching a file labelled 'Keon-Sawer Broadcasts' and scratching his head in bewilderment Calwell replies, 'Oh there you have me!'

The Hilversum broadcast

It was not only a broadcast emanating from Australia that caused chagrin and embarrassment to the Australian Government at this time, but also one from the Netherlands. Norman Makin, Acting Minister for External Affairs contacted Van Aerssen on 7 November complaining about a broadcast on Netherlands Radio Hilversum about the deterioration of Australian-Dutch relations and the lack of co-operation from the Australian Government.[27] Defending his government's conduct in relation to the *Esperance Bay* repatriation, the Indonesians and Netherlands establishments, and the *Stirling Castle* incident, which had all been condemned in the Hilversum broadcast, Makin stressed the Australian Government's preparedness to co-operate with the Dutch, but insisted that this readiness to co-operate had not obtained the results it should have. In particular he claimed that Netherlands officials did not take account of limiting factors and often showed impatience when a request could not be met. He also voiced his concern that some Netherlands officials did not use the correct channels of communication with the Australian Government and tended to exaggerate the gravity of particular sets of circumstances. Makin concluded —

> These things which are becoming so characteristic of the approach made by Netherlands officials to their day-to-day problems in this country do not make for smooth relations ... Our anxiety that there should be a lasting solution of present problems is no less than your own since the security and welfare of Australia depend so directly upon a settlement being reached ... I think that if this fact is kept in mind, the need for me to revert to the matter of our relations need not again arise.[28]

But as long as each side continued to consider itself in the right in any disagreement that arose, there was little hope that there would be any improvement in relations.

Unfinished business

While these embarrassing episodes were taking place, CENKIM was focussing its energy on getting the remaining Indonesians home. In a letter to the Prime Minister on 8 November, Secretary Bondan (now assisted by Molly Warner who had moved to Brisbane to work for the Republic) estimated that there were still approximately one and a half thousand Indonesians in Australia, comprising civilians plus militia and regular Army personnel who were refusing to work for the Dutch. (He made no mention of striking seamen in his calculations) Bondan pointed out the difficult conditions under which these people were living either from their own dwindling resources or at Australian Government expense and asked the Prime Minister to provide a second repatriation ship as soon as possible.[29] This letter was followed by another on 22 November, asking that a trade union representative be permitted to travel on any such ship to ensure that there was no repeat of the *Esperance Bay* situation when Dutch interference led to the enforced landings at Kupang. Can we detect Molly's English 'officialese' language skills at work in this excerpt? —

> We feel that prior to the departure of the next ship it would be well if the situation were clarified with respect to a guarantee that the agreement to return all aboard the ship to their homeland be carried out. This would imply that the question is one between the Australian Authorities and the Indonesians, and the Dutch would have no say in the matter, nor would any power other than the Australian Government and the Indonesians concerned.[30]

But at this stage, despite efforts to procure one, there was no ship available, and it was to be another three months before there was one.

A turbulent three months

The 3 short months since the proclamation of the Indonesian Republic, had been marked by an incredible amount of political activity by Indonesian nationalists and their supporters in Australia. Most of the action had taken place on the eastern seaboard where the Indonesians were concentrated. There was apparently some activity in Western Australia too, evidenced by a security services report about a meeting held in Perth on 21 November for the purpose of 'forming an organisation to assist in setting Indonesia up as a free sovereign state'.[31] About 200 people attended and apologies were received from a diverse range of people including clergymen, union representatives, a state politician and some individuals, some of whom sent along donations of money for the cause. The speakers came from the same range of people with the addition of some returned soldiers, and a resolution was taken to form a 'Hands Off Indonesia' committee. As was common in such reports, the investigating officer identified most of the individuals concerned, including the clergymen, as communists or 'communistically inclined'.[32] However union support in the west for the Indonesians was by no means unanimous. *Tribune* (18 Jan 1946) reported with disgust that when one of the Dutch ships which had been boycotted in Sydney sailed to Western Australia with a volunteer crew the West Australia Executive of the Labor Party instructed waterside workers to load it, which they did. This led the President of the WWF in Sydney to comment scornfully that the Western Australian Executive of the Labor Party had the distinction of being the only section of the Labor Movement in the world to help Dutch imperialism.

In suburban Sydney, someone else who did not support the Indonesians was Mr Osmond from Bondi who was doing some investigating of his own. In a letter to the authorities he reported that almost nightly a party of two to seven Indonesians gathered in rooms at the same address as his in Ebly Street, where the conversations he overheard revealed 'definite anti-British sentiment' and frequent 'subversive speech'. Indeed, Mr Osmond reported, 'some of the Indonesians who frequent this place openly brag that they are wholeheartedly in agreement with the extremist leader Soekarno'. Presumably these overheard conversations must have been in English for the eavesdropping Mr Osmond to understand them, whereas he would have had trouble with the short wave broadcasts from Java that he said were 'hungrily listened to nightly, followed by excited discussion in native tongues'.[33]

The last Sydney demonstration for the year was brought on by the desperate economic plight of the striking seamen – a few remaining Indonesians and the majority Indian. These were the occupants of the Lido to whom the Dutch would neither pay back-money owed nor provide any financial support in their present predicament. On 18 December, in desperation, nearly 300 of them, plus some union supporters, marched across the Harbour Bridge and stormed the office of their erstwhile employers, KPM, in George Street. The men demanded that some of the money owed them be handed over and deducted from their pay books. If the *Sydney Morning Herald* (19.12.1945) report was accurate, it must have been a chaotic scene when, 'jabbering in their native tongue and throwing their arms about, the men invaded every part of the office and ground floor ... girl clerks screamed and attempted to escape as wooden partitions were smashed down'. A conference which was hastily arranged between the demonstrators and some KPM officials, 'resolved itself into a babel of foreign tongues during which the coloured men were in a state of hysteria'. When the conference broke down, police took control of the situation and addressed the crowd through an interpreter, telling them to leave quietly as 'the big police boss' was carrying out the law. An agreement was made for some of the men's representatives to meet the KPM manager later, but they were told (by the company) that it would not be legal to give them any money, and the only result of their effort appears to have been more negative publicity in the press. No matter what the strikers did the Dutch were determined not to open the purse strings.

Developments in Indonesia

In Indonesia itself, momentous changes had taken place in this period. In September 1945, when Van der Plas arrived back in Jakarta aboard the first British ship to reach Java after the war, he had little appreciation of these changes and was eager to go ashore and pick up where he had left off before his evacuation to Australia. Commenting on this in later years, Laurens van der Post, a senior British officer who had been a prisoner of war and on release found himself in Jakarta and had met the ship, recalled hearing a broadcast Van der Plas made from Australia, shortly after the Japanese surrender. Commenting on this broadcast Van der Post said —

> What he had to say made me feel that he was speaking from a totally different planet. It was incomprehensible and frightening because the gist of it was that soon the Dutch and their allies would be back in Batavia to deal with all the 'war criminals' who had collaborated with the Japanese, to hang 'traitors' like the nationalists Soekarno and Hatta, and to restore Java and its chain of islands to the peace, prosperity and happiness that they

had enjoyed under the Dutch before the war. There seemed to be no suspicion on the part of Dr van der Plas that the Dutch presence in the old pre-war form would be unwanted in Indonesia and that everywhere the peoples of those islands were rising in revolt ... against any hint that the Dutch might come back as the lords and masters they had been for so many centuries.[34]

Writing to the Department of External affairs on 21 November, the Australian political representative in Jakarta, Mr MacMahon Ball, described the breakdown of law and order in the city, with increasing shooting and violence in the streets, particularly between the nationalists and the pro-Dutch Ambonese forces.[35] In other parts of Java, notably Surabaya, violent clashes had taken place between Indonesians and British forces, while in Eastern Indonesia (Timor, Dutch New Guinea, Kalimantan and Sulawesi) Australian troops were engaged in disarming the Japanese and establishing and maintaining law and order until the Dutch arrived. Their operations brought them into contact with the Republicans and led to support, both moral and practical, from some, but by no means all, of the troops.

There were changes too in the Republic's organisational structure when in November a new cabinet was formed, headed by the moderate Sutan Sjahrir as Prime Minister, while Soekarno continued as President and Head of State. The Republic hoped that this cabinet might be a more acceptable negotiating body to the Dutch and other parties than the Soekarno-Hatta cabinet because Sjahrir had worked underground during the war and therefore had never been tainted by any charges of collaboration with the Japanese.[36]

Australian opinions

Meanwhile, on the diplomatic and political front, the Australian Government's attitude to the question of Indonesian independence and the NEI had to this point been marked by apparent inconsistencies. Whilst maintaining that it was strictly neutral in a matter that should be left to the two protagonists to solve, nevertheless its actions, or in some cases lack of actions, suggested covert sympathy for the Indonesian cause. The refusal to train the Dutch troops, the refusal to intervene in the black bans, the handling of the first repatriation and determination to protect the Indonesians against Dutch recriminations for their political stance, together with the numerous bureaucratic spats with the Dutch over all manner of Indonesian-related issues all confirmed this impression. On the other hand, the Federal Opposition was totally consistent in its condemnation of the Republic and all who supported it.

And what effect did all of these events have on Australian public opinion? In December 1945 a national opinion poll was taken which showed that 60% of the population had actually read about the situation in the NEI in the press. Of these 41% favoured Dutch rule for the reason that the Dutch had done a good job and the Indonesians were not yet ready for self-government. Indonesian self-rule was favoured by 29% for the reason that the Indonesians had been exploited and 'self government is the right of all people,' 13% favoured joint rule and 17% had no opinion.[37] Clearly at this stage support for the Republic was not wide-spread among the Australian public and was confined to particular interest groups and individuals. If the Australian press coverage of incidents involving Indonesians in Australia and the independence issue itself formed the basis for public opinion, the minority support for the Indonesian cause demonstrated by this poll result was not really surprising.[38]

10

New Year, New Challenges

The year 1946 brought with it mounting aggravation for Dutch authorities as Indonesians found more ways to defy them. Early in the year there was another repatriation marked by controversy, and there were some unexpected developments on the waterfront. The Government continued to be the target of Opposition criticism for its failure to end the shipping bans, while its relationship with Dutch authorities deteriorated even further. The first anniversary of the proclamation of independence was a significant reminder that there was no turning back for the Republic.

Tit for tat

Despite their frustration with the Dutch authorities Australian officials never made adverse comments about them to the press, but the reverse was not the case and it was common practice for the papers to be fed information or comments from usually 'unnamed' Dutch sources, critical of Government action or inaction. For example in the *Age* (19.1.1946) a statement sourced from 'a Dutch naval officer' said, 'Australia is fighting an undeclared war against us,' or from 'a Dutch authority' speaking to the *Sydney Morning Herald* (15.2.1946) about lack of Government action on the black bans, 'We are bewildered and disgusted'. The Australian Government never publicly criticised the Dutch, and it was also very rare for any but the communist press to do so. Therefore, the appearance of some damning accusations in the *Melbourne Herald* (19.2.1946), later the subject of a feature in the *Midday Times* (9.3.1946), was very unusual. The article highlighted allegations made by British and Indian troops about Dutch atrocities against the Indonesians in Java. In addition, accusations about Dutch forces' insulting behaviour, incompetence and uncooperativeness were made by Australian ex-pows imprisoned with them, and by Australian troops who served with them in Dutch New Guinea. The Netherlands Minister, Baron van Aerssen, took great exception to these articles. Describing them as insulting and bad mannered, he requested the Government to investigate whether the allegations were based on any official report or had come from 'some ill-informed and irresponsible quarter'.[1] There was no joy for him when his request was dismissed on the grounds that there would be no enquiries about statements originating from any unofficial sources and for which the Government was not responsible.[2]

But revenge was at hand, and no doubt the Baron found some solace in the bitter attack launched on Australia in a Dutch publication, *Elsevier* (6.4.46). Recalling the important contributions made by the NEI forces and KPM ships to Australia's troops and war effort, the article took Australia to task for its ingratitude and its many 'hostile' acts towards to Dutch. These included reneging on the deal to train the Dutch troops, the shipping bans, 'propagandistically' influencing the Indonesian crews to leave their ships, and holding anti-Dutch demonstrations, with the 'Australians and Indonesians together'.[3] Referring to the people of Sydney watching 'one of the biggest demonstrations ever held in the country' on 25 September 1945, the author made the fanciful claim that Mr Forde, Minister for War, led the procession where banners bearing slogans such as 'Ditch the Dutch' were carried. But the most scathing part of this article was his attack on Australia's racialism. Claiming that Australians wanted the freedom of the 'dark brother' (meaning the Indonesians) completely, he observed, 'this is very strange, for it is the first time in history that Australia shows any sympathy for a people of a different colour'. Warming to his theme he continued —

> ... nowhere is race hatred so strong as in Australia. That is the reason why one sometimes comes across suspicious people who think it somewhat odd that Australia is now so idealistically standing up for the poor oppressed Indonesians.[4]

The Government received a translation of this article but there is no record of any complaints to the Netherlands Minister: not even the risible and unlikely claim that Mr Chifley sat staring out the window with his feet on the table and a pipe in his mouth when he received the

Minister in his office, provoked a reaction. The Australian authorities may have been more thick-skinned than their Dutch counterparts.

The second repatriation – HMAS Manoora

Irrespective of any displeasure it caused the Dutch, the Commonwealth was steadfastly committed to its policy of repatriating all of the Indonesians still remaining on Australian shores to Republican territory but hopefully doing this with the agreement of the NEI officials. At the beginning of 1946, Indonesians still in Australia comprised the remainder of the striking seamen and civilians, the majority of whom were in Sydney, the mutineers still detained in Casino, the ex-Tanah Merah political internees and their families who were in Mackay as well as a few others in Melbourne, Sydney and Brisbane, and some TB patients in the Princess Juliana Sanatorium at Turramurra, on Sydney's North Shore. The Dutch had planned to repatriate the latter on one of the KPM ships, the hospital ship *Tasman*, but were unable to do so when the Seamen's Union objected because some of the crew were Australian volunteers who were non-union members.

Unusual in the climate of strained relations between Australian and NEI officials, a very cordial letter was written to Mr Calwell on 7 January 1946 by Mr J. van Holst Pellekaan, Trade Commissioner for the NEI and one of its most senior officials still in Australia. Calwell had apparently agreed that the Commonwealth would accept responsibility for repatriating the TB patients along with all the other Indonesians, but asked for assurances that the NEI Government would not raise any objections to the entry of all these people into the NEI. Van Holst Pellekaan consulted his superiors in Jakarta and told Calwell he had 'ascertained without a doubt' that the NEI government had never previously objected to the repatriation of the Indonesians to their homeland, but some Dutch military officials under SEAC may have. He assured Calwell that in the future the NEI government would not raise any objections – provided they were fully informed of the names and numbers of Indonesians returned. He concluded —

> I understand that you are fully aware of all the difficulties caused by the fact of the great number of Indonesians now

staying in Australia and for whom my Government does not wish to assume any responsibility whatsoever and that you, therefore, are desirous of having these people removed from Australia at as early as possible date. I can assure you that the Netherlands Indies Government officials are looking forward to the date when such removal will take place and that any co-operation which you may wish to obtain from me and my colleagues in Australia will be rendered without delay.[5]

This assurance must have come as a relief to Calwell as by then plans were being formulated for the second repatriation, which was scheduled for February, this time on HMAS *Manoora*.

The Indonesians themselves, while welcoming this development, had not forgotten the fate of the 'extremists' on the *Esperance Bay*, and were adamant that there should be no repeat performance. Mohammad Bondan wrote to Calwell asking for a guarantee that all repatriates would be handed over to Republican control, without Dutch interference. CENKIM also requested that a union representative be permitted to accompany the ship to ensure that this happened. However, this latter suggestion was rejected because the Government had already decided that this time a representative from the Department of Immigration would accompany the ship to carry out this task.[6]

The planned repatriation time happened to coincide with the beginning of important discussions which were to be held in Jakarta between Prime Minister Sjahrir and Governor-General van Mook, under the chairmanship of high ranking British Government representative, Sir Archibald Clark-Kerr. The British had high hopes that these talks would produce some breakthrough in the search for common ground that might lead to the resolution of the Indonesian/Dutch dispute. When Van Mook heard that a ship load of approximately 700 Indonesians from Australia was expected to land in Jakarta around 20 February, right at the time these talks were due to start, he was unpleasantly surprised and asked the Australian Government to delay their landing for about a month. The reason given was that their arrival in February would 'prejudice discussions and adversely affect the situation'.[7] The request seems to have been overlooked, lost or ignored and plans proceeded.

New Year, New Challenges

The WWF Secretary, Ted Roach, also concerned for the welfare of the Indonesians, asked for assurances that there would be no repeat of the *Esperance Bay* incident. In a conversation on 8 February, Calwell promised Roach that nobody would be allowed to even board *Manoora* unless the Dutch gave a guarantee that they would not interfere. He also promised that the repatriates would be met by Republican representatives, and that the Australian Government would not allow any Indonesian to be handed over to the Dutch.[8] Also seeking reassurance were the Indonesians in Mackay, who wrote to Prime Minister Chifley asking for a full guarantee that 'the tragedy' of exile to Semau Island would not be repeated, before they would agree to repatriation.[9] As former inmates of Digul, and therefore knowing they were 'extremists' in Dutch eyes, there were reasonable grounds for their fears. The Prime Minister reassured them that there was no reason to anticipate any repetition of the previous incident and on receipt of this reply, they cabled the PM to say they would accept repatriation on *Manoora* and to thank the Australian Government and people for their sympathetic attitude.[10]

On 15 February, 234 Indonesians, including 41 who had come by bus from Melbourne and 15 who had been living and working in Adelaide, boarded the *Manoora*, which was berthed at Darling Harbour in Sydney. Also boarding was Mr T. Mungoven, the officer of the Department of Immigration, whose job was to escort the Indonesians home.[11] As with the first group of repatriates, this group too had a large amount of luggage and material goods,[12] understandable when they were returning to a country and families that had suffered the privations of the Japanese occupation.

The *Manoora* set sail for Brisbane later the same day without incident, and arrived on the 18 February. While she had been at sea, a battle was being waged between Prime Minister Chifley, and British and Dutch authorities, about the timing of the arrival in Jakarta of this second batch of repatriates. Again Mountbatten was involved, as was Van Mook and a new player, the senior British envoy, Sir Archibald Clark-Kerr. As mentioned above, Van Mook had previously made an unsuccessful request for the repatriates' arrival to be delayed for a month. Now, despite earlier assurances that the NEI officials would fully co-operate with the repatriations, they were again interfering in the plans of the Australian Government on the basis of their usual sensitivity about the imagined havoc of one kind or another that these returning nationalists could wreak. Van Mook had again managed to get the British on side. Chifley tried to deal with Mountbatten, but he had referred the negotiations on to Clark-Kerr. Chifley's annoyance was obvious as he had to cope with yet more Dutch meddling in his plans. He pointed out to Clark-Kerr that 'the decision to return these persons was made with the full agreement and actually the strong desire of the Netherlands Minister,' on the assumption that it was also Dr van Mook's desire.[13] As in the case of the *Esperance Bay* repatriates, Chifley was again dismissive of Dutch concerns about any disruption the Indonesians' arrival could cause saying —

> I appreciate the delicacy of the task confronting you. Nevertheless I find some difficulty in seeing how the arrival with Dutch and Indonesian consent, of a relatively small number of Indonesians, would give rise to any incident or otherwise embarrass the discussions now taking place. Indeed, in view of the Indonesians' desire for repatriation, you may consider that frustration of plans at this stage might well affect those discussions to a far greater degree than if they were allowed to proceed. Interruption of the movement would certainly create embarrassment and difficulties in Australia.[14]

Once again Chifley was crossing diplomatic and political swords with the British and the Dutch in order to keep a promise made to the Indonesians.

However Clark-Kerr was clearly not swayed by Chifley's arguments and preferred to believe what Van Mook told him. Suggesting that 'there must be some misunderstanding about the attitude of the Netherlands Minister,' he was adamant that no Indonesians be landed until the first stage of the negotiations between Van Mook and Sjahrir were complete and begged Chifley to arrange this, suggesting that some way should be found to slow up the voyage so that *Manoora* didn't arrive in Jakarta until the third week in March.[15]

Again Chifley was forced to compromise, though not entirely to the extent requested. He informed Clark-Kerr that in order to help out in the difficulty, the *Manoora* would be 'unobtrusively delayed'

New Year, New Challenges

and would arrive on 12 March, but any further delay was impracticable. He concluded, 'it is necessary for us to proceed on the assumption that your agreement will be forthcoming'.[16] This effectively closed the matter: the repatriation proceeded and no official agreement ever came from Clark-Kerr.

The *Courier Mail* (18.2.46) reported *Manoora*'s arrival in Brisbane commenting positively on the way the Indonesians had formed a central repatriation committee and other sub-committees to take care of all aspects of ship board life. In fact the previous night they had even held a concert on board to celebrate the six months' anniversary of the proclamation of the Republic. However, the next day's report was not so positive as it gave its readers the ominous news that 'thirty six sheathed knives, daggers and bayonets' regarded as dangerous weapons, had been seized by Customs searchers from some of the passengers who had boarded in Sydney. One Indonesian woman even had an ornamental *kris* in its scabbard confiscated from her luggage. Described as the 'prize seizure,' it was probably a family heirloom, and would indeed have been a prize for whoever ended up keeping it. Allegations were also made that guns were confiscated from some of the Indonesians who had boarded in Sydney. The contingent of 377 Indonesians, mostly seamen and former militiamen from various parts of Brisbane, including Gaythorne and Camp Colombia, and some from Casino, 'boarded quietly', and although no arms were found in their possession, two large cases of Communist literature were, including expensive volumes bearing the words 'U.S.S.R.' and 'Freedom'. To the relief of the owners, these were not confiscated.[17] A notable repatriate who boarded in Brisbane was Sardjono, former PKI chairman and long time Digul exile, who took up a leadership role in the PKI again on his return to Java.

The Digulists leave Mackay

Manoora sailed from Brisbane on 20 February and arrived in Mackay two days later. The Mackay *Daily Mercury* published a detailed article about the impending departure of the Indonesians, which it correctly said would mark the end of 'an episode in Mackay's history directly attributable to war,' – as indeed was the whole Indonesian sojourn a similar episode in Australia's history. Mackay was probably the country town which had the most intimate contacts with the

Indonesian graves at Mackay, Queensland.
Author's photo.

Indonesians because as previously mentioned they comprised civilian families living in the community among the local people, with their children attending local schools. The *Mercury* reported that 213 ex-Digulists were to depart on *Manoora* while 48 Indonesians who were not involved with the former political internees would remain behind until later repatriation on a Dutch ship. In the days leading up to their departure the repatriates had gone on shopping sprees and bought items such as garden tools, pharmaceuticals, mirrors, suitcases, clothing and bicycles for adults and children.[18] Their contributions to the local economy must have been sorely missed after they left.

The *Daily Mercury* (23.2.1946) remarked on contrasts between the 'evident gaiety and undisguised sadness in the demeanour of the Indonesians' as they prepared to board the *Manoora* for departure later that day. Mention was made of the amount of luggage they had, in particular the 'bicycles and more bicycles,' the checking of which kept customs officials busy, and of the children wearing 'glistening new shoes and brand new socks.' Gratitude was expressed by the Indonesians to the people of Mackay for their friendship and hospitality. Also at the wharf was Mr Mick Healy from the Queensland TLC, to ensure that the passengers were happy with arrangements and that there was no last minute meddling by the Dutch. When *Manoora* sailed from Mackay on the afternoon of 23 February, her commander, Captain Cousins, reported that altogether there were 821 passengers on board.[19] Siti Chamsinah, by now married to activist Jahja Nasution, and her family were among this group.

Arrival in Jakarta

As the *Manoora* steamed along at a leisurely pace in keeping with the undertaking to delay its arrival, the passengers enjoyed a far more congenial voyage than their predecessors on the *Esperance Bay* had. Some of them wrote glowing accounts of the trip to Mick Healy. For example, Soekanto, a former secretary of SARPELINDO, wrote about the Australian-Indonesian friendship on board and the helpfulness and co-operation of the ship's crew. When one of the children had a birthday, the Captain had a birthday cake baked for her, and that night the Indonesians put on a concert for the Australian crew and soldiers. The day before they arrived at Jakarta, the Captain gave a farewell party for all the children at which, 'the children got everything they could desire, ice cream, jelly, cakes.'[20] In return, the Indonesians presented Captain Cousins, Mr Mungoven, the ship's doctor, officers and crew with souvenirs – sarongs, table cloths, ties, (probably all of batik cloth made in Mackay) as 'a token of appreciation from the Indonesians of HMAS *Manoora*.[21]

Another passenger, Najoan, wrote about the representatives of the Republic and Prime Minister who boarded the ship when she arrived in Jakarta being 'unable to find enough words' to thank Mr Mungoven and Captain Cousins for the way the Indonesians had been treated. The warmth of feelings led to their expressing the hope that —

> ... once all was settled the Republic would invite the Australian Government to exchange representations soon in order to close friendly relations between the two nations. They would also thank the Australian Trade Unions for the stand they have taken to support the Indonesian Independence movement.[22]

Najoan also described the drama of the 'trigger happy Dutch MPs with their tommy guns ready' who 'dominated the wharf' when the ship arrived. However, with the help of some British officers Captain Cousins had them removed. Najoan concluded, 'This made the Dutch believe that the Australians were helping again the Indonesians, as if Australia had declared war on the Dutch.'[23] Such a sentiment would have been the last thing the Australian Government wanted to hear expressed at that time.

It was ironic that even though the arrival of the *Manoora* had been delayed at the request of the Dutch and British authorities, the all-important talks between Van Mook and Sjahrir under Clark-Kerr's chairmanship must also have been delayed because as fate would have it, they did not start until just before the Indonesians arrived. The *Courier Mail* (14.3.1946) reported that the talks had begun well. However, regarding the concurrent arrival of the Indonesians it noted that a senior official of the Republican Government was concerned that their presence at this juncture was 'just a little awkward' because they might not appreciate the difficulties of the political situation and might link up with the extremist elements which had been embarrassing Sjahrir. This alleged comment from a Republican official was in line with the Dutch and British concerns expressed earlier, but none of these forebodings were realized. The repatriates, particularly those from Digul, were probably more interested in getting back to their families and homes after such a long absence, than they were in trying to disrupt talks about which they would have had no knowledge.

Holding the line on shipping bans

After just over 3 months of being in force there was no sign of the shipping bans ending. The first challenge to union solidarity on this matter came from an unexpected source – the Australian Council of Trade Unions (ACTU). In January the Secretary of the ACTU, Mr Albert Monk, invited a number of the involved unions to attend a conference to consider how relief goods could be sent to Indonesia. Monk himself had just returned from a visit to the Netherlands where he had discussed the matter with the president of the Netherlands Federation of Trade Unions. Subsequently he had received a telegram from that body asking Australian workers to remove the bans and load ships with relief goods because of the serious famine and shortage of medicines in the NEI.[24]

As a result of this meeting, the unions agreed to make some concessions, namely facilitating a trial shipment of food and medical

New Year, New Challenges

supplies, with the proviso that a union observer accompany the ship to ensure non-discriminatory distribution of the cargo by the British, without any Dutch interference.[25] This plan failed for two reasons. Firstly neither Monk nor Dr Evatt would agree to it, suspecting that the CPA wanted one of its number (Ted Roach, assistant secretary of the WWF had been mentioned as a possibility) as observer in order to get first hand information about the situation in Indonesia and perhaps exploit this for some ulterior motive. Secondly, even when the unions suggested other names, including that of a respectable King's Counsel, The Netherlands Minister Van Aerssen emphatically rejected the idea of any Australian observer on a Dutch ship, declaring the idea was 'scandalous and insulting'.[26]

After this setback, a series of conferences during the next few weeks opened up a breach between what the *Herald* approvingly called 'the responsible trade union organisations' (the ACTU executive and the NSW TLC) under Mr Monk's influence, who wanted the bans modified, and the Communist influenced unions like the WWF and the Seamen's Union, who did not.[27] When the NSW TLC endorsed an ACTU recommendation to load the Dutch ships, an enraged Ted Roach issued a blistering attack declaring that the decision was —

> tantamount to asking our members to 'scab' on the Indonesian Seamens' Union, who, after striking in the interests of better conditions, and in support of freedom for their own people, declared the ships black and sought the support of the waterfront unions ... I want to say that the Indonesian Seamens' Union is a bona fide Trade Union and our support to them is based on fundamental traditions of Australian Trade Unionism and the right wing intrigues designed to force our members to 'scab' will fail.[28]

Mountbatten to the rescue

Despite these undermining actions by the ACTU and the NSW TLC, the constant attacks from the press and the Parliamentary Opposition and attempts at persuasion from the Government, the striking unions held firm and resolved that the bans would stay in place until the Indonesians themselves asked for them to be lifted. It was time

211

to try a new tactic and unexpectedly this took the form of dramatic intervention by no lesser personage than the Supreme Allied Commander Southeast Asia, Lord Louis Mountbatten himself, when he made his first visit to Australia on 24 March, 1946.

After talks in Canberra with Government officials including Prime Minister Chifley, Mountbatten arrived in Sydney on 29 March and the same day attended a meeting with the Minister for Supply and Shipping, Senator Ashley, his Department's Secretary, Mr Chippindall, the Commonwealth Director of Shipping, Mr Hetherington, Messrs. Monk, King and Kelly of the ACTU, Mr Elliott of the Seamens' Union and Mr Roach of the WWF. Mountbatten was accompanied by his aide, Rear-Admiral Douglas Pennant, who laid out Mountbatten's case.

In his preamble he explained that the British never tried to take sides in the NEI, and that most Indonesians were law abiding and good – although there were some fascist trained and minded youths who were out to cause trouble. The British only fought these people when they interfered with designated British tasks such as rounding up the Japanese, repatriating prisoners of war and internees and maintaining law and order. He said that things in Java were going 'extremely well,' and negotiations between Prime Minister Sjahrir and Dr van Mook were proceeding smoothly.[29] The aide painted a picture of harmonious relations between Sjahrir's Cabinet and the Dutch, suggesting that the British did virtually nothing without consulting Sjahrir first. However, one problem was the hold up in Australian ports of six Dutch ships desperately needed to relieve British ships currently transporting food and helping maintain law and order in Indonesia – ships urgently required back in Singapore for SEAC operations.[30]

When Rupert Lockwood interviewed Mr Elliott and Mr Roach about this meeting in later years, they each recalled that when Mountbatten spoke he was very affable and appeared to direct his appeals at them, aware that they were the key to solving the impasse because their unions had called and maintained the bans.[31] They said Mountbatten was perfectly amenable to the idea of sending union observers on a trial relief shipment, but his main interest was in getting the ships themselves back in action. When told that the unions would not release the ships unless Prime Minister Sjahrir approved, Mountbatten undertook to try to arrange for a union representative to be flown to Java for discussions with Republican leaders, or else to engage Sir Archibald Clark-Kerr to lobby for Sjahrir's support of a plan for Dutch ships to bring supplies and then be released for use in the area.[32] The next day both the *Sydney Morning Herald* and the *Age* portrayed Mountbatten as the hero coming to save the day, with optimistic predictions that the bans would soon be lifted as a result of his intervention.

But these predictions did not take into account the stubbornness of the Netherlands Minister and it transpired that the optimism was misplaced. Van Aerssen still would not countenance union observers on Dutch ships, with the result that no relief ship could be sent. Neither at that stage was Sjahrir willing to support a lifting of the boycott, for various strategic reasons of his own. Thus, like others before him, Mountbatten failed to end the now 6 months' long bans. The result was that ships, vehicles, munitions and stores owned by the Dutch in Australia were still denied to the war effort against the Indonesian republic.[33]

No confidence

While the *Manoora* had been steaming towards Jakarta with the second contingent of repatriates, and various attempts to end the shipping bans were failing, a fierce debate was taking place in the House of Representatives as the result of a motion of no confidence in the Government, particularly in its handling of the bans and Australia's relationship with the NEI Dutch. The motion was moved by the Opposition Leader on 6 March.[34]

It easy to imagine Menzies in the full rhetorical flight for which he was so well known as he embellished all of his previous arguments about the Government's passivity and silence in the face of the bans to the detriment of the Australia-Dutch relationship and to trade opportunities, the Communists on the waterfront dictating foreign policy, the evils of the arch collaborator Soekarno, and implications for Australia's security if the Dutch were ousted. Pouring scorn on what he called 'the one overt act' performed by the Government, that is the repatriation of Indonesians then under way, he accused the Government of committing —

'BORROWED PLUMES'
'News Item: The Prime Minister, Mr Chifley, said that, after the departure of Lord Louis Mountbatten, "something had gone wrong with the negotiations" for the despatch of Dutch ships.'
'Mr Forde:* Just hide your pipe, Ben, and they won't know you from the supremo.'
* Mr Forde, Deputy Prime Minister and Minister for the Army.

Cartoon: Sydney Morning Herald, 6 April 1946

the unspeakable act of folly of sending back to Indonesia at the most critical period of these negotiations (the Van Mook-Sjahrir talks) hundreds of Indonesian natives who have been in Australia for months, during which time they had been constantly indoctrinated with Communist nonsense ... these men who have been indoctrinated in this fashion with a few superficial ideas of a revolutionary kind acquired in Australia have been sent back ... at a very delicate moment in these discussions, in order no doubt to add fuel to the fire ...

Not letting the facts get in the way of an attempt at political point scoring, Menzies exposed his own ignorance of the Indonesian nationalist movement in his nonsensical suggestion that the Indonesians' revolutionary ideas were a result of Australian Communist indoctrination.

In his counter-attack accusing Menzies of political propaganda in making what was in effect a 'preliminary election speech,' A general election was due to be held later that year) Chifley deplored the subject of the relations between the Australian Government and the Dutch being discussed in the House and asserted that his own relations with the Netherlands Minister had always been 'harmonious'. Recapitulating the history of the shipping bans Chifley insisted, as he always had, that the trouble arose out of the refusal of Dutch nationals – in this case Indonesians – to work Dutch ships, and that whatever the merits or demerits of their case, his Government was not prepared to take any action against the Indonesians' Australian union supporters which had the potential to involve the whole industrial movement and shipping trade of the country in industrial dispute. On the matter of the *Manoora* repatriates, Chifley omitted to mention his irritation with Van Mook's interference but praised the co-operation of the Netherlands Minister in Australia and read a message of appreciation from Sir Archibald Clark-Kerr for the efforts Chifley was making to help him by delaying their arrival. Countering Menzies' concerns about loss of trade with the NEI Chifley said astutely —

> I should think that 70,000,000 Indonesians might be very good customers ... I have not been thinking in those materialistic terms, but if I had been, I should have thought that after the final wash up this country would be as liable to get trade from the Indonesians as from the Dutch.[35]

The motion was defeated. So was Menzies' Opposition Party when the Labor party was returned to Government in the general elections of September 1946. This was despite the Opposition's attacks and constant efforts to suggest that the Communists in the WWF were dictating foreign policy in the face of Government weakness.

Shipping news – Dutch turn the tables

In June, much of the Opposition's attack on the Government was still centred on the shipping bans. Attention was focused on the plight of the *Piet Hein,* a warship from the Royal Netherlands Navy, which had some unspecified time earlier limped into Fremantle in need of repairs. When these were denied because of the bans she

'A FEW INAPPROPRIATE WORDS'
The Prime Minister, Mr Chifley, says it was 'most inappropriate' to send the Netherlands warship Piet Hein to Australia for repairs in view of existing trouble in Australia with Dutch ships.
Mr Chifley: 'You should be ashamed, Piet Hein, coming here worrying this gentleman after all the trouble he's had keeping your friends out!'

Cartoon: Sydney Morning Herald, 22 June 1946

sailed on to Melbourne with the same result. Her arrival in Sydney was mentioned briefly in the *Sydney Morning Herald* (13.6.1946) with the news that because unionists refused to handle the ship the repairs could not be done. As a result, the ship had left for New Zealand in the hope of finding help there.[36] Nobody thought to ask why the Dutch authorities had brought a warship to Australia for repairs when their merchant ships were already being refused such services under the terms of the black bans.

However, the gloom generated by this state of affairs vanished when shortly afterwards the Dutch had the last laugh. In July, desperation as a result of the bans led them to stage a brilliant coup, described as 'Right Wing Treachery' by the *Maritime Worker* (20.7.1946) and 'Dutch Ingenuity' by the *Sydney Morning Herald* (17.7.1946). Whatever the case, it must have been a great boost to their morale, and more importantly, it resulted in their six KPM ships, three from Sydney and three from Brisbane, outwitting the waterside workers and getting away. According to the *Maritime Worker*, the 'treacherous' right wing Sydney Coalers Union had not joined in the strike, so the three ships in Sydney, *Stagen, Merak,* and *Van Swoll*, had no problem obtaining coal. In Brisbane, however, the unions only permitted *Both, Bentokoe* and *Van Outhoorn* to load enough for basic electricity and refrigeration during their enforced stay in port. But when in July there was a large-scale general waterside strike in Brisbane and the coal supply dried up, the Dutch ships were allowed to load firewood in its place. Using their own service personnel and some Lascars, they managed to load large quantities of wood without arousing the suspicions of the watersiders. Then, in a co-ordinated movement, the *Stagen*, with enough coal on board to fuel the Brisbane ships, and crewed by 40 Australian ex-servicemen, slipped out of port and headed north, accompanied by the other two Dutch ships, crewed by Lascars.[37] Just before this, 'following a concerted and secret plan', the Brisbane ships had slipped their moorings and made their way down the Brisbane River, unnoticed by the watersiders there. They anchored in Moreton Bay to await the arrival of the *Stagen*, bringing coal for them.[38] When she did arrive it took ten days to transfer the coal, after which all six ships headed for Indonesian waters, still undetected by the watersiders.[39] With the 'escape' of these ships, the last of those which had been involved since the boycott was first imposed, this phase of the bans was virtually over by default. The Dutch had themselves achieved what Mountbatten and everybody else had failed to do – effected the release of their own much needed ships.

Despite this, the *Maritime Worker*, (which described the Sydney Coalers' actions as 'working class treachery,') took pride in the fact that the waterside workers had instituted the bans and could be 'happy in the fact that this 10 month ban has been responsible for rallying world wide moral and practical assistance to the Indonesian cause.[40]

Eye spy

After the second repatriation the Commonwealth Investigation Branch estimated that there were still about 350 Indonesian civilians in Australia, including the TB patients at the Queen Juliana Sanatorium in Turramurra, a number of people described as 'political strikers,' a handful of former pearl divers, and some loyal NEI civilian employees in Mackay.[41] In addition to these civilians there were also both dissident and a few loyal servicemen still in Casino.

Both the Australian and the NEI security services maintained their scrutiny of the 'political strikers' – the remnants of the striking merchant seamen and ex-Digulists who formed the membership of the Indonesian Independence Committees in Melbourne and Sydney and CENKIM in Brisbane. An Australian security enquiry into the Melbourne Committee identified its membership as six former Digulists and three former KPM seamen and decided that although it worked 'under the direction of the Australian Communist Party' and continued to spread anti-Dutch propaganda in pamphlets and public addresses, it was less active than formerly.[42] It was further noted that the AIA had been formed in Melbourne for the purpose of furthering the aims of the Independence Committee and that its activities would 'receive all possible attention'.[43] A Dutch security report on the situation in Sydney noted that as the result of an ideological split there were actually two independence committees in Sydney, one whose members were nationalists and anti-Dutch and the other whose members were nationalists, anti-Dutch and Communists. All were former KPM seamen. This report also mentioned the Sydney AIA and its alleged 'pro-communist' membership.[44]

A Commonwealth Investigation Branch report on the Indonesians in Brisbane revealed that there remained only four main members of CENKIM, three of whom were ex-Digulists and the other a former KPM shipping clerk. It also was noted that SARPELINDO still existed 'in theory,' with Simon Pinontoan, the KPM man from CENKIM, keeping it going mainly for propaganda purposes. Mention was made that Mr George Greaves, first secretary of the Brisbane AIA, was being watched, because Bondan had referred to him in correspondence- apparently enough justification to arouse the suspicion of the security authorities.[45] So we see that in each eastern state there was an on-going link between the remaining Indonesian activists of the Independence committees and the AIAs, and this link was a matter of continuing interest to the security services.

The fight goes on

Although their numbers in Australia were so depleted after the second repatriation, the remaining Indonesian activists still managed to make their voices heard. At a 'Hands Off Indonesia' meeting which attracted 1,500 people to the Sydney Town Hall on 15 April, one of the speakers was Jan Walandouw, former KPM employee, whose letter to his friend George Worang, extolling the carefree delights of his life in Sydney, appeared in our story earlier. There was no hint of political concern in that letter written in February 1944, but by April 1946 Jan Walandouw, now president of the Sydney Independence Committee and married to an Australian, was under Dutch scrutiny and labelled by them as a Communist and anti-Dutch.[46] He had become a 'bad boy.' Walandouw thanked the waterfront unions on behalf of his people and declared that 'the name of Australia would long be remembered in his country'.[47] On 21 April, an Indonesian who claimed to have escaped from the camp at Casino, also addressed a large meeting in the Sydney Domain. His name was not announced because the Dutch were allegedly searching for him. Dressed in a civilian suit he 'spoke in halting English from a step ladder draped with a red flag,' and thanked the Communists for helping the Indonesian cause, before being whisked away by his Australian friends, to avoid capture.[48]

The TB patients

Another group of Indonesians still in Sydney after the February repatriation were 25 TB patients in the Dutch-run Princess Juliana Sanatorium (for Indonesians) located in the north shore suburb of Turramurra. Most of these patients were merchant seamen, some were from the NEI forces and some had been in Tanah Merah. The first hint that all was not well in the sanatorium came in a letter from the secretary of SARPELINDO on 19 March to the NSW Minister for Health, claiming that Dutch doctors were neglecting their Indonesian patients and had not been near the sanatorium for the past four months and pleading for Australian doctors to visit.[49] Further correspondence by SARPELINDO president Mailangkay on 7 May alleged deplorable conditions which had been allowed to develop since the opening of the Sanatorium in 1944. He complained that there had always been a shortage of orderlies and qualified medical staff, that there was now no regular laundry service and that the hospital canteen had been closed down so it was impossible for the patients to obtain the 'necessities and comforts they may desire or require'. Mailangkay concluded, 'If the Dutch are too inhuman to recognise their rightful duty and responsibility it is up to us to approach the Australian Government to move in the matter and see that something is done for them in the name of common decency and humanity'.[50]

There is no record that this happened but on 21 August, Dutch authorities took steps which may or may not have been a consequence of these complaints: they made an unsuccessful attempt to transfer the Indonesians to another Dutch-run establishment, the Queen Wilhelmina Hospital near Centennial Park, allegedly because as a result of pressure from local residents they had been asked to vacate the Turramurra premises.[51] Inquiry officer H. Hay from the Commonwealth Investigation Branch, present at the time, reported that just when all arrangements for the transfer were completed and the patients had indicated their willingness to comply, Mrs Burns of the AIA – 'an associate of the extremist element of the Indonesians' and 'a well known trouble-maker' – intervened, and the Indonesians refused transfer to the Dutch hospital. Nineteen of the 23 patients had then left the Sanatorium with all their luggage and been taken to the premises of the Chinese Youth League in Dixon Street, Chinatown. The NEI medical officer, Dr van Leent, considered that although most of the patients were recovering, they should not be mixing with the general public for health reasons. NEI authorities blamed four of the patients for the recalcitrant attitude of them all. In particular they singled out one Johan Idroes as the most dangerous because he had a criminal record in the NEI (in fact he was an ex-Digulist) and was very friendly with that 'well known Communist', Mrs Laura Gapp.[52]

Mr Peters, an officer of the Department of Immigration, who had spent the day trying to reason with the Indonesians, said they had been fearful that if they went to the Queen Wilhelmina Hospital they would lose their leave privileges and right to have visitors, and their food would not be properly cooked. They said they would rather go to gaol or 'back to the jungle' – clearly a reference to Digul- than go to a Dutch hospital. Peters was obviously fed up as he spoke of the 'stupid obstinacy' and 'flimsy excuses' of the Indonesians.[53]

The exasperated Dutch authorities thereupon made one last offer to repatriate these men on one of their hospital ships, the *Tasman*, in Melbourne at the time. Notifying the Commonwealth of this offer, the Dutch Consul in Sydney warned that if the Indonesians refused the offer and if Australian authorities then refused to 'conduct these patients on board,' NEI authorities would wash their hands of them and reject further financial or any other kind of responsibility for them.[54]

Predictably, no Australian force was used, and the Indonesians did refuse to be repatriated on a Dutch ship, preferring to wait for another ship under Australian control to take them home. In the interim they solved their own accommodation problem when after a few days they left Dixon Street and took possession of the then unoccupied premises of the Dutch *Oranje* Clinic in Kent Street, Sydney. When Dutch authorities asked the police to evict them they refused on the grounds that the Indonesians were squatters taking over a vacant building, apparently not illegal in those days.[55]

The Dutch kept their word and refused any aid to these sick Indonesians, who were being maintained by SARPELINDO, the AIA and the Sydney branch of the Indonesian Independence Committee. These helpers had managed to obtain the necessary food coupons for them from the Rationing Commission and to persuade the Department of Commerce to release rice supplies, but finding the money to pay for the food was a constant problem.[56] In an impassioned appeal to the Seamen's Union of Australia for financial assistance for those whom she called 'these cruelly ill-used and helpless invalids', the secretary of the AIA, Enid Hampson, described their plight thus —

> ... since 29 August the Dutch authorities have refused the patients food, medicine and medical attention, nor will the KPM Shipping Co. hand over their deferred pay amounting to several thousand pounds. The men's meagre savings are now exhausted. Yet they hold written assurances from the KPM that they will be properly cared for ashore during their illness... some of the men are dangerously ill and worry over their hapless situation is preventing their recovery.[57]

It must indeed have been a miserable time for the TB patients, all crammed together in the room that constituted the *Oranje* Clinic, and also a worrying time for the friends trying to look after them.

On 4 November Miss Hampson tried another tack in her quest for help when she wrote to the Prime Minister asking him to authorise the re-opening of the abandoned and well-equipped Turramurra sanatorium, and using it for the treatment of both Australian and Indonesian TB sufferers. In her emotive appeal she claimed that the position of the Indonesians was desperate and that they were facing starvation.[58] A different kind of appeal was made to the Department of External Affairs by the Australian Red Cross Society, which in accordance with its policy of 'giving short term emergency service irrespective of the cause of the need,' was also assisting the Indonesians 'because their need was immediate and vital'. However, the Red Cross felt that the time had come for a formal solution to the problem and asked the Government to bring this about.[59] In fact, by the time this request was made, 15 November, the end of the Indonesians' ordeal was in sight, as arrangements were then well underway for the imminent third repatriation.

The first anniversary of independence

The initial reaction of the Dutch in Australia to the Indonesian rebellion had been to claim that it was confined to a relatively small number of extremists in Java and would be a short-lived affair. It must have been galling for them then when the first anniversary of the Sukarno-Hatta declaration of 17 August 1945 rolled around and was celebrated as the first anniversary of independence.

In Australia the event was marked by gatherings of Indonesians and their supporters in Brisbane, Sydney and Melbourne. Predictably proceedings were closely monitored by the vigilant inquiry officers of the Commonwealth Investigation Branch who forwarded reports to Canberra. From officer H. Hay in Sydney we learn that the Paddington Town Hall was the venue for the Sydney celebrations held on 18 August 1946. About 500 people attended, of whom about 40% were Australians, the remainder being Indonesians and a few uniformed Dutchmen.[60] The speakers included Jan Walandouw, Henry Mailangkay and Andrew Sorongan, secretary of SARPELINDO, and Jim Healy, WWF Secretary. From Hay's point of view, the whole event appears to have been rather an anticlimax. He described the speeches, 'which were not received with any fervour,' as now familiar 'reiterated platitudes' and claimed that 'there was a general apathy to the celebration as far as the Australians attending were concerned'. Even some of the 'moderate' Indonesians were allegedly 'disgusted' by the speeches and by the fact that only the Chinese and the Republican red and white flags were displayed – the absence of a British flag was felt to be a 'slight on Australia'.[61] Those attending the function may not have viewed it the same way as this security officer.

The celebration in Brisbane seems to have been a more spirited affair. Described as a 'social evening,' it was held on 19 August at the Rationalists Hall and attended by about 100 people, most of whom were Indonesians.[62] Among the 25 or so Australians were G. Sleeth, the CIB inquiry officer keeping an eye on proceedings, Mr Englart, Secretary of the Brisbane Branch of the WWF, Max Julius, the lawyer who had represented the striking seamen in court, and Molly Warner, now living in Brisbane and working to assist Bondan (whom she would soon marry) and the work of CENKIM. When Raden Abimanjoe spoke on behalf of the Indonesian community in Brisbane, Mr Sleeth listened closely and was no doubt relieved to report that 'no reference was made to the British Empire in relation to political matters in the islands and no utterances were made that could be construed as subversive'. Molly Warner, introduced as 'the leading lady in Australia behind the Central Committee of Indonesian Independence in Australia,' also spoke in an effort to elicit donations to help the work of the cash strapped CENKIM, which according to Sleeth would probably cease to function without the 'moral support and general backing' of the Communist Party. Sleeth obtained a photo of a group of Australians and Indonesians taken on the evening and identified every Australian as 'Communist', especially Molly Warner who was 'constantly in the company of Indonesians'.[63]

Such sentiments about the dependence of CENKIM on the communists, similar to those made by Opposition leader Menzies, illustrate the security officer's superficial understanding of the determination and political experience of the Indonesians themselves in their fight for independence. They may have welcomed financial support but had the strength of their own convictions and beliefs to sustain their struggle, particularly those nationalists who had endured exile in Tanah Merah, with or without the 'moral support' of the Communist party or anyone else.

11

People to People

To this point in the story the tone of most of the propaganda in the public domain in Australia was anti the Republic and its Australian supporters, with the mainstream press openly siding with the views of the Opposition and sympathising with the Dutch over the shipping bans and Indonesian demands for independence. Apart from *Tribune*, pro-Republic propaganda material was limited to pamphlets, for the most part produced by the Communist Party. So it was quite a coup when, for the first time, the medium of film was utilised as a powerful propaganda weapon in support of the Indonesian revolution. This was the result of a joint Australian-Indonesian people to people enterprise, ironically, with the co-operation and expertise of a Dutchman.

Meanwhile the Government remained as determined as ever to repatriate the remaining Indonesians as quickly as possible. To this end it would have been expedient for it to co-operate with any strategy the Dutch formulated for return of the rebels to Dutch territory, thereby painlessly removing one source of irritation between the two allies. But the Government did not take the easy way out. It was resolute in its determination to shield the rebels from Dutch reprisals by adhering to humanitarian principles in execution of the first two repatriations and continued to be so with those still to come. One consequence was that it found itself dealing with another result of the people to people relationship between Indonesians and Australians, the war brides.

Indonesia Calling

When Phyllis Johnson went to the wharves to rally support for the Indonesians she always announced her presence by loudly shouting, 'Indonesia Calling'. It was fitting then that this catch cry, deriving

*Joris Ivens, Dutch film-maker.
Photo: Penjoeloeh, 6 August 1945.*

from broadcasts made from the Republic, was the title of a propaganda film made in Australia in support of Indonesian independence by the internationally renowned Dutch film-maker Joris Ivens who had previously made political propaganda films in Poland, the Soviet Union, Belgium, USA and China.[1] Political documentaries were a rarity in Australia in those days and this one was particularly so, being made by a Dutchman and dealing as it did with a foreign cause being fought for on Australian soil.

The circumstances that brought Ivens to Australia initially were in no way connected with making this film. In September 1944 he had been appointment as Film Commissioner to the NEI Government. The contract he was offered spoke of the Dutch desire to liberate the NEI and of 'the great Western ideal of freedom and democracy,' and his first task was to document the liberation.[2] To that end he flew to Brisbane in March 1945, continued on to Melbourne, and took up residence at the Menzies Hotel to await the liberation. This he understood to mean not only liberation of the NEI from the Japanese but also of the Indonesians from colonial rule. After all, the press release announcing his appointment and the film he would make talked about how Dutch and Indonesians would 'operate on a footing of complete equality, mutual respect and admiration'.[3]

Shortly after his arrival, to his consternation Ivens' application for accreditation as a war correspondent was refused by US authorities, probably because of his left wing leanings. This meant he was denied permission to enter the war zone to shoot the film he had been hired to make. He was still cooling his heels in Melbourne when the Japanese were defeated and Soekarno proclaimed Indonesia's independence. Therefore he was on the spot when a few weeks later the first Indonesian seamen walked off their ships and the build up of support for them and the Republic started in Australia. It must have soon become obvious to him that the Dutch were going to oppose any efforts by the Indonesians to gain independence from them, and that their talk of 'equality, mutual respect and admiration' was apparently mere rhetoric.

In September Ivens moved to Sydney to a flat in Elizabeth Bay,[4] and in November, in protest against the Dutch attitude, resigned from his appointment as Film Commissioner. The other members of his film unit soon followed suit. In a press statement he explained, 'I cannot reconcile my conscience with the job that the Dutch Government wants me to do ... as an artist I will not do any film work that would be against my principles and convictions ... the people of Indonesia have a right to expect national independence'.[5] We can assume that during this time Ivens probably had contact with the Indonesians and their union supporters in Sydney, and would have been aware of the various Indonesia-related incidents, the waterfront action and protests going on around the country. From all of this the idea of making a propaganda film on behalf of the Waterfront Unions of Australia and under the auspices of an independent body called the Australasian Film Syndicate, must have evolved. Ivens himself said in later years, '... the idea came to make some shots of what happened, newsreel shots practically, not even a film, but I couldn't just let what happened go '.[6]

The resulting documentary was made largely clandestinely on a shoestring budget, by Ivens and some sympathetic supporters volunteering their expertise free of charge. Actor Peter Finch provided the narration and it was shot mainly on the Sydney waterfront. The making of the film must have actually been underway before Ivens resigned because the Commonwealth Investigation Bureau had been aware of it a few weeks beforehand when Inspector Alexander reported to his superiors in Canberra his suspicion that the film was really being made for Communist propaganda purposes and that 'well known Communist, Stan Moran,' was in one scene.[7] In an article in the *Sun* (22.11.1945) it was noted that 'Mr Harry Watts, English film director and Mr Joris Ivens, famous Dutch film director ... both said they knew a film was being made but did not know who was making it'. This proved the clandestine nature of their involvement.

While *Indonesia Calling* was to some extent a documentation of real events as they happened, and using Indonesian, Australian Indian and Chinese 'actors,' it was also a recreation of real events that had already happened. In particular it highlighted the boycott of the Dutch ships and the dramatic turning back of the *Patras* after it was pursued by a launch manned by Indian and union sympathisers who shouted through a megaphone to persuade the Indian crew to join the strikers. The oft-repeated message of the film was the justice of the Indonesians' cause and in particular the solidarity of the unions and Australian friends with them. The narration expressed such sentiments as —

> Here in Australia we know the Indonesians well. For years they have lived in our country as our friends and fellow townsmen. The women learned the names of our vegetables and mothers found that children were much the same in any language. There were the Indonesian soldiers and seamen. Our boys knew them as good fighters against a common enemy, Japan.[8]

Indonesia Calling is acknowledged by contemporary scholars of film as one of Ivens' most important documentaries. There was controversy about the film even before its public premiere at the Kings Cross Newsreel Theatre in Sydney on 9 August, 1946. Describing it as 'an anti-Dutch film version of the watersiders' black ban on Dutch vessels,' the *Sunday Telegraph* (4.8.1946) reported that the Commonwealth Censorship Board had approved its showing in Australia, but banned its export on the grounds that it would 'offend the people of a foreign country'. The motion picture trade organ, *Film Weekly*, condemned the film as one-sided propaganda, 'with almost every line containing a stinging indictment of the Dutch'. Despite, or perhaps because of this bias, at its premiere *Indonesia Calling* was 'enthusiastically received by a large audience comprising trade unionists, members of cultural, civic and student organisations'.[9]

Understandably, the Royal Netherlands Legation in Australia did not share this enthusiasm. Baron van Aerssen protested to the Prime Minister about the film's screening in Australia, and the possibility of its export, on the grounds that it was prejudicial to the good relationship between the Dutch and Australian people.[10] Chifley passed on Van Aerssen's concerns to the state premiers because any decision to show or not show a film was a state, not a Commonwealth matter. In response, NSW Premier McKell echoed the sentiments of the other state premiers when he said that because the film was largely a factual account of events which were all well known to the public through the newspapers, there were no objections to the film being screened in NSW and there would be no banning.[11] Having had no luck with his request to the Prime Minister for some sort of intervention, Minister Van Aerssen, tried another tack and appealed to Dr Evatt. Expressing his anger that the 'insulting film' had been exhibited in NSW, and his objections to a forthcoming screening of it in Canberra.[12] Despite these objections and the Opposition's accusations that the film 'had the hammer and sickle on it' and was 'detrimental to Australia' the Government insisted it would be an abuse of its own power to invoke censorship of the film and prevent its export.[13]

While Rupert Lockwood's claim that *Indonesia Calling* was shown to 'millions throughout the world'[14] may be an exaggeration, it certainly was shown outside of Australia. *Tribune* (8.12.46) reported that it had been screened in New York, on Broadway no less, and warmly received by the public and the press as a 'superb movie with mature political understanding'. One New York paper, *PM,* commented, 'It seems the Australian, Chinese, Indian and Indonesian workers took the Atlantic Charter at its word'. It was also eventually screened in Indonesia, allegedly smuggled aboard a repatriation ship.[15] Lockwood notes that Marion Michelle, the camera operator, wrote in later years how the film was shown in village after village of Republican Java on open-air screens. Mohamed Bondan also mentions several screenings in Yogyakarta but that sadly that copy of the film vanished after Dutch attacks on the city in 1948.[16]

No doubt *Indonesia Calling* was a great morale booster for the

Republicans in Indonesia, and it would also have enhanced Australia's image as a champion of their cause. There was probably no one to explain that the Australians depicted in the film represented the views of some of the pro-Indonesia/anti-Dutch pressure groups but not the official view of the Government or of the majority of Australians. The images of white Australians shoulder to shoulder with their non-white comrades must have come as a surprise to any international audience with knowledge of Australia's entrenched racial policy and probably disconcerted any Australian viewers who supported it, while the glimpses of 1940s post-war Sydney, particularly the harbour, provide a fascinating backdrop to the events the film portrays.

Whatever else it did, *Indonesia Calling* provided a source for later generations of Indonesians and Australians to learn of the shipping bans and the related actions of Australian, Indian and Chinese supporters of Indonesian independence, and is a lasting historical record of the Australia-Indonesia bond of those years.

Political negotiations between the Republic and the Dutch in 1946

While this activity on behalf of the Republic was taking place in Australia the main game was being played out of course in Indonesia itself. The Jakarta negotiations (which had coincided with the arrival of the repatriates on the *Manoora*) between Sjahrir, arguing for Dutch recognition of Indonesian independence, and Van Mook, arguing for the formation of a Commonwealth of Indonesia as part of the Kingdom of the Netherlands, had got off to a fairly slow start, with neither side prepared to compromise. However, under the mediation of Sir Archibald Clark-Kerr, there was a breakthrough in April 1946, when Sjahrir proposed, and Van Mook agreed, that the Republic would be accorded *de facto* recognition in Java and Sumatra and would co-operate with the Netherlands in establishing a Federal Indonesian Free State, linked to the Netherlands in a political union, cemented by a treaty.[17] However, when both sides travelled to the Hague in April to finalise an agreement with the Netherlands Government, it rejected the proposals and the concept of any treaty which would alter the status of the NEI as an integral part of the Kingdom of the Netherlands. When the Dutch made a counter proposal that *de facto* recognition of the Republic would only apply to Java, the Republicans rejected it and the negotiations broke down.

They resumed again in October in Jakarta, with an urgent desire on both sides to reach some agreement before British troops were withdrawn at the end of November and replaced by 3 Dutch army divisions. The Republicans feared 'a bloodbath' if there were no political settlement, and the Dutch negotiators, who had become aware of the growing strength of popular support for the Republic, also feared 'disastrous conflict'. Under a new mediator, the United Kingdom Special Commissioner to Southeast Asia, Lord Killearn, the negotiators moved to Linggadjati near the Javanese town of Ceribon, to resume their discussions. The result was the Linggadjati Agreement, (also known as the Ceribon Agreement) initialled by the two sides on 15 November 1946, and due to be signed and come into effect the following January. Under the terms of this agreement, the Dutch would recognize the Indonesian Republic as the *de facto* authority in Java, Madura and Sumatra, while the Netherlands and the Republic would co-operate in the formation of a sovereign, federal United States of Indonesia, comprising the Republic, Kalimantan, and East Indonesia, which would be an equal partner in a Netherlands-Indonesian Union under the Dutch crown. Although the Linggadjati Agreement left many issues still unresolved, there was optimism on both sides that negotiation and compromise had averted bloodshed. In the Australian Parliament, Evatt expressed his satisfaction that 'the danger of conflict and instability in an area of great strategic importance to Australia had apparently receded'.

With a blueprint for rapprochement between the Dutch and the Republic now in place the Australian Government, particularly the Department of External Affairs, wanted to leave its options open with regard to its representation in the NEI. Just after the Linggadjati Agreement was concluded, Mr Ballard, the Australian Political representative in Jakarta, was sent instructions that clarified Australia's interests: it was loath to establish direct representation with the Dutch if this would prejudice 'an effective exchange' with the Indonesian Republic. Ballard was therefore instructed to assist and advise the Indonesian authorities on an informal basis till it was known how the Agreement would work out, with the object of strengthening Australian influence because 'Australian relations with Indonesia will be of supreme importance'.[18] Despite its so-called neutrality in the dispute between the two powers in the NEI, the Australian Government appeared to be at least recognising the strength of the Indonesian Republic and positioning itself favourably should this strength prevail.

The third repatriation. November 1946
While the Government was tentatively exploring new ground in its relations with the Indonesian Republic, there was no let up in its efforts to remove Indonesians from Australia. HMAS *Manoora* was used again in September to repatriate to Java 508 Dutch evacuees, including 98 loyal Indonesians prepared to return to Dutch controlled territory and some 20 Australian brides of Dutchmen. On her return to Sydney from this voyage, she was then made available for the third repatriation of the rebels. When they were informed of the plan Bondan gave assurances that CENKIM would fully co-operate with the Australian authorities and urge all remaining Indonesians to go home on this third repatriation ship if possible.[19]

Mr Calwell meantime was addressing the problem of the Indonesian TB patients, describing them as 'a menace to the health of the community as long as they remain in Australia,' when he wrote to the Minister for the Navy requesting accommodation for them on the *Manoora*. Disclosing his eagerness to see the last of all the Indonesians, Calwell mentioned his and the Prime Minister's desire to repatriate as many of them as possible, 'as their presence here has been a source of much embarrassment and trouble'.[20]

Embarkation in Sydney took place on 16 November, but not without some aggravation from Mailangkay, Walandouw and another member of the Independence Committee, Sorongan. These three had gained a reprieve from this repatriation because they were married to Australian women, but were at the wharf and acting, according to one official, as though 'they were in charge of the operation'.[21] Walandouw the chief culprit among the three, who were 'all communists and distinct troublemakers', even declared that he was 'the president of the Indonesians and he would instruct them not to embark'. Despite this irritation, embarkation went ahead and *Manoora* sailed from Sydney on 19 November. Once again Mr Mungoven was on board to escort the repatriates and ensure that they were delivered safely to Republican authorities. He reported that 76 Indonesians from Melbourne and Sydney had embarked.[22] To what would have been Mr Calwell's undoubted relief, the Sydney contingent did include the TB patients, who wrote a letter to 'Dear Friends of Indonesia' while they were at sea, expressing their joy at being on the way home to their 'beloved fatherland' after their suffering, and their gratitude to the friends who had helped them to survive after their ejection from the Turramurra hospital, mentioning some now familiar names in our story, such as Messrs. Campbell and Peel, Mrs Reid and Miss Hampson of the AIA and the omnipresent Mrs Laura Gapp. 'Your names will be remembered by us as long as we live,' they wrote '... we hope you will enthusiastically continue the work we have started to foster and strengthen friendship between Indonesia and Australia'. They also urged their friends to 'be propagandists to eliminate the racial prejudice which exists in Australia'.[23]

Manoora arrived in Brisbane on 20 November, a few days after Mr Pie of the Queensland State Parliament had complained about the Indonesians in Chermside occupying huts which should have been made available for 'good Queensland families' needing accommodation.[24] He would have been pleased then to learn that these men were scheduled for imminent departure. The Brisbane contingent comprised 230 men from Chermside, another 8 from Brisbane, 1 from Darwin, 2 from Northern Queensland, I from West Maitland Gaol (NSW) and 1 Australian born coloured wife of one of the Indonesians.[25] On 21 November, Mr Bird the Immigration officer personally escorted the Chermside men to the ship, noting that the camp had been cleaned by the Indonesians and 'was in much better appearance than when it was taken over'. *Manoora* left Brisbane at 4pm that day, *en route* for Thursday Island, where she picked up a further nine Indonesian passengers who had commandeered a boat in Merauke in an attempt to get to Brisbane to join CENKIM, before continuing north.[26]

Mr Mungoven reported that *Manoora* stopped off at Kupang for about an hour to disembark two passengers, and then continued on to Jakarta, arriving at 7.30 am on 1 December. 'Up to the arrival in Batavia,' he enthused, 'the voyage had been an excellent success, the behaviour of the Indonesians had been splendid and they were most contented and happy, while the ship's organisation and co-operation (again under Captain Cousins) could not be faulted'.[27] But there was soon a dramatic turn of events and an unexpected adventure for Mr Mungoven, when, after obeying a signal to remain outside the harbour, *Manoora* was boarded by a number of Dutch officials and an Indonesian representative of the Red Cross. But to everyone's consternation there was no sign of any British officials. The Dutch officials announced that the Indonesians were to be embarked onto a small Japanese vessel, the *Nansi Maru* and taken to Ceribon, a port about 150 miles away. Naturally, the Indonesians were very suspicious about this and refused to leave the *Manoora* until they heard some assurance from their own Republican people that these arrangements were genuine and approved by them. Captain Cousins sent radio signals to shore but was unable to contact anybody the Indonesians trusted. Finally, in a desperate effort to break the impasse, Mungoven offered to accompany the Indonesians to Ceribon in the *Nansi Maru*, at which point they agreed to go.

Conditions on the Japanese boat were primitive, with everyone, including Mr Mungoven, sitting on the dirty iron deck for a journey that took almost 24 hours, with no room to lie down, sanitary arrangements that were 'indescribable,' no life saving equipment and worst of all, no food of any kind on board, despite assurances to the contrary by the Dutch officials. When they arrived at Ceribon, Mr Mungoven and the members of the Indonesian Committee were taken ashore by launch and interviewed by some Republican officials, who, it transpired, had no knowledge at all about the arrangements for the repatriates arriving in Ceribon. Eventually, the Indonesians were all given a meal and then landed and handed over to their own people, while Mr Mungoven was lodged at the home of the Resident of Ceribon, who then arranged for his safe passage by train to Jakarta the next day, where he rejoined the *Manoora* as soon as he could. In his report he described his trip to Ceribon as 'a rather unenviable experience which I would not care to repeat'.

Thus, like the others, the third repatriation was not without incident. Nevertheless, the ever-grateful CENKIM once again thanked Calwell effusively. Bondan wrote —

> We are very appreciative of the fact that, in spite of a continuing attitude of hostility on the part of a section of the Australian

community able to publicise its views very widely the officers of your department and members of the Australian Government concerned have been unwavering in fairness towards our people, and still endeavour to secure just and democratic treatment towards those who support the Indonesian Republic.[28]

By the end of 1946, there were only a few hundred Indonesians still left in Australia, the majority of whom were the remainder of the Casino contingent. These men were finally released on 14 December, and like their predecessors, taken to Chermside camp in Brisbane to await repatriation, and presumably annoy Mr Pie even further. They were joined a couple of weeks later by another 19 who were sent up from Long Bay Gaol in Sydney, where they had been held as illegal immigrants.[29] There were also a few married to Australians who were using delaying tactics to put off their inevitable departure as long as possible.

The final repatriation, May 1947
Once again, HMAS *Manoora* was assigned the task of taking the Indonesians home, this time on what would be the final repatriation voyage. Typically the actual departure was preceded by 4 months of wrangling between Australian and NEI authorities, this time mostly about the point and manner of disembarkation of the repatriates. The Australians did not want a repeat of the previous debacle when repatriates had been hustled off willy-nilly from Jakarta to Ceribon on a Japanese boat, with no arrangements in place for their reception there. The crux of the problem this time was that the Australians wanted the *Manoora* to sail straight to Ceribon, disembark the Indonesians there and hand them over directly to Republican authorities. The Dutch however, wanted them to travel via a Dutch controlled port first, so they could be searched for weapons, and possibly so that any undesirables could be removed.[30] Mr Ballard, the Australian Political Representative whose job it was to negotiate with the Dutch in Jakarta about these arrangements, was instructed to assure them that the Indonesians would not be allowed to carry any weapons, and to seek an undertaking that there would be no Dutch interference or attempts to intercept the Indonesians at any time between their embarkation in Australia and their disembarkation in Ceribon.[31]

Meanwhile Republican authorities gave assurances that they would take responsibility for the landing and care of the repatriates in Ceribon and for their part were assured that the Australians would not accede to a Dutch request for a list of the names or ultimate destinations of the repatriates.[32] No headway was made in breaking the deadlock with the Dutch until the Australians offered a sweetener in the form of an undertaking to carry 2, 500 tons of their stored cargo from Sydney. Thereupon the Dutch relented and agreed to accept Kupang, where the *Manoora* intended to land some Dutch Timorese, as the Dutch controlled port which they had insisted on from the beginning of the negotiations. With Dutch co-operation finally promised *Manoora* was readied for departure from Sydney on 1 May, with Mr Mungoven once again supervising the repatriation.[33]

The final voyage was quite straightforward in that there were no controversial incidents as there had been on the previous repatriations. In Sydney *Manoora* was loaded with Dutch cargo by Dutch labour and 45 Indonesians were boarded. These included KIM members, Walandouw, Malangkay and Sorongan and 3 others on whose behalf Mr Clarrie Campbell had unsuccessfully appealed to Calwell for an extension of their stay in Australia because they were all married to Australian women and were fathers or expectant fathers.[34] *Manoora* sailed on 1 May and arrived in Brisbane on 3 May, where a further 372 Indonesians – ex Casino via Chermside – were embarked.[35] From Brisbane she proceeded to Darwin, then to Dili where she dropped off some Timorese who had hitched a ride with the Indonesians. From Dili she sailed to Kupang where seven Kupanger pearl divers landed. There Dutch naval and army officers boarded to finalise arrangements for her arrival in Ceribon, which took place on 16 May. With the assistance of the navigating officer from the Dutch destroyer which was patrolling the port, the Republicans were contacted and asked to send launches to disembark their people. This they did, and the last repatriation was completed. *Manoora* carried on to Surabaya, the destination of the Dutch cargo she was carrying.[36]

Thus, the Indonesian 'invasion' of Australia, which had started early in 1942 virtually came to an end some five years later. After this just a few remained, including some former pearl divers who had returned to Broome to work, and in Brisbane Bondan (now married to Molly) and Slamet, because they were winding up the affairs of CENKIM. One of its many activities had been to act as a conduit between the Australian Government and the Indonesians themselves in the negotiations and arrangements for the repatriations. With the repatriations over, the work of CENKIM too was almost over.

The war brides

While the story of the many Australian women who married American servicemen stationed in Australia during the war is well known, there was another smaller group of war brides whose story is less familiar – the courageous women who crossed racial, cultural and religious barriers to marry Indonesians. In the White Australia of the 1940s, a country with perhaps the most discriminatory racial policy in the world, many of these women faced prejudice from society at large and from their own friends and families as well as societal and economic hardship as a result of their choice of husband. For example they, and in fact any woman who married a foreigner, were required to register themselves as 'Aliens by Marriage' and surrender their British nationality. There are no figures available for the number of Australian women who married loyal Indonesian members of the NEI forces, but one estimate prepared by the Department of Immigration in July 1947, noted that about 40 of the Indonesians who refused to work for the Dutch had 'white Australian wives' and about 10 had 'coloured Australian wives' The majority of these women married merchant seamen, including petty officers whom they met at the Indonesia Club in Sydney.[37] Others married former Digul men.

Their experiences in later life very much depended on which 'category' of Indonesian they married. When the war ended and the Indonesians started going home, their wives naturally expected to go with them. For those who had married servicemen still loyal to the Dutch, this apparently did not present any great problem. A Department of Immigration note mentioned that they had the opportunity of going on Dutch ships or planes and did not need to apply for Australian passports as they were Dutch subjects by marriage.[38] However, those who married Indonesian rebels had a harder time of it. As mentioned above, some 'coloured' Australian wives had been passengers on the *Manoora* in November 1946 and again in May 1947, but 'white' wives were not permitted to accompany their husbands at that stage. Mr Calwell explained in Parliament in April, before the final repatriation, that it had been intended to allow the wives and children of the Indonesians to accompany them (at Government expense) but this decision had been reversed following a request from the Indonesian Republican authorities not to let any Australian women go to Indonesia yet. He added that at a future date when conditions improved any wives who still wanted to go could do so, but at their own expense.[39]

Calwell had been guided in his decision by information from the Australian representative in Jakarta, Mr Ballard. He mentioned the difficult living conditions, high cost of living, primitive facilities and the fact that the Indonesian-Australian Association, recently established by repatriates from Australia, had recommended that the wives delay their arrival until conditions and security improved.[40] This decision was a blow to the women, who had been told on 21 March that they would be able to join their husbands on the *Manoora* for the final repatriation in May. But, in the middle of their preparations, they received an order on 10 April that permission had been withdrawn. Mrs Jean Batjo, one of the wives, sent Calwell an impassioned letter, signed by herself and nine others, protesting —

> No consideration at all was given to the welfare of wives and children left stranded by this order and that (*sic*) no mention is made of the possibility of or date for us rejoining our husbands. Without exception our Indonesian husbands have been good citizens whilst in Australia. We are devoted to them and our children and being fully aware of the difficulties awaiting us desire with all our hearts to accompany them ... We beg you to enable us to proceed with our husbands on the Manoora as originally ordered, or failing this, grant our husbands an extension of leave to remain in Australia until such time as you may think fit for us to accompany them. By doing this you will help us to preserve our happy established family groups save untold hardship to wives and children and earn our true gratitude.[41]

The matter was raised again in Parliament on 30 April when Mr Beazley drew the attention of Mr Calwell to an article in the *Canberra Times* about the plight of the wife of one Indonesian, A.J. Maramis, who had been arrested and held in gaol pending his deportation the next day on *Manoora*. Maramis had met Lotte Reid, staunch Sydney AIA member, at the Indonesia Club and the couple were married in January 1947. Considering that Mrs Maramis and other wives should be allowed to join their husbands, Beazley appealed to Calwell, '... does not the honourable gentleman regard the right to choose whom one will marry as a fundamental human right which should not be interfered with by preventing Australian women joining their Asiatic husbands, however mistaken the Government may feel their marriages to be'?[42] Calwell merely reiterated his earlier statement about his decision being in the best interests of the women's safety and comfort and made it clear that there would be no exceptions.

Apart from the unhappiness caused by being separated from their husbands, the wives left behind faced great economic hardship. As the Indonesian Ministry for Foreign Affairs had pointed out to the Australian Political representative in Jakarta back in July 1946, there was a difference between the wives whose husbands were still loyal and employed by the Dutch and those whose husbands were repatriated on *Esperance Bay* and *Manoora*. The loyalists still received their regular salaries and could therefore support their wives and were soon reunited in Indonesia. However, the men who had refused to co-operate any longer with the Dutch had become unemployed, and could not make provision for their wives in Australia after they were repatriated.[43]

When CENKIM received word that the wives would not be permitted to join the final repatriation voyage, Bondan wrote to Calwell pleading for financial help for 'these unfortunate women and their children'. Pointing out the logistical difficulties of the husbands sending money from Republican Indonesia in the circumstances at the time, Bondan even optimistically floated the idea of some sort of centralised accommodation such as a hostel being provided for the women and children in one of the capital cities.[44] This did not eventuate and for the most part the women seem to have been forced to share accommodation with each other or board with friends or family. Whatever financial assistance they did receive was largely due to the efforts of CENKIM, which negotiated on their behalf with Republican authorities in Indonesia and with the Immigration Department in Australia.

Jean Zakaria's story

A poignant story of one of the women left behind is that of Mrs Jean Zakaria who was pregnant when her husband, an ex-Digul man, was repatriated on the final *Manoora* voyage. Unfortunately he died before she could join him, so she never made the trip to Indonesia. Jean Edgar, as she was before her marriage, was a member of the Victorian AIA and met her husband at *Roemah Indonesia* at the Hotel Metropole. Zakaria went to Melbourne to work for NIGIS after he was released from 36AEC but left when the Republic was proclaimed and worked for the Indonesian Independence Committee. Their relationship was bitterly opposed by Jean's mother and sister, even to the extent of their visiting NEI authorities and Australian Immigration officials in Melbourne and asking them to deport Zakaria.[45] Despite this opposition the couple married in December 1946. In 1947, the Commonwealth Investigation Service, which was monitoring Zakaria's movements, reported that he and his white Australian wife moved to Brisbane, where he became one of the leaders of CENKIM prior to his repatriation.[46] Jean returned to Melbourne where she gave birth to a daughter in October. Her poverty with no husband to support her meant that she had to depend on her mother and sister for help, and they minded and helped raise the baby when Jean was forced to get a job. Zakaria died some months afterwards without ever seeing his daughter, and Jean later remarried.

Jean Zakaria called her daughter Nooraya Zakaria, but the child's aunt and grandmother changed it to Patty and she was known as Patty Edgar, until she changed her name back to Nooraya Zakaria when she turned 18. Her mother rarely spoke about her father and all Nooraya knew was that he had been a freedom fighter for his country. She felt that her mother had never stopped loving him nor recovered from the circumstances of their separation and his death. Nooraya tried by various means to find information about her father. Unbeknown to her, someone from his family had been trying to trace her mother for a number of years. Finally, through an incredible set of circumstances and some good detective work, Nooraya was finally able to travel to Jakarta to be united with her large welcoming extended Indonesian family. [47]

From the Republic, through Prime Minister Sjahrir himself, CENKIM obtained permission to use some of the interest accruing from the funds deposited in the Victory Loan on behalf of the *Esperance Bay* repatriates – the funds that Molly Warner had been asked to handle when she farewelled the *Esperance Bay* from Brisbane. At the time, the ship's committee had given permission for this interest to be used for CENKIM's work and as Bondan pointed out to the Department of Immigration when reporting this development, this was only a short-term emergency measure because the funds did not belong to the Republic, but to the individual owners who would eventually have to be repaid.[48] Most of the wives who were helped by families with accommodation and child minding were able to work and did not need help from CENKIM, while others who had no help and no job were paid an average allowance of £1/10 a week, until the funds were exhausted. In October 1947 Bondan wrote to the recipients urging them to contact the Social Services and Child Welfare departments because the CENKIM payments were about to dry up.[49]

CENKIM had also made representations to the Australian Government on behalf of the wives and children, but observations by social workers who visited those who lived in Sydney and Brisbane show that they were a resilient and optimistic group of women, and the majority were reluctant to ask for 'charity'.[50] In the end the Government did decide to help out those in serious need, with Mr Chifley saying in November, 'It has been decided that in view of the unfortunate circumstances in which certain of these women are placed that unemployment, sickness or special benefit as appropriate will be paid'.[51] It was not until April 1948, almost a year after the women were prevented from leaving on the last repatriation voyage, that grants of travel facilities for wives were finally made, but only after each woman who still wanted to go had acknowledged receipt of a written statement which set out all the difficulties likely to be encountered. They also had to accept that if they resided in Indonesia they and their children would be regarded as Indonesian nationals.[52]

Young wives' tales

While the wives of the rebels were still trying to get to Indonesia to join their husbands, stories started appearing in the press about the experiences of the wives already there. For example the *Sunday Sun* (19.1.1947) reported that 15 Australian girls married to loyal Indonesians had refused to land in Jakarta and decided to come home 'after seeing their bare footed sarong clad in- laws waiting to greet them on the wharf'. In the same report and Australian who had been interned in Java by the Japanese commented, 'Washing is done on rafts or river banks, with all the women of the family doing their share. I can't imagine Australian girls being exempt'. The *Canberra Times* (1.4.1947) carried a story about Australian wives wanting to come home, with one woman claiming that when she arrived in Jakarta she found that her husband had another wife and four children whom he had neglected to tell her about. On the other hand a different picture was painted by Maramis (*Sunday Sun* 19.1.1947) when he described the conditions his Australian wife could expect. 'Many brides will go to better class suburbs ...' he said. 'The brides will have electric stoves radios and live almost a European life.'

J. Lahawia

One young woman from Casino, Mrs J. Lahawia, had met and married a loyal Indonesian soldier in NICA when she was 17 years old, went to Indonesia and found herself in Macassar living in primitive married quarters in an army camp. A solicitor engaged by her father to plead for Australian Government aid to repatriate her explained that 'she was in a pathetic state' and 'she was of course rather foolish to have contracted the marriage but at 17 I can imagine she had not the slightest idea of the sort of life she was going to lead'.[53] In the nine months it took for the government to agree to help her financially with a loan for her repatriation which finally took place in 1948, her husband was hospitalised with a nervous breakdown, it was confirmed that he would not be allowed to join his wife in Australia and her second child died shortly after birth. But despite these wretched circumstances, final approval to repatriate her was only given after a signed guarantee undertaking to repay the travel costs was received from her mother.[54]

Jean Batjo

Mrs Jean Batjo who had formerly pleaded with Calwell to allow the wives to join their husbands finally arrived in Java in October 1948, but returned to Australia, disillusioned, 8 months later, 'shocked with village life'. 'The man who was so affectionate and well mannered in Sydney had 'gone native', she said and complained about the standard of village housing and that 'colourful Java has too many smells and hazards' for Australian girls.[55]

Enid Achmad

While some of the wives who did go to Indonesia were not able to handle the conditions they faced, other remarkable women embraced their new circumstances and country and stayed for many years or for the rest of their lives. One of the latter was the former Enid Hamilton of Sydney. She met her husband, Eddie Hoesin Achmad, Inspector-General of Government shipping for the NEI navy, at the Indonesia Club. They married at St Barnabas Church, Broadway in September 1945, despite her family's objections – she was a Christian and he was a Muslim – and the advice of her local minister of religion. Her family and friends were so unhappy that nobody wanted to come to the wedding. As one of those who struck against the Dutch, Eddie was repatriated to Java but Enid was unable to join him until 1950, when the Indonesian Government paid her way. Her husband has long since passed away, but Mrs Achmed still lives in Jakarta with her family, and speaks fluent Indonesian and accented English.[56]

Jean Wachjo

Jean met her husband Maurice Lancelot, a NEI army intelligence officer in Cairns. He attended the Anglican church where she played the organ. At the time, he was undergoing training at the 'House on the Hill,' mentioned earlier in connection with training for espionage work. He became the sole survivor of a Japanese-ambushed intelligence gathering operation in New Guinea and was later decorated for bravery. Whilst the Japanese were searching for the spot where he was hiding, they actually found a bible Jean had given him, which fell out of his pocket – but they never found him. When Maurice was later posted to Brisbane he used to travel to Cairns to see

Jean, and finally asked her to join him in Brisbane. To the disgust of her parents she did this, and when they married in Brisbane in September 1944, her parents were so 'ashamed' and her brothers so 'shocked' that she was marrying an Asian that they did not attend the wedding. The couple lived in a flat in Brisbane and Jean soon became pregnant with their first child, a son.

When the war ended they left Australia when Maurice was posted to Ambon to oversee the Japanese prisoners of war who were still there, and a new world opened up for Jean, a world she loved. His next posting was to Jakarta where he eventually left NICA and joined the new Republican Army. Life here was not so pleasant and very frightening in the middle of the revolution. Many of the Republicans were suspicious of the former NICA men, who were sometimes intimidated and even murdered. Perhaps this was why he changed his name from the European sounding Lancelot, to the Indonesian sounding Wachjo. However they survived and raised a large family in the new independent republic. Maurice later left the armed forces and became a businessman, with varying degrees of success. Jean spent 27 years in Indonesia but returned to Australia when she and Maurice were divorced. Some of her children and their families now live in Jakarta and some in Australia. Jean travels back and forth to visit them as often as she can.[57]

Sheila Soegito

When late in 1945 Sheila Fitzgerald, a Sydney girl working in Melbourne, accepted an invitation from a friend to make up a foursome to play tennis, she had no idea that her whole life would radically change as a result. Neither did she know that her soon-to-be tennis partner, Lieutenant Soegito, an Indonesian officer in the NEI airforce visiting Melbourne from Brisbane, had dropped into Myers Emporium where she was working, to look her over beforehand. Romance blossomed between them and they were married in Melbourne in August, 1946. Sheila's family, who at that stage had not met Soegito, did not attend the wedding as they were disgusted that their daughter was marrying a 'black man.' Indeed, her father was so incensed that he rang from Sydney and threatened to kill any minister who agreed to marry them. Soegito, who was working as a code officer at NEI headquarters in Camp Columbia, returned to Brisbane after the

People to People

Above: Mrs Jean Wachjo on her wedding day.
Photo: Jean Wachjo.

Below: Mrs Sheila Soegito on her wedding day.
Photo: Sheila Tattersall (formerly Soegito).

wedding, and was posted back to Jakarta. Sheila followed soon after, right into the unrest of the Revolution.

She recalls the tanks rattling along the streets, outbursts of shooting and the atmosphere of fear on the one hand, and the challenge of coming to grips with the daily practicalities of living in a culture of which she had no knowledge. Her husband had not prepared her even for the basics of how to use an Indonesian bath and toilet – procedures quite different from those she was used to. Whilst still in the KNIL forces, Soegito was posted to Hollandia in Dutch New Guinea where they spent 2 years and then to Biak. They returned to Jakarta when the Indonesians gained their sovereignty, and along with many other former Indonesian officers in KNIL, Soegito joined the new Indonesian Armed Forces.

In Jakarta after independence was achieved the Soegitos lived in an apartment quite close to the Presidential Palace, and Sheila had a 'wonderful and exciting life' there. Her husband was officer-in-charge of the air force base, and life was a whirl of parties, dances and receptions at the Palace. When VIPs came to visit, Sheila would often be called upon to help with their programs because she spoke English. Thus she met the actor John Wayne, accompanied the future Prime Minister of Britain, James Callaghan, on a trip and met Sir Edmund Hillary, among other noteables.

The only shadow in her life in Indonesia was that she had two miscarriages. When she came back to Sydney after an illness, and 20 years of life in Indonesia, her husband, who had by then left the airforce and joined a building firm, followed and stayed for a short time. But when he returned to Indonesia and suggested it would be best if she stayed in Sydney she slowly realised that the marriage was over, probably under her mother-in-law's influence, because she wanted her son to have children. After some years Sheila remarried, but remembered Soegito, who has since died, and those extraordinary 20 years of her life with nothing but affection.[58]

The remarkable Molly Bondan

No anecdotes about the experiences of women who married Indonesians would be complete without reference to Molly Bondan who has already played a prominent role in this story as founder of the AIA in Sydney and dedicated worker for CENKIM after she moved to

Brisbane following the departure of the *Esperance Bay*. In October 1946 she married Bondan, so they became partners in life as well as partners in the work of CENKIM. Her own comments about that work give us a good idea of how important she thought it was. Writing to Clarrie Campbell on 12 November, 1946 she said —

> Between you me and the gate post, I sometimes get rather scared at the size of the job we are at present tackling, particularly when I remember to think we can afford no mistakes, and that maybe the quick success of the struggle up north depends on what we are doing here now. And then I wonder how on earth we are going to find time - or the competent people - to do everything we should do. When at times, on top of all that we have ... the axe of the 'prohibited immigrant' with its consequent forced repatriation at any time hanging over our heads, I begin to think we should have a hundred Clary (sic) Campbells or Bondans to get the work done.[59]

She could well have added 'a hundred Molly Bondans', as it is doubtful that the work of CENKIM could have proceeded so ably without her hard work and of course her English language skills put to such good use in official correspondence and newsletters. Her letters to Campbell give us delightful glimpses of Molly, not only the indefatigable, feisty worker for the Republic, but also the personable woman and wife. For instance, telling Campbell that one of the main CENKIM members, Simon Pinontoan had been repatriated on the second *Manoora* voyage she wrote —

> ... the little devil could do nothing but murmur the names of delicious (to him!!) Indonesian feeds from the time the arrangement was concluded until the ship sailed: indeed his last remark to me as the ship sailed off was lovingly to repeat the name of a kind of vegetable salad!!! The bloody little gutser.[60]

and later —

> ... While writing this the washing has boiled over, and now there's another lot on - Sunday is wash day and the damn flat

Social evening, 19 August 1946, Brisbane, celebrating the first anniversary of the foundation of the Republic of Indonesia.
Photo: National Australian Archives, A 6122 138 part G.

needs a scrub too. Then there are letters to do this afternoon and tonight (hooray) we are going to see 'Indonesia Calling' – the Eureka Youth League are showing it. Neither Bondan nor I have seen it yet, so this is a red letter day.[61]

Molly was eventually able to accompany Bondan to Indonesia in November 1947, when he and Slamet, the remaining two CENKIM leaders, were repatriated. We will follow their journey in the next chapter. With the departure of virtually all the Indonesians the focus now shifted entirely from the people-to-people to the political sphere.

12

Now is the Hour

As long as a permanent solution to the Dutch/Indonesian dispute remained inconclusive the Indonesians' grass roots supporters in Australia continued to exert whatever political pressure they could on the Dutch. Then, when the fragile accord reached in the Linggadjati Agreement crumbled and armed conflict erupted and escalated in Indonesia, the Australian Government found it increasingly difficult to sit on the fence of neutrality. Events finally forced it to take sides openly and emerge as a champion of Indonesia's right to independence.

Stalemate on the waterfront

Bans on loading and servicing Dutch vessels bound for Indonesia had been maintained since their imposition in September 1945, although in practice there were limited opportunities to apply them once the last of the wartime Dutch merchant ships had managed to get away in 1946. When in January 1947 Dutch officials themselves asked the unions to lift the bans entirely, Jim Healy of the WWF suggested they make their request through the Republican Government, implying that if the Republic was agreeable the unions would comply.[1] No doubt at this time the apparent rapprochement between the Dutch and the Republicans exemplified by the Linggadjati Agreement led everyone concerned to believe that the end of the dispute was in sight and therefore the bans would soon be lifted. But in February the ACTU received a message from the newly established All Indonesia Central Trade Organisation, SOBSI, which put an end to any conciliatory thoughts. Requesting that union support continue, SOBSI claimed that despite the Agreement, the Dutch were still carrying out acts of aggression with the aim of crushing the Republic.[2]

Another impediment to having the bans lifted was the naval blockade the Dutch had imposed on ports in Republican territory

'SLAVE OF THE LAMP'

Cartoon: Courier Mail, 1 April 1947

since late 1946. As a result the Republic was powerless to engage in any trade independently of the Dutch and unable to import any military equipment to strengthen its forces. Sjahrir told the Australian Consul Van Mook had proposed that they (Sjahrir and Van Mook) make a joint appeal to the unions requesting the shipment of NEI government goods still stockpiled in Australia. However, Sjahrir was not disposed to help the Dutch until they were prepared to reciprocate by freeing Republican ports.[3] With no request to the contrary from the Republic the unions decided to stand firm.

The Honorary Trade Commissioner

By the end of 1946, trade was on the minds of both the Australian and the Republican Governments and each had been independently exploring ideas on how to establish trade relations. The Australian Government, encouraged by the legitimising of the Republic implicit in the Linggadjati Agreement, encouraged its representatives in Jakarta to establish informal contacts with the Sjahrir government to explore such matters, while at the same time CENKIM was encouraging the Republican Government to set up import/export enterprises in Australia. Heavily involved in the CENKIM dealings was Clarrie Campbell, already a prominent player in this story. He was an unusual character – unusual because it seems he was able to marry his socialist beliefs with the hard-nosed capitalism that made him a successful businessman and Managing Director of United Lubricants. Through his participation in both the Indian and Indonesian Seamen's Unions, and on the executive of the AIA, Campbell was in the forefront of political agitation on behalf of the Indonesian Republic in Sydney. Whether he was motivated by altruism or business opportunism he was now looking for a new dimension to his involvement. On CENKIM'S recommendation he wrote to Sjahrir suggesting that trade between the two countries be commenced 'through official channels' and offering in the interim to become the Honorary Trade Commissioner for the Republic in Australia. His offer was accepted and he was appointed in December 1946.[4]

Word of this must have been made public in some way, because Campbell soon began receiving approaches from various quarters expressing interest in trade with Indonesia. The Western Australian Chamber of Commerce for instance had importers and exporters looking for opportunities.[5] In the first three months of 1947 Campbell also received a spate of letters from individuals looking for opportunities to work in and for Indonesia. These were adventurous people prepared to face the rigours of life in a foreign country – an Asian country in the middle of a revolution at that – and lend their expertise to the new Republic. For example, on the basis that he had travelled in Java, knew the Malay language and the ways and culture of the people, Mr L. Robinson expressed interest in 'a job in Java with the (non-existent) Economics Branch of the Australia Indonesia Association'.[6] Then there was Mrs Lorraine O'Farrell, a journalist with the *Sunday Telegraph*, who sought a position that would enable her 'to help the Indonesian republic in whatever way possible'.[7] Another very enthusiastic applicant was the journalist, John Thompson, who had been one of the first Australian journalists to visit Java immediately after the Japanese surrender, as War Correspondent for the Australian Broadcasting Commission. After his recall to Australia in January 1946 he wrote a book (*Hubbub in Java)* about his experiences; experiences that had clearly made him sympathetic to the Indonesian cause. In March 1947 Thompson expressed these – radical for their times – sentiments —

Personally I would like to study Java, Sumatra, Bali and Celebes for years and I would like the youngster to grow up with a mixed Austral-Asiatic background. It would be a very good basis for living in tomorrow's world. Qualifications: I am very fond of the Indonesians. [8]

A week later he wrote again, telling Campbell that applications for Indonesian jobs were 'pouring in' including one from one of his wife's best friends, a teacher who Thompson proposed could establish 'an intelligent Austral-Asiatic school' for the children of the expatriates he expected to flood into the country.[9] There was also a significant number of technicians and tradesmen employed in the Queensland sugar industry in towns such as Tully, Innisfail and Cairns, who were keen to work in Indonesia. A Mr Miller, who seems to have been recruiting on Campbell's behalf, sent him a list of 15 names of people 'keenly interested to work in Indonesia' while others contacted Campbell directly.[10] This correspondence is a reminder that Australian community support for the Indonesians was not just limited to the waterside unions and the Communist Party.

Whether Campbell started recruiting people on his own initiative, whether the Republic asked him to or whether the applicants themselves took the initiative is not known. Nor is there any evidence of an influx of Australians actually going off to work in Indonesia at that time. Based on the optimism and high hopes expressed in their letters there must have initially been some disappointed people when it all came to nothing, but this may well have turned to relief when armed conflict broke out between the Dutch and the Republicans a few months later.

Nothing came of Campbell's attempts to set up trading ventures either. It was probably a premature plan anyway, with no appropriate structures in place in either country, and with shipping bans in Australia and the Dutch blockade of Republican ports still in place. Perhaps another reason was that the Australian Government never accorded him any kind of official accreditation or recognition as a basis for negotiations. He did manage to meet with Evatt, who apparently expressed the fear that the Dutch would 'grab' for themselves anything Australian interests managed to get into the country. In a letter to CENKIM on 8 February, Campbell wrote of his frustration and the difficulty of finding out just what goods were needed by the Republic —

> I do wish we could get an answer to our December letter (to the Republic) so it would be known just what is wanted. Machines and machine parts could mean anything, agricultural machines could be suitable here and useless there. Motor tyres have scores of sizes, radios could be A.C. or D.C. and so on, and it is not until you get down to fundamentals that clarity is required.[11]

In order to get this clarity, Campbell decided he should travel to Indonesia as quickly as possible so he could confer with authorities there. In May 1947, coinciding with his visit, it happened that the first congress of SOBSI was being held in East Java. As trade unions had been suppressed under Dutch rule, this was a red-letter occasion. In the interests of establishing close contact with the Australian union movement, SOBSI had invited Australian delegates to attend the congress and those chosen by the ACTU were appropriately enough, the WWF officials who had been most involved with the Indonesians, Healy and Roach. By the time the Congress got under way, Campbell was already in Indonesia and took the opportunity to attend, even though trade discussions were not on the agenda and he was not a delegate. In fact, not only did he attend but he aroused the ire of the Australian delegates by addressing the Congress on political matters which were not in his domain, before they had even arrived in Java.[12] When reports reached Australia that Campbell had taken it upon himself to inform the Congress that Australian unionists were planning a world-wide ban on Dutch ships, the Federal Opposition condemned this revelation and Dr Evatt had to explain in Parliament that Campbell had no Government accreditation and that even the ACTU had repudiated his statement about a world-wide ban on Dutch shipping.[13]

Whether it was because of his inability to make any headway on trade matters, his gaffe at the SOBSI Congress and the subsequent criticism from the ACTU, or the appointment by the Republic of Dr Oesman Sastroamidjojo as its *de facto* representative to Australia, Campbell resigned from his position as Honorary Trade Representative on 30 May,[14] and from then on his involvement in Indonesian matters fades from our story. Dr Oesman arrived in Australia on 11 June, bearing personal letters to Chifley and Evatt from Sjahrir, praising the kindness of the Australian Government in dealing with his compatriots and their hardships in Australia and expressing his optimism about prospects for future peaceful and prosperous relations between the two countries.[15] But peace in Indonesia itself, was still a long way off.

The First Police Action and reaction of the Australian Government

On 20 July 1947, in contravention of the Linggadjati Agreement which had finally been signed and become effective in March, Dutch armed forces launched a major offensive against the Republic, an offensive they claimed was merely a 'police action in which military police were charged essentially with police duties'.[16] During the prolonged negotiations and stalling over the formal signing of the Agreement, the Dutch had apparently been building up their military strength in preparation for such a strike, which appeared aimed at regaining complete sovereignty over the NEI.[17] The result was that with the element of surprise on their side plus their superior weaponry, the Dutch forces gained control of Republican ports in Java (thereby also gaining control of valuable export commodities awaiting the lifting of the Dutch blockade) while in Sumatra they seized significant plantations and oil and coal fields. Caught unawares, the outmanoeuvred and poorly armed Republican Army retreated to the mountainous areas to wage guerilla warfare.[18]

Bondan immediately contacted Chifley to clarify the gravity of the situation. Taking it upon himself to speak on behalf of the Republic even though CENKIM had no official status with the Republican Government, Bondan spelt out the extent of what he called 'warfare'. Based on information obtained by monitoring radio broadcasts from Yogyakarta, (the Republican capital) he claimed that 100,000 Dutch combined land, sea and air forces had launched an attack on military and non-military objectives throughout Java and Sumatra at midnight of July 20 and that heavy fighting was going on in all demarcation areas. Asserting that this was proof the Dutch had no intention of accepting the territory accorded to the Republic under the Linggadjati Agreement, Bondan called on the Australian Government, as one of the 'guardians of democracy,' to refer the dispute to the United Nations Organisation, an appeal Soekarno had also made to anyone who could do so, in a dramatic speech the previous evening.[19]

The Government, had in fact already announced its intention to raise the Dutch/Indonesian dispute with the Security Council or the U.N. General Assembly, four days before the Dutch offensive took place. After it was launched, and while the governments of the U.K. and the U.S. were still procrastinating and looking for other solutions, the Governments of Australia and India each independently brought the whole dispute to the United Nations Security Council, with the principle aim of securing a cease-fire and stopping bloodshed while the dispute was arbitrated. This marked the beginning of major changes in the direction and emphasis of Australia's foreign policy.

Surabaya Sue and the university students

After news of the police action appeared in the Australian press one of the few public protests came from students of the University of Sydney. The catalyst for this was an extraordinary woman called Muriel Pearson *aka* K'tut Tantri, dubbed 'Surabaya Sue' by the Australian press and security officials. She was a native born Scot who worked as a journalist in the United States before travelling to the NEI in the 1930s. There, in fairy-tale fashion, she was adopted as a daughter by a Balinese king, and lived in his palace as a member of his household. Vehemently opposed to the Dutch colonialists, she refused to leave Bali with them when the Japanese invaded and was later interned and tortured by the Japanese in the mistaken suspicion that she was an American spy. When the war ended, she allied herself with the Indonesians against the returning Dutch, probably the first Western foreigner to do so in Indonesia itself. She involved herself in the Revolution by joining the guerillas in the hills and broadcasting anti-Dutch propaganda, which resulted in the Dutch putting a price on her head. Later she moved to the Republican capital Yogyakarta and worked for Soekarno as his translator and English language speech-writer, and also broadcaster on the Voice of Free Indonesia radio station, whose messages were monitored by CENKIM in Brisbane.[20]

In 1947 she left Indonesia for Singapore and after wangling an entry permit from the Australian High Commissioner there, set out in June for Australia, where her arrival immediately attracted the attention of the Commonwealth Investigation Service because of her very public pro-Indonesia leanings and activities such as her address to students of the Sydney University Labor Club on 24 July.[21] Outlining the Dutch violation of the Linggadjati Agreement, she painted a graphic picture of the desperate plight of the Indonesian fighters, '... ill equipped to fight against the planes and tanks of the Dutch. Their army is dressed in rags and has little more than bamboo spears ... there are few doctors or hospitals and they are acutely short of medical supplies'.[22] She pleaded for Australians to send medical aid, and the meeting ended with discussion about staging some sort of a protest.

Wasting no time, the next day students and others (including wharf labourers) held a demonstration outside the offices of the Dutch Consulate-General in Margaret Street in the city, with violent consequences resulting from the heavy handedness which typified the way the police used to deal with any possibly communist inspired demonstrations. The front page story in the *Sydney Morning Herald*, (26.7.1947) described the 'wild fight' as police broke up the demonstration and arrested people. The crowd of many onlookers and about 200 participants (among them Surabaya Sue) had assembled in Wynyard Park for a peaceful protest and speeches against Dutch policy in Indonesia, after which a number of students marched up Margaret Street towards the Dutch Consulate in the Kembla Building, carrying banners and placards with anti-Dutch inscriptions. When they tried to enter the building they were prevented by plainclothes policemen (who did not identify themselves) who tore down banners when students refused to surrender them. That was when the trouble started. As the *Herald* described it —

> During the disturbances banners and placards were torn down, poles on which they had been carried were used as weapons, punches were exchanged, men and women were hurled on the roadway and water was poured over the struggling mob from a high building.

Back on the campus more than a thousand students attended a meeting defending the right to peaceful demonstration and urging an inquiry to find out what had provoked the violence of 'The Battle of Kembla'.[23] Opinions expressed in the student newspaper *Honi Soit* varied from condemnation of the police for their violence from Labor Club supporters, to compliments from conservatives linking the demonstration and the Republican cause with the Communists. H. Brunen's sentiments were a good example of the latter point of view —

> Any doubts Sydney may have about the efficiency and ability of its police force must have been dispelled by those who had the pleasure of seeing the collection of long-haired nigger-lovers who staged the disgraceful exhibition outside the Dutch consulate on Friday having their skulls cracked, being laid low in the gutter and then being escorted away as guests of the Government in police vans. The insolence of the Labor Club supporters who purport to represent student opinion on this question is completely intolerable to all those who acclaim Dutch action in Java as a long- delayed move to free the country from the grip of the Communist 'Republican' Government, most of whose members actively collaborated with the Japanese during the occupation.[24]

More union pressure

Characteristically it was the unions who took the most decisive action in retaliation against the Dutch offensive. Following the 'police action,' SOBSI had issued this plea —

> ... we appeal to all democratic and progressive people everywhere, and especially to the working class in all countries of the world to boycott all that is Dutch in all harbours, stores, roadways and other places throughout the world in the event of the outbreak of war in Indonesia. The working class of Indonesia have faith in and are relying on the working class of the international world.[25]

On 5 August the Australian unions responded when in Sydney the ACTU (backing the waterside unions this time) convened a conference of 18 Federal unions associated with land and sea transport, and passed a unanimous resolution condemning the Dutch 'war of aggression against the Indonesian people' and calling on trade unionists to refuse to move Dutch goods or to perform maintenance work on any Dutch vessels, vehicles or aircraft in Australia, until a request to the contrary from the Indonesian trade union movement.[26] Ted Roach later claimed that within a couple of days of these extended bans being applied, workers in British Colombia, the Suez Canal, India, Siam, New Zealand and other countries quickly took similar action, to protest at the 'brutal and unprovoked attack by Dutch Militarists'.[27]

An unsigned memorandum (27.11.1947) emanating from a Dutch source, probably the Netherlands Ministry in Canberra, gives rare access to what Dutch authorities were saying to each other privately about the bans and their effects. It was noted that public opinion in the Netherlands was perturbed by the 'antagonistic attitude' of certain Australian trade unions, particularly after the extension of the boycott following the police action, and also that 'Australia was not an unbiased nor unprejudiced observer of events'.[28] The memorandum further acknowledged that in addition to whatever the propaganda effects of the bans in publicizing the Republican cause, the hold up of their cargos in Australia was really hurting the Dutch financially. As this excerpt put it —

> It needs no comment that the continuation of the boycott places a heavy financial burden on the Netherlands at a time when the foreign exchange position is extremely difficult. The storage, maintenance, administration etc. of the supplies involve expenditure of large amounts plus the upkeep of a relatively large civil personnel. The supplies were in the main purchased and paid for in 1945, hence the loss of interest and the risk of deterioration of goods is very considerable ... No gesture of goodwill could be more telling nor have greater effect than if the Australian Government were to use their influence for the termination of the shipping ban.[29]

The unions would have been heartened had they had access to this document.

The decision to extend the boycott set off another round of

Now is the Hour

attacks by the Federal Opposition, during which all their old arguments about Communist unions dictating Foreign Policy, betrayal of gallant white Dutch allies, the Japanese collaborator Soekarno and the so-called Communist-led and inspired Indonesian Revolution were aired. They even criticized the Government for referring the dispute to the United Nations, implying that this was only done as a result of union pressure.

Chifley defended the Government's action in referring the matter to the United Nations as a step towards stopping bloodshed and reiterated that the Australian Government was not taking and never had taken sides in the dispute. He reminded the House that as a result of the Government initiative, the UN Security Council had now set up a Committee of Good Offices to arbitrate the dispute. The Indonesian Republic had shown its esteem for Australia by nominating it (with Justice Kirby as spokesman) as its representative, the Netherlands had nominated Belgium and together, Australia and Belgium had nominated the United States as the third member. This positive move did not dampen the Opposition's enthusiasm for repeating the same old arguments and criticisms *ad nauseum* for weeks to come.

Whatever Chifley said about his government not taking sides in the dispute, the Republican Government saw things differently. In a radio message on 10 August, Prime Minister Sjarifuddin (who had recently replaced Sjahrir) thanked Chifley profusely for 'defending the Indonesian cause before the forum of the United Nations'. Noting the assistance given by Australians to Indonesians in their struggle for freedom and democracy, he expressed his 'deep gratitude to the Government and people of Australia who have repeatedly proved their sympathy for the Indonesian cause.'[30]

Bearing in mind these sentiments, had he seen it the Indonesian Prime Minister would no doubt have been puzzled by the results of an opinion poll taken in August 1947. True, the number of those supporting restoration of Dutch rule had fallen substantially from 41% in the December 1945 poll to 23%. This was possibly a reaction to the Dutch police action, but at the same time, support for Indonesian rule also dropped, from 29% to 18%. Support for joint rule rose from 13% to 15%, but the winner was 'abstain,' up to 44% from 17%.[31] These results suggested that rather than being sympathetic to the Indonesian cause the vast majority of the Australian public

259

was uninterested or disinterested in the conflict to the north, even though the newspapers were full of it.

Medical Aid for Indonesia

While the students demonstrated, the unions extended their bans and the politicians and diplomats wrestled with the dispute at national and international levels, some Republican supporters in Sydney responded to the outbreak of hostilities following the Dutch offensive on a more practical and humanitarian level. On 13 August an association called Medical Aid to Indonesia was formed with the stated aims of conducting an appeal for medical aid and obtaining and dispatching medical supplies and medical and nursing personnel to the Republic.[32] As was its wont with any Indonesia-related organization, the Commonwealth Investigation Service, ever vigilant against possible communist plots, immediately launched an investigation into the activities and office bearers of the new association. It should come as no surprise that it reported that the organization was under communist control and suspected that the body would be used for propaganda purposes.

Given that at the time this judgement was made (12 September) the association had only just been formed, no activities had taken place, and the only one proposed at the time was a fund raising button day on the streets of Sydney, the report provides a good illustration of the paranoia about communism that existed in the post-war period in Australia. Perhaps the fact that the CPA was going to 'organize all branches in an endeavour to sell 12,000 buttons at sixpence each' was cause for alarm. However, it was the alleged political leanings of the office bearers that sealed the communist label for the association. For example, the Right Reverend Moyes, Bishop of Armidale, who was a patron, was highly suspect because he was on the executive of an organisation called Christian Social Order Movement, 'believed to have Communist tendencies'. Vice-President Reverend William Coughlan, an Anglican clergyman of Woolwich, was suspect for the same reason. The office-bearers included doctors, lawyers, journalists, unionists, public servants and academics, and the unlikely claim was made that all had some degree of 'communist tendencies'. It was anticipated that similar organizations would be formed in Melbourne and Brisbane and the conclusion drawn that it was highly likely there was a connection between Medical Aid for Indonesia and the Indonesian Republic.

Not much is known about the longevity or success of Medical Aid for Indonesia, but *Tribune* (2.11.1947) did report the safe arrival of some medical supplies it somehow sent to Republican territory, and the thanks from Vice-President Hatta.

The sting in the tail

With the arrival in Australia in June of Dr Oesman Sastroamidjojo, acting as *de facto* Ambassador for the Republic of Indonesia, the work of CENKIM was gradually wound down until it ceased altogether in the latter half of 1947. This meant that there was no longer any reason for the Government to allow Bondan and Slamet, the two remaining members, to stay in Australia any longer. Despite the ban on Australian wives accompanying their Indonesian husbands, an exception was made in the case of Molly Bondan who heard the joyous news that she would be able to accompany her husband, two days after she returned home from hospital with their new-born son, Alit.[33]

In keeping with its policy of repatriating Indonesian nationalists to Republican territory, the Department of External Affairs informed the Netherlands Legation of its intention to follow this procedure with the Bondans and Slamet, and requested its co-operation. An assurance of this came on 21 October, when the Legation informed the Department that no restrictions would be placed on the repatriates, who would be allowed to travel freely to their final destination.[34] With this assurance the way seemed clear for the repatriation to proceed without incident and on 29 October the *News Weekly* reported that a big social event had been held in Brisbane to farewell 'Messrs. Slamet and Bondan, the remnant of the great Indonesian influx'. But on 7 November, just as the travellers were about to commence their journey, the Australian Consul in Jakarta, Mr Eaton, reported that Dutch authorities in Jakarta were raising 'technical issues' revolving around what they termed 'normal foreign landing routine'. Clearly disconcerted by this hitch, the Department quickly instructed Eaton to remind the Dutch authorities that their colleagues in Canberra had already given positive assurances and therefore the movement would be proceeding as planned.[35] Yet again NEI authorities in Jakarta were interfering in an agreement made between their Dutch counterparts in Australia and the Australian Government, and demonstrating their unwavering resentment towards the rebels and determination to make their situation as difficult as possible.

The first stage of the journey took the Bondan party to Darwin to wait for a connecting plane to transport them to Yogyakarta, their destination, with a fuelling stopover at Surabaya *en route*. After being issued with NEI entry visas by the Dutch Consul in Darwin, on 27 November 1947 Molly, Bondan and Slamet with nine weeks old Alit sleeping peacefully, took off from Darwin in an Australian Dakota with an Australian crew, bound for the Republic.[36] For Bondan and Slamet, who had spent 9 years in Boven Digul and then a further 4 years in Australia, the prospect of going home must have been an overwhelming joy, and for Molly, finally seeing her new homeland, the country for which she had worked so tirelessly for the past two years, was eagerly anticipated.

It was when the plane reached Surabaya for the refuelling stop that the NEI authorities played their hand. The most colourful (and amusing) account of what happened comes from Molly herself in a letter she wrote to Dr Burton, Secretary of the Department of External Affairs, a few days later. 'Our reception at Soerabaja airfield was in the best Nazi tradition, except that their guns were hidden in valises,' she wrote scornfully. 'Slamet was even refused permission to go to the toilet until I made a loud and wrathful fuss.'[37] The party was separated from the other passengers, all their luggage was unloaded from the plane and they were then taken off to a hotel in town, 'not a bad place – better beds than Darwin (excuse the dig!) – but dirty. Good food. But we were all under strict room arrest and had two armed guards on constant duty, one even trotting like a sheep dog at our heels when any one of us went to bathroom or lavatory'. The next day all the luggage was searched, and the day after, passengers, 'including the baby's pants, unfortunately just wet at the time,' and luggage, were searched again.

Describing the 'total haul' from the two searches, Molly listed such 'seditious' material as four books on Marxism, Sun Yat Sen on China, T.E. Lawrence on Arabia, classical music records, CENKIM files, and even 'the letters of the poor damn fool Australian wives

Now is the Hour

to their husbands, lipstick kisses and all'. She described the farcical nature of the search and the excessive number of personnel who conducted it as follows —

> You'd have thought we were arch enemy and king pin in the struggle against the NEI Government instead of three poor devils of very handicapped coots who'd been living on the smell of a rice husk and putting out a very second rate rag by way of propaganda, by the fuss they made.

On 13 November, the Department of External Affairs heard of the incident in a report from Mr Eaton in Jakarta. Flight Lieutenant Banyan, captain of the Dakota, had immediately informed Eaton of the forced disembarkation of the repatriates and their luggage when he arrived in Jakarta after being allowed take off from Surabaya without his passengers. The Department was appalled and instructing Eaton to lodge an immediate protest, cabled back immediately —

> This comes to us as a shock since besides certain admittedly unsatisfactory written assurances, we had most explicit verbal assurances from the Netherlands legation that the persons concerned would not be interfered with ... In our view the Dutch have been equivocal to the point of dishonesty, since they knew perfectly well that we had undertaken to return the persons to Indonesia and not into the hands of those who have previously kept them in political internment in New Guinea, and that we would not have let them go if we had not been sure that we could rely on Dutch co-operation.[38]

The protest was effective. Dutch authorities conveyed an apology to Eaton, blaming the whole incident on a misunderstanding between the Netherlands Legation in Canberra and the NEI authorities in Jakarta. Moreover, they undertook to bring the repatriates to Jakarta and accommodate them at Netherlands expense until it was convenient to transport them to Yogyakarta,[39] and this they soon did.

There may have been some truth in the Dutch explanation for the incident, but it is hard to accept that it was only a misunderstanding between two sets of officials. It seemed par for the course that during every repatriation, Dutch authorities, either in Australia or in Indonesia or both, had put some sort of obstacle in the path of a smooth operation. Frustration that these people they saw as rebellious native troublemakers who had dared to defy them were out of their reach, and with the help of the Australian Government were sent safely to Republican territory, must have been intense. Interfering with the repatriation of Bondan and Slamet, who through CENKIM had been the effective leaders of the Indonesian revolution in Australia, was an attempt to inject one last sting in the tail. But as with the earlier incidents, this too became merely an irritant, and the repatriation was completed successfully.

We return to Molly's letter to Burton (written from Jakarta while they waited for transport to Yogyakarta) for the final words on this incident. Never one to let an opportunity for anti-Dutch propaganda pass her by, she wrote —

> Of course, we have known all along that, quite apart from the broken agreement with the Australian Government which stinks of chicanery and trickery (as I have told several of the searchers), the action of the Dutch authorities here merely belittled the standing of their own officials in Australia who probably concluded details of the arrangement. And quite frankly, we were calculating on you getting good and mad! Politically also, I don't mind admitting that the thought more than crossed my mind that the longer the Dutch detained us, the better for the Republic.[40]

This remarkable woman devoted the rest of her life to working in various capacities for her adopted country. She and Bondan arrived safely in Yogyakarta where they lived during the Revolution, and where Molly worked in the Indonesian Department of Foreign Affairs. After independence, the family moved to Jakarta where among other tasks she wrote Soekarno's English speeches for him. In the 1950s she became well known to some of the first Australian Volunteer Graduates who came to work in Indonesia. Bondan died in February 1981, and Molly nine years later, in January 1990. The same year she was posthumously presented with a prestigious award from the Indonesian Government in recognition of her services to the Republic.[41]

The escaped criminal

There was one other case involving the repatriation of an Indonesian nationalist which illustrated the determination of the Australian Government to honour its agreement to return such people to Republican territory. This involved one Soegoro Atmaprasadja who had been sentenced in January 1947 to four years imprisonment in Dutch New Guinea for 'complicity in riots against the NEI Government'. He had escaped, been recaptured and then escaped again to Australian New Guinea, where he had been detained and then sent to Darwin to await repatriation. Before this could happen word came from the Netherlands legation in Canberra that he would not be allowed to fly on to Yogyakarta but would be arrested in Surabaya when the plane stopped for fuel, because he was considered to be an escaped criminal. The Australian authorities, wanting to procure safe conduct to the Republic for him, then removed him from the plane he had just boarded. He remained in Darwin for some months where he became 'something of an embarrassment to the Northern Territory Administration'.[42] While Soegoro himself was 'perfectly law-abiding' and had been given some employment, there was a four-way tussle about what to do with him: the Northern Territory Administrator was pleading for his removal, the Minister for Immigration, Mr Calwell, was insisting that he be immediately sent to Indonesia or any other country that would have him, the Dutch were insisting that he be surrendered to them to serve his sentence, and the Department of External Affairs was appealing to the Dutch to pardon him 'since his offence was merely political and not criminal,' and trying to think of ways to get him to Republican territory. Finally, about a year after he was stranded in Darwin, a solution was found when Soegoro, a well educated man, was sent to New Delhi to fill a vacancy in the Republic's office there.

Although this incident was merely a mopping up operation in the saga of the Indonesian repatriations, the file on the Soegoro case reveals an interesting insight into the shifting attitude of the Australian Government to the Republic. A good example is this July 1948 memorandum —

> ... if Soegoro were to be shipped back to Indonesia through a Dutch-controlled port, he would be seized and thrown into

'ARE YOU COMING IN, OR HAVE I GOT TO RESCUE YOU?'
'A Dutch spokesman says Dutch forces have taken "Police action" for the purpose of "liberating" Indonesian Republican territory.'

Cartoon: *Courier Mail,* 22 December 1948

goal. If this were to happen, it could not fail to destroy the trust which the Government of the Republic of Indonesia reposes in the Australian Government. After the efforts we have made to repatriate Soegoro and our undertakings he would not be allowed to fall into Dutch hands, and in view of our declared policy of support and sympathy for the Republican Government and its followers, it is considered that such a proposal cannot be entertained.[43]

Taking sides

What had happened between Prime Minister Chifley's assertion in September 1947 that Australia was not taking sides in the dispute, and this 'declared policy of support and sympathy for the Republican Government' referred to ten months later? It is neither intended nor possible here to provide a detailed narrative of all the events, complex negotiations, proposals, counter-proposals and Australian Government involvement which culminated in the eventual Dutch transfer of sovereignty to Indonesia. Such narratives are beyond the scope of this discussion and are available elsewhere. Suffice to say,

Now is the Hour

'RIGHT ON OUR DOORSTEP'
Cartoon: *Sydney Morning Herald*, 21 December 1948

through its spokesmen on the Good Offices Committee, (First Justice R. Kirby and from March 1948, Mr Tom Critchley, an official from the Department of External Affairs) the Australian Government's sympathy with and championing of the Republic's point-of-view became more marked, even when this led to differences of opinion with their fellow Committee members from Belgium and the United States.

Eventually though it was the action of the Dutch themselves which really turned the tide, not only of Australia's, but of world opinion, against them and towards the Indonesians. The eventual cease-fire after the first police action was consolidated in an agreement known as the Renville Agreement, signed between the disputants in January 1948. But although hostilities ceased, no solution to the problems of disputed territory and make up of the proposed United States of Indonesia, acceptable to both sides, had been found. The Renville Agreement also failed when the Dutch launched another police action in December 1948. This time their forces crossed over the recognized demarcation lines between their territory and Republican territory, entered Yogyakarta and detained the Republican leaders, including Soekarno and Hatta. At this stage, any pretence the Australian Government had made of maintaining neutrality disappeared. It strongly condemned the Dutch action, viewing it as a challenge to the authority of the United Nations, and urged 'vigorous action in defence of the Republic'.[44] Chifley's own views were forthrightly expressed in a letter to a senior British official in January 1949 —

> The Dutch seem to have stirred up considerable antagonism as a result of their latest police action in Indonesia. I had a heart to heart talk with Teppema (The Dutch Minister in Australia) in Canberra recently and told him I thought his government has made a colossal blunder ...[45]

Although the Dutch had taken control of Republican areas of Java and Sumatra, there was strong resistance and fierce sustained fighting from the Republican forces. There was also widespread international condemnation of the Dutch, particularly from the United States. The United Nations, which had not had much success in solving the dispute, called for a cease-fire and release of the Republican leaders and prisoners.[46] Another initiative was taken by the Indian Government when it held a conference of Asian countries in New Delhi in January 1949 to discuss the issue. Perhaps as a sign of its changing role in its geographical region and in appreciation of its perceived anti-colonial views through its now overt support for the Indonesians, Australia was also invited to participate, and did so.[47] The resolutions passed at this conference were strongly pro-Indonesian, and were symptomatic of the direction in which world opinion was turning.

Interlude – the Annie O'Keefe case

At the time of these delicate international negotiations in which the Australian Government was involved on Indonesia's behalf, a situation arose in Melbourne which caused it great embarrassment. This was the highly publicized attempt by Immigration Minister Calwell to deport an Indonesian woman and her children from Australia, for reasons based firmly on application of the White Australia Policy. The background was that an Ambonese schoolmaster, Samuel Jacob, his wife Annie and their seven children had been among a small party who had fled the Japanese to a small island near Ambon, from where they had been rescued by HMAS *Warrnambool* in September 1942 and brought to Australia. The NEI authorities had settled the family in Melbourne at the Bonbeach home of an Australian landlord, John O'Keefe, and an eighth child was born shortly afterwards. Samuel Jacob, who had been working for the Dutch as an administrator when the Japanese invaded, quickly volunteered his services as an intelligence officer for the Allies, and was accepted. He completed a number of dangerous missions behind enemy lines, for which he was decorated for bravery, but was killed in a plane crash while on duty, in September 1944.

Mr O'Keefe, a bachelor, kept an eye out for the welfare of family, now living on a pension from the Dutch government, until in June 1947 he married Mrs Jacob and cared for the children as his own. Their lives were shaken in January 1949, when Mr Calwell ordered Mrs O'Keefe, 'a full blooded Indonesian,' and her children, to leave Australia by 28 February. This was in line with Calwell's determination to return all remaining coloured people who were evacuated to Australia during the war, to their native lands.[48] The problem was that naturally enough, after five years' residence, an Australian husband and with her children at school and in the work force, Mrs O'Keefe had no desire to leave and return to an uncertain future in the unsettled conditions that existed in Indonesia.

Once this case became public knowledge, and the deadline for the family to leave voluntarily or face deportation approached, Calwell was targetted by the Parliamentary Opposition.[49] Arguing for sympathetic treatment for the family, at least until the children had completed their education, Opposition speakers accused the Government of offending 'the peoples of Asiatic countries' through its inflexible application of the White Australia Policy, though they were at pains to assure everyone that they were not critical of the policy itself, merely its harsh application in this case.

Calwell defended his actions vehemently, referring to previous repatriations he had organized and the gratitude of the Indonesians. But his emotions got the better of him when he shouted, 'We can have a white Australia, we can have a black Australia but a mongrel Australia is impossible, and I shall not take the first steps to establish the precedents which will allow the floodgates to be opened'. Menzies condemned the speech as a shocking one which 'revealed a singularly unbalanced mind'.

Undeterred, Calwell's harshest criticism was for the Dutch, whom he accused of aggravating the whole situation. The diplomatic kid gloves had long been removed as the antagonism between Australian and Dutch authorities had escalated in the post-war years. Calwell bluntly accused the Dutch Government of 'wishing the family on Australia,' (an unfortunate choice of words in such a sensitive matter) and of trying to embarrass the Australian Government in retaliation for its participation in the New Delhi conference and for its interest in Indonesia.

The Dutch angrily denied this, and given the bad blood now existing between the two governments, they probably relished the Australians' discomfiture over this case, which was attracting a lot of negative publicity. On 8 February, the Australian Consulate in Jakarta sent the Government a collection of comments on the O'Keefe affair, taken from Dutch and regional Indonesian newspapers. The most virulent was from the Dutch paper, *Dagblad*, employing the favoured weapon of the Dutch press in attacks against Australia – accusations of racialism —

> There is no better example of the Australian contempt for coloured people than the expulsion of the Indonesian wife of an Australian by the orders of Immigration Minister Calwell. It may be true that several Australian newspapers had protested against this barbaric act, but it is an ascertained fact that the Government to which Calwell belongs which is making blunders one after the other, and carrying out the White Australia Policy very consistently as far as her internal affairs are concerned, is tolerated by the great majority of the Australian people.[50]

Later came this assessment —

> This crime towards a coloured person is the most convincing and recent proof of the fact that Australia's approach towards the coloured races of Asia is guided by the motive of fear, and once more fear, without any trace of sympathy for those in possession of the dark pigment. Of course this fact will not remain unnoticed in these countries with which Chifley's government with almost moving insincerity declared to be so closely allied.[51]

Now is the Hour

Other negative reactions came from the press in Borneo, Singapore and South Sumatra and the Sultan of West Borneo threatened to retaliate by deporting all Australians from Borneo if the O'Keefes were deported. Australian legations in the Hague, New Delhi and Karachi all came under local pressure to justify the Government's decision.[52]

In Australia, the press criticized Calwell and took a sympathetic attitude to the O'Keefes. The *Sydney Morning Herald* featured different aspects of the case right through February, for example the editorial of 7 February pulled no punches with its heading, 'How to make enemies for Australia in the East.' It attacked Calwell for embarrassing the Government with his 'tactless, provocative handling of alien problems,' and declared that 'officiousness, intolerance and lack of humanity had marked the handling of this deplorable affair'. The *Herald*, which along with the Federal Opposition and most other newspapers had never shown any particular sympathy for the plight of the other Indonesian refugees in Australia and had been glad to see the last of them, sank into hypocrisy when it spoke about 'the rejection and deportation of these friendly aliens who found sanctuary in Australia six years or so ago.' Perhaps it was the fact that all of the other Indonesians had gone that enabled the press and the Opposition to display such generosity of spirit to the O'Keefes.

The drama escalated as the deadline for voluntary departure approached, with the *Herald* publishing emotive photographs of the O'Keefe children, the home where they lived and their preparations for leaving. After all this, it must have come as a surprise to everyone to read on 15 February that the O'Keefes planned to fight the deportation, and on the same day it was announced that their solicitors would issue a High Court Writ against the Commonwealth to fight the deportation.

The case of Annie Maas O'Keefe v A.A. Calwell and the Commonwealth of Australia came up for hearing on 28 February before the Full High Court of Australia, and continued until 2 March.[53] The legal arguments were complex but rested on the Crown's case that Mrs O'Keefe was a migrant and therefore 'within the category of persons liable to be prohibited from remaining in the Commonwealth,' or on her case that she was an evacuee from the NEI and not a migrant so was therefore, 'not subject to the deportation power of the Immigration Act'.[54]

On the 18 March the verdict was handed down: by a majority of four to two, Mrs O'Keefe was granted an injunction restraining the Minister for Immigration from deporting her. The *Sydney Morning Herald* (19.3.1949) hailed this victory as a 'rebuff for Mr Calwell'. In a comment that typified the sophistry which had been used to justify the White Australia policy since its inception, by pretending that it was actually nothing to do with race, the editorial said —

> Mr Calwell, by his ill-judged zeal in trying to push out of this country all of the few wretched aliens who had been involuntarily planted here by the war, has converted the sore point into a raw wound. Whereas intelligent Asiatics were willing to concede that Australia had a justifiable economic basis for her immigration policy, there is now a dangerous tendency to see it as an offensive manifestation of racialism.

The O'Keefe case was one of the earliest legal challenges to the Immigration Restriction Act. It became a *cause celebre* which the Australian Government could have done without at that particular time. Calwell saw himself as doing his duty and upholding the immigration laws of the country as he had always done. But his rigidity in a case which tugged at the collective heart strings of the nation and received such wide spread unfavourable publicity did present a negative picture of Australia as a racist country at a time when, for its first venture into foreign policy independent of the United Kingdom, it was lining up with Asian countries against a European power.

In February 1949, while the O'Keefe case was in the public eye, another opinion poll was taken about the Indonesian situation. This showed some slight variation compared to the previous one in 1947 and also indicated that the Government's now overt political support of the Republic was out of step with public opinion. Despite the second Dutch police action, the number supporting Dutch rule in Indonesia rose 5% to 23% while support for Indonesian rule rose only 1% to 19%. Support for joint rule fell 4% to 11%, and though falling by 2% to 42%, the winner was still 'abstain'.[55] It seems amazing that such a large percentage of the Australian public still did not or could not formulate an opinion about the power struggle taking place on their doorstep.

Now is the Hour

Merdeka at last

As a result of intense negotiations in Jakarta, Dutch soldiers were withdrawn from the Republican capital, Yogyakarta, in June 1949. Soekarno was released and returned there in July, and a cease-fire order came into effect in August. In August also the Dutch initiated a Round Table conference in the Hague between Republican Indonesian, non-Republican Indonesian and Dutch delegates, together with the representatives from the UN Commission for Indonesia, with Australian Tom Critchley as first chairperson. Painfully – particularly for the Dutch – and painstakingly, the many differences between the parties were thrashed out and the conference concluded in November, with an agreement that the Netherlands would unconditionally transfer sovereignty of its former territory (except for West New Guinea) to the Republic of the United States of Indonesia, comprising the Republic of Indonesia and a number of Dutch-sponsored states.[56]

In common with most of the Australian press, the *Sydney Morning Herald's* response to the news was lukewarm. In an editorial (3.11.1949) that was largely devoted to praise for the Dutch as colonial administrators, a note of foreboding was struck —

> If stresses inherent in a rambunctious nationalism imposed upon a teeming colonial population are too severe for the structure that has so painfully evolved in Indonesia, we in Australia may yet have heavy cause to regret the premature passing of Dutch authority.

On 1 December, at the request of the WWF, the ACTU convened a Sydney meeting of representatives from the 17 unions involved in the shipping bans. Jim Healey reported that in light of the Hague settlement, the Council of the WWF had formed the opinion that it was time to lift the bans, and a resolution to this effect was passed unanimously. The resolution included the following appraisal —

> Despite the many attacks by political and trade interests opposed to our policy and the many distortions and hostile attacks published in the Australian press, we are satisfied that not only was our action justified but that it assisted materially

'THINGS ARE HAPPENING NEXT DOOR'

Cartoon; Courier Mail, 10 September 1949

in attracting world interest and support for the struggle and aspirations of the Indonesian people.[57]

The validity of this claim cannot be disputed and the unions' pride in it is justified. As mentioned previously the Dutch themselves acknowledged that the four year ban really hurt them economically, although the waterside workers may not have known that at the time. The bans had also cost Australia 60 million pounds worth of trade in Indonesia according to the estimates of Sydney exporters,[58] but the unionists always claimed that the motives for their actions were noble and justified any negative effects on trade. Their insistence that their action had been an important factor in helping the Indonesians achieve their independence was eventually vindicated: when the bill for the transfer of authority to the Republic was passed by the Dutch parliament on 9 December, the Minister for Foreign Affairs, Mr Stikker, acknowledged that foreign influence had exerted pressure on the Netherlands and cited the boycott by the Australian waterside workers as one of the major factors.[59]

On 27 December 1949, the Indonesian Prime Minister, by this time Dr Hatta, received the documents for transfer of sovereignty to the Republic of the United States of Indonesia from Queen Juliana

Now is the Hour

The Indonesian flag is raised at Kemayoran Airport, 28 December 1949.
Photo: Sheila Soegito.

at a ceremony held in the Hague. The next day, at around 11.30 am, two Dakota aircraft landed at Kemayoran airport in Jakarta bringing President Soekarno, his family and entourage from Yoyakarta. It was the first time he had set foot in the capital since 1945.[60] After a ceremony at the airport when the Dutch flag was lowered and the Indonesian flag raised, and a triumphal drive through wildly cheering crowds to the Presidential Palace, Soekarno appeared on the balcony as thousands of jubilant Indonesian voices chanted, '*Merdeka*! *Merdeka*! *Merdeka*!' The scene was described by the Australian Department of External Affairs representative at the transfer of sovereignty in Jakarta as 'a tremendous demonstration of affection for the President'.[61]

The Australian government, now led by Mr Menzies after the defeat of the Labor Party in the December 10 election, recognized the new republic immediately. After four years of constantly heaping insults on Soekarno and the nationalist movement, we can assume that it must have been galling for him to take this step. However, as would be expected, pragmatism, diplomacy and political expediency prevailed and the new Minister for External Affairs Mr Spender sent the following message to Dr Hatta —

Soekarno arrives in Jakarta as President of the Republic of Indonesia, 28 December 1949. Photo: Sheila Soegito.

The Australian Government and people send to the Government and people of the United States of Indonesia warmest congratulations and best wishes on the inauguration of the Republic. As a new neighbour Australia has a deep and constant interest in the well-being and prosperity of Indonesia and we look forward to most intimate and friendly relations with you.[62]

With no credit to itself, the new Menzies Government had in fact already inherited a legacy of 'friendly relations' with Indonesia thanks to the efforts of the Labor Government and those ordinary or extraordinary Australians who had supported the Republic. Maintaining those relations has challenged successive governments from both countries ever since. But that was all in the future on the day Soekarno made his triumphant return to Jakarta and Australia's stocks were high. It happened that among the welcoming party at the airport was Australian war bride, Sheila Soegito, present with her husband, by then a high-ranking officer in the Indonesian Air Force. By a twist of fate, Sheila was the first European woman the President greeted on this historic day, a fitting symbol of the fledgling relationship between his country and hers – a relationship born of the upheavals of wartime and people to people relationships between ordinary Indonesians and ordinary Australians.

Conclusion

The presence of several thousand Indonesians in Australia in the 1940s was a significant element of Australia's wartime and immediate post-war history. It was significant at three levels; grass roots, national and international. It was also unique because it was and is the only instance of a significant number of men, women and children belonging to a discrete ethnic group coming to Australia, staying for a few years, and then voluntarily departing, without any intention or attempt to settle permanently. Another unusual factor was that these sojourners in the White Australia of the time were Asians, whose colour was of no concern to the ordinary Australians whom they befriended – even if it was sometimes alluded to prejoratively by some politicians and the conservative press, particularly during the struggle for Indonesian independence. It was unique too, because one of its consequences was that a foreign revolution was fought in part on Australian soil.

At the grassroots level many Australians and Indonesians enjoyed friendships which widened the intellectual and cultural horizons of both. For the majority of them it would have been the first time they had mixed as equals with people of different skin colour, instead of in the master/servant, superior/subordinate roles that had been the norm for whites and non-whites in each of their societies. Initially these friendly relations may have happened because the Indonesians in the NEI forces and on the merchant ships had both curiosity value and respectable credentials as native subjects of the 'gallant Dutch allies,' for whom Australians on the homefront wanted to do their bit as part of the war effort. Some newspapers contributed to a positive impression when the Indonesians first came, by publishing informative articles about some of the exotic cultures and traditions of the 'natives' of the NEI, usually painting a rosy picture of their contented lives under the benign rule of the Dutch colonists. Although 'coloured,' the Indonesian were accepted in a way the Chinese or Aborigines, with whom white Australians had a long-standing history of racial tensions, prejudice or paternalism, had never been accepted. Even in country towns, with populations traditionally more conservative than their city cousins, there were friendships and social intercourse between some of the local people and those Indonesians who were free to come and go in the community, even if they were regarded with suspicion by others.

People-to-people relationships of the kind pioneered in those early years have persisted to the present day, regardless of the complex and volatile nature of the political relationship between the two countries. At the personal level, Indonesians and Australians tend to get on well together, despite the ethnic, cultural, religious, social, political, linguistic, and all the other differences between them. They visit each other's countries, study each other's languages, marry each other, enjoy cultural, educational and sporting exchanges and engage in business, trade, tourism and the variety of activities one would expect between close neighbours. On the other hand the extreme and irrational reactions of some Australians after the guilty verdict in the Schapelle Corby case in May 2005 are an example of how fragile those links can be in a situation where Australians' opinions of Indonesia are based on ignorance and emotions whipped up by irresponsible media. People-to-people engagement based on knowledge and understanding of each other is and always will be an important element in the complex bilateral relationship between the two countries.

The impact of the Indonesian presence in Australia at the national, official level was also significant. During the war and after the declaration of Indonesian independence, to some degree it exercised the minds and energy of two Prime Ministers, various Cabinet Ministers, parliamentarians from both sides of the House, as well as bureaucrats, policemen and security agencies. The editors of national newspapers who helped shape public opinion were also in the mix. Like it or not, all were eventually swept up to some extent in a unique event in Australian history – a foreign revolution being fought in part on Australian shores, as a direct result of the Indonesians being in the country.

The Indonesians were not passive observers: they took the initiative in their campaign against the Dutch in Australia and in enlisting the support of Australians. This happened almost immediately when the first strikes of merchant sailors took place in 1942. Although these first strikes were about pay and working conditions, they were a demonstration of defiance against the Dutch and a curtain raiser to the crucial 1945 walk-offs, also initially about economic injustices but soon with a strong political dimension in support of the Republic. In both strikes, it was Indonesians soliciting the support of the Australian waterside unions which ultimately led to the black bans. The fact that the waterside unions were under Communist control and that Communism was ideologically opposed to colonialism was a significant element in this support. In a domino effect, it was then the Government's response, or as their critics would have it, lack of response to these bans, which so infuriated the Dutch authorities. In addition, the refusal of Australian officials to take punitive action against the Indonesians when requested on a number of occasions by the NEI authorities further estranged the two allies. The final straw was the Government's insistence on repatriating the nationalists to Republican safe havens where they could not be punished by NEI authorities for their political activities. From the Dutch perspective, all of these responses by the Australian Government seemed to indicate that while professing neutrality in the dispute, it was in fact supporting the Indonesians. The Federal Opposition shared the views of the Dutch and used them as ammunition in their parliamentary propaganda against the Government.

Throughout all these activities, Indonesian activists in Australia were in direct and frequent contact with officials, Government Ministers and even the Prime Minister: the petitions from the political internees, the constant flow of information, propaganda, requests, advice and expressions of thanks from CENKIM meant that it would have been difficult to ignore them. This pro-active behaviour meant that some Australian officials had a chance of hearing both sides of the Dutch/Indonesian dispute and as the wry comments in some of the records show, as time passed and their irritation with the Dutch authorities increased, they did not always take Dutch accusations of criminal behaviour against the nationalists at face value. There was a growing awareness in official circles that the Dutch tended to label every Indonesian politically opposed to them as an extremist, and this awareness influenced the Government in the way it dealt with the Dutch and the Indonesians, and with their dispute as it was played out in Australia.

At the international level the first manifestation of the significance of the Indonesians in Australia was the effect of the shipping bans, which were directly attributable to their actions. The greatest effect was in attracting international interest to a dispute which might otherwise have gone largely unnoticed for some time, buried among all the pressing matters needing to be dealt with in the aftermath of World War II. By its nature, the publicity drew attention to the rights of the Indonesians and their case for independence – a side of the argument that may not have found an audience without the bans. The Dutch themselves acknowledged the significance these bans had in influencing their eventual decision to transfer sovereignty to the Indonesians.

Similarly at the international level, we cannot divorce the Indonesian presence in Australia from the eventual political support the Australian Government gave the Republic by taking its case to the United Nations. Because the Indonesians were in the country the Australian Government was able to observe at first hand the interaction between the NEI authorities and their native subjects and did not always like what it saw. Relations between the Australian and Dutch authorities deteriorated as a direct result of conflict between the latter and the Indonesians, and the Australians' refusal to intervene as the Dutch expected them to. It is reasonable to propose that these factors may have influenced to some degree the Government's attitude shifting from neutrality, to covert, to overt sympathy for the Indonesians which carried onto the world stage, marking a momentous change in Australia's foreign policy. Before the war, Australia had been subservient to the mother country, to Britain, and had not asserted an independent voice in its own foreign policy. The Indonesian case changed all that when for the first time in its history the Australian Government formulated and followed its own policy, without seeking the approval of the UK Government. This particular policy, which in fact marked the genesis of Australia's engagement with Asia, married the idealism of the Labor Party's humanitarian anti-colonial views with the pragmatism of ensuring Australia's security by establishing and developing good relations with the newest political power in the region.

We cannot rewrite history, but it is hard to resist the temptation

Conclusion

to ask 'what if ...?' when we consider the story of the Indonesians and the Dutch in Australia. If certain circumstances had been different there may well have been different outcomes. The Dutch brought a lot of their problems upon themselves. If they had respected the Indonesian merchant sailors, paid them properly and not persisted in treating them like coolies the first and subsequent strikes may not have occurred. If they had kept their promise, loosened their grip on the purse strings and paid the contentious 6s 6d to the militarized labourers of the 36AEC there would not have been the build-up of resentment that later made these men so receptive to nationalist propaganda from the ex-Digulists. The decision to withhold some of the seamen's pay until they returned to Indonesia had a similar effect. It seems that in these instances parsimony prevailed over fairness and common sense. Overall, in their dealing with the Indonesians the Dutch were unable to break their own colonial mould even in such changed circumstances in a foreign country. This led to many Australians from different walks of life sympathizing with the Indonesians as a result of what was perceived as Dutch arrogance and bullying.

Another error of judgement the Dutch made was helping to instigate the evacuation of the Digulists. Here was a situation where most of the experienced, hard-line Indonesian nationalist activists in the NEI were gathered together and brought en masse to Australia from Digul. After their time in Cowra, where there was plenty of time to regroup and plan their strategies, they were then released and dispersed to various places where Indonesians were congregated – free to disseminate their propaganda and politicise hundreds of their compatriots. They helped organise SARPELINDO and set up the Independence Committees including CENKIM, They were in Casino in the Militarized Labour Battalion that first went on strike and among the members of the Technical Battalion who mutinied. They even infiltrated NIGIS, with the blessing of Dr van der Plas, who employed them. Their influence spread to sections of the wider community when they established relationships with sympathetic Australians and enlisted their support. If they had been left in Tanah Merah it is quite possible that there would not have been such widespread resistance to the Dutch by the Indonesians in Australia.

The final factor was one over which the Dutch had no control, but which eventually worked against their interests. This was the fortuitous circumstance that the Labor Party was in Government during the time the Indonesians and Dutch were in Australia. Judging from his parliamentary rhetoric there is little doubt that if Mr Menzies had been Prime Minister, his Government would have supported the Dutch to the hilt. If the same events had unfolded a likely scenario would have been that force would have been used to try to end the shipping bans, and against Indonesian rebels invading Dutch establishments. It is certain that the rebels would have been deported to Dutch territory, and the Australian Government would not have taken the Indonesian cause to the United Nations and supported the Republic.

But, as fate would have it, Mr Menzies was not in power, and it was the Chifley Labor Government that took Australia into its first independent political relationship with an Asian country. The extent of Australian support to the Republic has been exaggerated ever since by both countries. Reference to it has become part of the formulaic niceties that form the prelude to diplomatic and political speeches on certain occasions. Nevertheless the giving of that support was significant at that period in each country's history, and the memory of it gives some hope of better outcomes whenever the contemporary relationship between Australia and Indonesia is under strain.

However significant Australia's role was in contributing to Indonesia's struggle for independence, the Indonesians coming to Australia had an important impact on Australia's own process of maturing in the post-war world. This was the first time many Australians involved themselves directly in wider issues, shaking off their previous xenophobic mentality, looking outwards to their own region of the world with something different from the usual fear of the 'yellow peril' and invasion theories, and actually engaging with Asian people, with the 'other,' and challenging the racism embodied by the White Australia Policy. When the dust settled, Australians and Indonesians had irrevocably become part of each others' histories.

Endnotes

Introduction

1. Nonie Sharpe, *Saltwater People: The Waves of Memory*, Allen & Unwin, NSW, 2002, p. 64.
2. C. C. MacKnight, *Voyage to Marege: Macassan Trepangers in Northern Australia*, Melbourne University Press, Melbourne, 1976, p. 28.
3. C.S.R. Archives. File D3/02 Noel Butlin Archives, Australian National University.
4. Queensland State Archives. QSA File AGS/N. 360.
5. Adrian Cunningham, On Borrowed Time: The Australian Pearlshelling Industry, Asian Indentured Labour and the White Australia Policy. 1946-1962, Unpublished Master Of Letters Thesis, Department of History, ANU, 1992, pp. 9-17.
6. Barry York, Studies in Australian Ethnic History. Number 2. Admitted: 1901-1946. Centre for Immigration & Multicultural Studies, Research School of Social Sciences, Australian National University, Canberra, (n.d.) (n.p.).
7. *Sydney Morning Herald,* 19.9.1921.
8. ibid. 10.4.1922.
9. David Walker and John Ingleson, 'The Impact of Asia', in Neville Meaney (ed), *Under New Heavens,* Heinemann Educational, Australia, 1989, p. 312.
10. Richard J. Moorehead, *The Cruise of the Goodwill Ship,* Ruskin Press, Melbourne, 1933, p. 160.
11. Moorhead, p. 133.
12. Jack Ford, *Allies in a Bind. Australia and the Netherlands East Indies in the Second World War,* Australia Netherlands Ex Servicemen & Women's Association Qld Branch, Queensland, 1996, p. 21.
13. *Sun News Pictorial* 14.2.1941.
14. Cited in Edward Duyker, *The Dutch in Australia,* AE Press, Melbourne, 1987, p. 85.

Chapter 1

1. *Sydney Morning Herald* 9.3.1942.
2. Rupert Lockwood, *Black Armada. Australia and the struggle for Indonesian independence, 1942-1949,* Australian Book Society, Sydney, 1975, p. 60.
3. Yorke, pp. 92-95.
4. NAA (ACT) Series A 6591 Item 42/1/1296.
5. NAA (ACT) Series A 981/1 Item Nethe 66.
6. NAA (ACT) Series A 981/1 Item Nethe G6 .
7. The *Advertiser,* 10.3.1942.
8. *Daily Telegraph,* 10.3.1942.
9. CPD Vol 170 25.3.1942, p. 376.
10. Ford, p. 66.
11. *Daily Telegraph,* 10.4.1942.
12. NAA (ACT) Series A 989/1 Item 43/600/5/1/5.
13. *Daily Telegraph,* 10.4.1942.
14. G. Wallace Campbell, Correspondence 1997.
15. Kate Darien Smith, *On the Home Front: Melbourne in Wartime 1939-1945,* Oxford University Press, South Melbourne, 1990, p. 211.
16. The terms 'Indonesian' and 'Javanese' were often used interchangeably, irrespective of what part of the archipelago people came from. A number of informants referred to Indonesians whom they had met as ' Javos,' 'Jarvos,' 'Javies' or even 'the Javas'.
17. *Daily Telegraph,* 18.4.1942.
18. NAA (NSW) Series C 123/1 item SIT 19156.

19 NAA (ACT) Series A 1928/1 Item 1181/37.
20 Julius Tahija, *Melintas Cakrawala*, PT Gramedia Pustaka Utama, Jakarta, 1997, pp. 42-53, and Jean Tahija, *An Unconventional Woman*, Viking, Victoria, 1998, pp. 71-84.
21 Jean Tahija, p. 83.
22 Allison Ind, *Spy Ring Pacific*, Weidenfield & Nicolson, London, 1958, pp. 103-105.
23 Vera Bradley, *I Didn't Know That*, Boolarong Press, Brisbane, 1995, p. 165.
24 Guy Black, ibid, p. 165.
25 Alan Amos, ibid, p. 166.
26 Alan Powell, *War by Stealth*, Melbourne University Press, Melbourne, 1996, p. 66.
27 Gordon Wallace, *Up In Darwin with the Dutch*, Surry Hills, Victoria, 1996, pp. 11-13.
28 Errol Lea-Scarlett, *Queanbeyan District and People*, Queanbeyan Municipal Council, p. 207.
29 Jim Gibney, *Canberra 1913-1953* cited in Newsletter No 45, 18 Squadron NEI-RAAF Forces Association, 1994.
30 CPD Vol 170 14.5.1942 p. 1276.
31 NAA (ACT) Series A 1695/1 Item 1/305/ORG.
32 ibid.
33 Wallace, p. 11.
34 ibid. pp. 26-27.
35 Cited in Wallace, p. 43.
36 James Gibson, correspondence, 1996 and interview, Traralgon, 1999.
37 Ford, p. 89.
38 Brian Fitzpatrick and Rowan J Cahill. *The Seamen's Union of Australia 1872-1972*, SUA, Sydney, 1981, p. 169.
39 Correspondence with the late Moh Hodrie 1966 and interview Madura, 1997.
40 Lieuw Pronk, *KPM A Most Remarkable Shipping Company 1888-1967*, North Turramurra, 1998, p. 98.
41 NAA (Vic) Series MP 508/1 Item 115/703/597.
42 Ford, p. 89.
43 Algeemene Rijk Archief (ARA) inventaris van de Archief van het Gezantschap Ambassade te Australie 1842-1945. Invent No 58.
44 ibid.
45 NAA (Vic) Series MP 508/1 Item 255/714/331.
46 NAA (NSW) Series SP 1714/1/0 Item N 45633 Part 3.
47 ibid.
48 ibid.
49 ibid.
50 Correspondence Mrs Eva Cusack (Cowra) 17.2.1997.
51 NAA (NSW) Series SP 1714/1/0 Item N 45633 Part 1.
52 NAA (NSW) Series C 123/1 Item 20332.
53 NAA (Vic) Series MP 508/1 Item 255/714/597.
54 NAA (NSW) Series C 123/1 Item 20332.
55 Fitzpatrick & Cahill, pp. 169-170.
56 Anhar Jamal, *Di Bawah Salib Selatan: Gerakan dan Usaha Mempertahankan Kemerdekaan Indonesia di Australia (1942-1947)* Skripsi Sarjana PSUI, Jakarta, 1990, p. 76.
57 NAA (ACT) Series A 472/1 Item W11647.
58 NAA (ACT) Series A 472/1 Item W11647.
59 ibid.
60 *The Sun News Pictorial* 30.4.1943.
61 This section is based on an unpublished article, "The Boat People of Port Melbourne", written by Rev Freeman's son Wilfred D'Estena Freeman in August 1995 for the archives of the Uniting Church, and on interviews with two of the Rev Freeman's daughters, Miriam Nichols and Bonita Ellen in Melbourne, 1997.
62 NAA (Vic) Series MP 287/1 Item 2541.

Endnotes

63 John Guthrie interview, Melbourne, 1997.
64 *Argus* 23.5.1942.
65 H. Abdul Rachman, correspondence, May 1995.
66 R.M. Roeslan, correspondence, June 1996.
67 Miriam Nichols, interview 1997.
68 Nancy Loan, interview, Adelaide August 1997.
69 John Treloar, interview 1996.
70 Ted Fryer, interview 1996.
71 Lilian Perston, interview 1996.
72 Wendy James, correspondence, 1997.
73 NAA Series 981 Item NEI 66A.
74 *Penjoeloeh*, NIGIS, Melbourne, 21.8.1942.
75 *Penjoeloeh*, NIGIS, Melbourne, 1.10.1942.
76 ibid. 24.12.1942.

Chapter 2

1 *Penjoeloeh*, 19.2.1943.
2 NAA (Vic) Series MP 742/1/0 Item 92/1/256.
3 ibid.
4 ibid.
5 NAA (Vic) Series MP 742/1/0/ Item 92/1/256.
6 Ibid.
7 Moh Hodrie, correspondence, 1997.
8 NAA (Vic) Series MP 742/1 Item 247/1/829.
9 AWM 86/1/263 Part 2.
10 AWM 60 86/1/263 Part 1.
11 NAA (Vic) Series MP 742/1 Item 92/1/256.
12 Elva Beck and Jan Ritchie, correspondence, 1997.
13 AWM 60 86/1/263 Part 2.
14 Elva Beck, Jan Ritchie and Laureen Collins, correspondence, 1997.
15 Gordon Hooton, interview, 1997.
16 AWM 60 86/1/263 Part 2.
17 Allan Brownlee, correspondence, 2003.
18 ibid.
19 AWM 60 86/1/263 Part 2.
20 ibid.
21 NAA (Vic) Series MP 742/1 Item 92/1/256.
22 AWM 60 86/1/263 Part 2.
23 ibid.
24 ibid.
25 AWM 6086/1/263 Part 1.
26 NAA (Vic) Series MP 742/1 Item 255/2/676.
27 Cited in J de Jong *Het Koninkrijk der Nederlanden in der Tweede Wereldoorlog*, Rijksinstituut voor Oorlogsdocumentatie, Netherlands, 1986, p. 132.
28 ibid.
29 NAA (Vic) Series MP742/1 Item 92/1/256. Mr C. Duce, a local resident whose trucks were used by the army disputes this opinion. He commented that the Javos loading and unloading his trucks were 'strong little blokes and very hard workers'. Interview, Brisbane 1998.
30 NAA (Vic) Series MP 742/1 Item 255/2/676.
31 Queensland State Archives Bundle A/734 78 File No. 1268 M 10.
32 NAA (Vic) Series MP 742/1 Item 255/2/676.
33 NAA (Vic) Series MP 742/1 Item 255/2/676.
34 De Jong, p. 132.
35 NAA (Vic) Series MP 742/1 Item 92/1/256.
36 AWM 60 86/1/263 Part 1.

37 Margaret Wright, correspondence, 1997.
38 ibid. and Moh Hodrie, interview, Surabaya, 1997.
39 Ernie Hills and Trevor Mc Ivor, 'The Kite Flying Jarvos,' in Don Talbot and John Larkin (eds) *Toowoomba – Strange and Unusual Tales*, Toowoomba, Queensland, 2003, pp. 70-71.
40 Paul Etherington (ed), *The Diaries of Donald Friend*, Vol 2, National Library of Australia, Canberra, 2003, p. 224.
41 *Penjoeloeh*, 14.4.1943.
42 ibid. March-November 1943.
43 R Miller, interview, Sydney, 1997.
44 *Penjoeloeh*, 12.11.1943.
45 George Worang, interview, Bandung, 1997.
46 NAA (Vic) Series MP 742/1 Item 244/1/260.
47 *Penjoeloeh*, 10.12.1943.
48 Richmond River Historical Society, *Wartime on the Richmond*, Lismore, 1995 p. 12.
49 Worang, interview, Bandung, 1997.
50 *Wartime on the Richmond*, p. 12.
51 Lew Hughes, interview, Casino, 1996.
52 *Wartime on the Richmond*, p. 18.
53 Matina King, interview, Lismore, 1996.
54 Information in this and the next two paragraphs taken from 'Hindsight' ABC Radio National, 10 November 2002, presented by Graham Irvine, based on his own research.
55 NAA (ACT) Series 1838/278/Item 401/3/6/1/4/Part 1.
56 Des Darragh, interview, Casino, 1997.
57 *Wartime on the Richmond*, p. 12.
58 NAA (Vic) MP Series 742/1 Item 115/1/385. A similar complaint was made in September 1946 about Indonesians from Brisbane consorting with 'coloured persons' (Torres Strait Islanders) residing in Brisbane and Tweed Heads.
It even was claimed that two Indonesians had lived for some time among the coloured population of Cudgen and Tweed Heads with the express purpose of spreading Communist propaganda among them. See NAA (ACT) Series A 6322/40 Item 138 .
59 ibid.
60 NAA (ACT) Series A 433/1 Item 47/2/1949.
61 ibid.
62 RM Roeslan, correspondence, 1977 and interview Yogyakarta 2002. See also J de Jong, pp. 125-126.
63 Roeslan interview, 2002. A member of the family of the Sultan of Yogyakarta, Roeslan was given an entry in *Who's Who in Australia* XII 1944, a distinction then reserved for 'titled persons ... serving Australia with or beyond the Commonwealth.
64 *Penjoeloeh*, 10.12.1943.
65 Jan Walandouw, letter to George Worang, 27.2.1944. Jan Walandouw's status as a 'good boy' came to an end when he later became an active nationalist and president of the Sydney branch of the Indonesian Independence Committee.
66 H.V. Evatt, *Foreign Policy of Australia*, Angus & Robertson, Sydney, 1945, pp. 106-107.
67 NAA (ACT) Series A 989 Item 43/600/5/1/2.
68 ibid.
69 Margaret George, *Australia and the Indonesian Revolution*, Melbourne University Press, Melbourne, 1980, p. 18.
70 NAA (ACT) Series A 989 Item 43/600/5/1/2.
71 NAA (ACT) Series A 989 Item 43/600/5/1/2.
72 NAA (ACT) Series A 989 Item 43/600/5/1/5.
73 ibid.
74 NAA (ACT) Series A 989 Item 43/600/5/1/5.

Endnotes

Chapter 3

1. Jean GelmanTaylor, *Indonesia: Peoples and Histories,* Yale University Press, New Haven, 2003, pp. 283-286.
2. This terminology is used by Peter Lowensteyn in his on line essay, *Political Activism in Traditional and Colonial Society: Indonesia between 1908 and 1928*: www.lowensteyn.com/indonesia.
3. ibid.
4. Anthony Reid, *The Indonesian National Revolution 1945-1950,* Longman, Victoria, 1974, p. 6.
5. Harry J Benda and Ruth T. McVey (eds), *The Communist Uprisings of 1926-1927 in Indonesia: Key Documents,* Southeast Asia Program, Cornell University, Ithica, 1969, p. xxii.
6. J. D. Legge, *Intellectuals and Nationalism in Indonesia. A Study of the Following Recruited by Sutan Sjahrir in Occupation,* Cornell Modern Indonesia Project, 1988, p. 38.
7. This was the title of a propaganda pamphlet published by the Indonesian Independence Committee in Melbourne, n.d. but content suggests 1945 or 1946.
8. Takashi Shiraishi. 'The Phantom World of Digoel', in *Indonesia,* No. 61, Cornell University, 1996, pp. 94-95.
9. ibid. p. 96.
10. Cited in Rudolf Mrazek, *Sjahrir, Politics and Exile in Indonesia,* Cornell University, Ithica, 1994, p. 130.
11. Shiraishi, p. 98.
12. I.F.M. Chalid Salim, *Lima Belas Tahun Digul,* Penerbit Bulan Bintang, Jakarta, 1977, pp. 100-103.
13. *Pandji Poestaka,* 1927, (n.d.) pp. 562-563.
14. ibid. p. 379.
15. Sharaisi, p. 98.
16. ibid. p. 100.
17. Salim, pp. 269-279.
18. ibid. pp. 344-346.
19. Sharaisi. pp. 115-116.
20. ibid. p. 297.
21. Van der Plas to Van Mook (1943) quoted in Mrazek, p. 131.
22. Richard Chauvel, *Nationalists, Soldiers and Separatists: the Ambonese Islands from Colonialism to Revolt,* KITLV Press, Leiden, 1990. p. 75.
23. ibid. pp. 123-124.
24. Siti Chamsina Nasution, *Femina,* Jakarta, August 1995, personal correspondence, and interviews in Jakarta 1997 and 2002.
25. J.M. Pluvier,' Dutch-Indonesian Relations 1940-1942. in *Journal of Southeast Asian History,* Vol 6, No.1, University of Singapore, 1965, p. 35.
26. L.L. Snyder, *Fifty Major documents of the Twentieth Century,* Anvil, Princeton, 1955, p.p 91-93.
27. Cited in S, Abeyasakere, *One Hand Clapping: Indonesian nationalists and the Dutch, 1939-1942,* Monash papers on Southeast Asia, no 5. Centre of Southeast asian Studies, Clayton, Victoria, 1976, p. 64.
28. *Citra dan Perjuangan Kemerdekaan: seri Perjuangan Ex Digul,* Direktorat Jenderal Bantuan Sosial, Departemen Sosial, Jakarta, 1977, p. 103.
29. ibid. p. 104.
30. AWM Series 54 Item 605/3/3.
31. ibid.
32. NAA (ACT) Series 989/1 Item 1943/40/13.
33. NAA (ACT) Series 989/1 Item 1943/40/13.
34. ibid.
35. ibid. Van der Plas was often at pains, as he was in this letter, to perpetuate the idea that the internees /Indonesians were of inferior intellect.
36. NAA (ACT) Series A 989/1 Item 1943/40/13.

37 Salim, pp. 434-435.
38 NAA (ACT) Series A 989/1 Item 1943/40/13.
39 ibid.
40 ibid.
41 NAA (Vic) Series MP 742/1 Item 255/2/676.
42 ibid.
43 NAA (ACT) Series A 816/1 Item 54/301/244.
44 Salim, p. 463.
45 See Robert James Hamilton, 'Psychopaths, communists and criminals: Brigadier Simpson and the internees of Tanah Merah', in *Journal of the Australian War Memorial, No. 24, 1994,* p. 25. Given the close proximity of these islands it is easy to understand the confusion, and the internees may even have been transferred from Horn Island to Thursday Island for departure by ship.
46 One of these soldiers, Ray Block, recalls that the Australians were sympathetic to the 'prisoners', and that the Dutch masters' arrogance and insistence on being addressed as 'Tuan' irritated the Australians greatly. Lola Burke, correspondence, 1997.
47 Siti Chamsinah, interview, Jakarta, July 1997.
48 Molly Bondan, *Spanning the Revolution,* Pustaka Sinar Harapan, Jakarta, 1992, p. 186. This unique *gamelan* is conserved in the Department of Music at Monash University, Melbourne.
49 NAA (Vic) Series MP 742/1 Item 255/2/298.
50 Pat Noonan, 'Merdeka in Mackay. The Idonesian Evacuees and Internees in Mackay, June 1943-February 1946', in Bob Hering (ed), *Pramoedya Ananta Toer 70 Tahun,* Edisi Sastra Kabar Seberang Sulating Maphalindo, 1995, p. 242.

Chapter 4

1 Noonan, p. 242.
2 NAA (Vic) Series MP 742/1 Item 255/2/298 This is an extract from a petition written to the International Red Cross by the Tanah Tinggi men on 29th July, while they were interned at Cowra.
3 ibid p. 247.
4 Terry Hayes, *The Daily Mercury,* 14.8.1999.
5 *Mackay Mercury,* 21.6.1943.
6 NAA (Vic) Series MP 742/1 Item 255/2/298.
7 This whole passage is from NAA (NSW) Series SP 1714/1 Item N 45633 Part 4.
8 Molly Bondan, p. 18.
9 NAA (Vic) Series MP 742/1 Item 255/2/676.
10 Siti Chamsinah, interview, Jakarta, 1997.
11 NAA (ACT) Series 989/1 Item 1943/925/1/97.
12 Anonymous, *Three Hundred Communists from Indonesia 1943* pp. 81/43.
13 ibid.
14 Lionel Boorman, former Intelligence officer, interview, Sydney, 1998.
15 Siti Chamsinah, interview, Jakarta, 1997.
16 NAA (Vic) Series MP 742/1 Item 255/2/676. Van der Plas visited the camp on 25 June. see NAA (NSW) Series SP 1714/1/0 Item N45633 Part 4.
17 NAA (NSW) Series SP 1714/1/0 Item N45633 Part 4.
18 State Archives of NSW *Reports on War Deaths in NSW 1939-1948.* See also Register of Deaths, held in Cowra Courthouse.
19 NAA (NSW) Series SP 1714/1/0 Item N 45633 Part 5.
20 James Baillie, *You Can't Help Bad Luck, unpublished MS, (n.d.)* pp. 4-5.
21 NAA (Vic) Series MP 742/1 Item 255/2/676.
22 After the war the son of Salamah, one of the few women interned after the revolt in West Sumatra in 1927, returned to Cowra and had a headstone erected over his mother's grave. (Interview with Athol Kendal, Stonemason, Cowra 1997) The graves gradually fell into disrepair and were neglected for

Endnotes

many years until in November 1997 they were identified, and subsequently restored by the Indonesian Government. At a ceremony at the site attended by officials from the Indonesian Government and the Cowra Council, the 13 Indonesians who are buried there were acknowledged with the official designation, *Pejuang Kemerdekaan*, Freedom Fighters.
23 James Baillie, correspondence, 1998.
24 ibid.
25 NAA (Vic) Series MP 742/1 Item 255/2/676.
26 ibid.
27 NAA (Vic) series MP 742/1 Item 255/17/36.
28 Salim, p. 443.
29 Molly Bondan, pp. 193-194.
30 NAA (Vic) Series MP 742/1 Item 255/2/676.
31 ibid.
32 ibid.
33 ibid.
34 ibid.
35 NAA (Vic) Series MP 742/1 Item 255/2/676.
36 *beyond the legal power or authority of the person concerned.* ibid.
37 ibid.
38 NAA (Vic) Series MP 742/1 Item 255/2/298.
39 ibid.
40 NAA (ACT) Series A 472/1 Item W16960.
41 ibid.
42 ibid.
43 Molly Bondan, p. 197.
44 A.Ely, *Indonesian Exile Report,* Noel Butlin Archives P81/43.
45 ibid.
46 Lockwood, pp. 23-24. These 'sick prisoners' must have been some of the Tanah Tinggi contingent, who were all transferred to Liverpool in September, 1943.
47 NAA (ACT) Series A 989/1 Item 1943/40/13.
48 ibid.
49 NAA (Vic) Series MP 742/1 Item 255/2/676.
50 ibid.
51 NAA (ACT) Series 989/1 Item 1943/40/13.
52 ibid.
53 ibid.
54 NAA (ACT) Series A 989/1 Item 1943/40/13.
55 NAA (Vic) Series MP 742/1 Item 92/1/256.
56 ibid.
57 Jamal, p. 23.
58 NAA (NSW) Series SP 1714/1/0 Item N45633 Part 6.
59 ibid.
60 NAA (ACT) Series A 989/1 Item 43/40/13.
61 ibid.
62 NAA (Qld) Series BP 234/1 Item SB 1944/221.
63 ibid.
64 FX Lasman, correspondence, 1997. His two year old sister, Soelistimah was among those who died.
65 Mongkalmata, *Penjoeloeh* 14.4.1944.
66 Noonan, p. 249.
67 Queensland State Archives. Register of North Mackay State School 1944.
68 Noonan, p. 250.
69 Laxman, correspondence, 1997.
70 Noonan, p. 250. The Dutch also provided a 'Muhammedan' spiritual leader.
71 Noonan, p. 254.

72 Siti Chamsinah, interviews, Jakarta 1997 and 2002. Jahja Nasution, who died in 1962, continued to be a political activist after they returned to Indonesia.
73 NAA (Vic) Series MP 742/1/0 Item 255/2/676.
74 ibid.
75 ibid.
76 NAA(NSW) Series SP 196/2 Item 556/2/1039.
77 ibid.
78 NAA(NSW) Series SP 196/1 Item 556/2 1039 (Box 6).
79 Transcripts of the hearings are found in NAA (NSW) Series C32981, various items.
80 ibid.
81 NAA(ACT) Series 989/1 Item 1943/40/13.
82 NAA (Vic) Series MP 742/1 Item 255/2/676.
83 ibid.
84 ibid.
85 Ford, p. 212.

Chapter 5

1 *Penjoeloeh*, 18.8.1944.
2 Jamal, p. 13.
3 De Jong, p. 138.
4 *Penjoeloeh*, 18.8.1944.
5 NAA (ACT) Series A 6122/40 Item 136.
6 NAA (ACT) Series A 6122/40 Item 136. One of the main tasks of the Australian Security Service during World War II was the surveillance of communists or suspected communists, despite the fact that Russia was an ally.
7 ibid.
8 ibid.
9 NAA (ACT) Series A 989 Item 1944/600/5/1/8.
10 NAA (ACT) Series A 989 Item 1944/600/5/1/8.
11 NAA (ACT) Series A 6122/40 Item 136.
12 ibid.
13 Soe Hok Gie, *Orang-orang di Persimpangan Kiri Jalan*, Bentang, Yogyakarta, 1977, p. 39.
14 Noonan, p. 250.
15 ibid.
16 Dr A.H.Nasution *Sekitar Perang Kemerdekaan Indonesia*, Jilid 3, Angkasa, Bandung, 1977, p. 157.
17 Ford, p. 376.
18 NAA (ACT) Series A4331 Item 49/2/8187. This cable written four months before Soekarno proclaimed independence, was quite possibly the first approach made to the UN on the issue of Indonesian independence – an issue that would occupy a great deal of its attention in the immediate post-war years.
19 ibid.
20 ibid.
21 Nasution, p. 158.
22 Noel Butlin Archives Centre, ANU Canberra. E183/26/39.
23 NAA (ACT) Series A367/1 Item C54160.
24 ibid.
25 Information in this and the next two paragraphs is based on Jamal, p. 72-76.
26 Hilman Adil, *Hubungan Australia dengan Indonesia: 1945-1962*, Penerbit Djambatan, Jakarta, 1993, p. 43.
27 *Guardian* 8.6.1945.
28 Terry Hogan, *The Labour Movement and the Indonesian Republicans in Australia, August 1945-March 1946*, B.A (Hons) Thesis, University of New England, Armidale, 1972, p. 14.
29 CPD Vol 182 18.5.1945, p. 1901.

Endnotes

30 Joan Hardjono and Charles Warner (eds) *In Love With a Nation, Molly Bondan and Indonesia,* Published by Charles Warner, Picton, 1995, pp. 18-20.
31 ibid. pp. 21-23, 30.
32 Noel Butlin Archives P81/41.
33 ibid.
34 Reprinted in *Pantja Raj a* (Batavia) 15.11.1945.
35 Phyllis Johnson, interview, Sydney 1998 and NAA (ACT) Series 6122/40 Item 136.
36 Noel Butlin Archives P81/41.
37 ibid.
38 Hardjono and Warner, p. 33.
39 ibid. p. 37.
40 NAA (ACT) Series A 472/1 Item W29545.
41 Hardjono and Warner, p. 219.
42 Algemene Rijksarchief. Ministerie van Buitenlandsche Zaken, Inventaris No: 56/70.
43 NAA (ACT) Series A 472/1 Item W29545.
44 ibid.
45 Lockwood, p. 90.
46 ibid p. 74 .
47 *Pantja Raja,* December 1945.
48 Margaret Kartomi, 'The First AIA'. *AIA Journal,* August 1981, p. 9.
49 See Eric Marshall, *It Pays to be White.* Alpha Books, Sydney, 1973.
50 Kartomi, p. 8-11.
51 NAA (ACT) Series A 989 Item 43-44/600/5/1/5.
52 Ford, p. 288.
53 Ford, p. 289.
54 NAA (ACT) Series 373/1 Item 9971.
55 ibid.
56 Ford p. 293.
57 ibid.
58 NAA (Vic) Series MP 742/1 Item 244/1/260.
59 ibid.
60 NAA (ACT) Series A 1838/2 Item 401/4/3/1.
61 ibid.
62 ibid.
63 Ford, p. 409.
64 NAA (ACT) Series A 1838 Item 401/4/3/1.
65 NAA (ACT) Series A 1838 Item 401/4/3/1.
66 de Jonge. p. 611.
67 George Mc Turnan Kahin, *Nationalism and Revolution in Indonesia,* Cornell University Press, Ithaca, New York, 1963, p. 104.
68 B. Anderson. *Java in a Time of Revolution, Occupation and Resistance 1944-1946,* Cornell University press, Ithaca, new York, 1972, pp. 68-82.
69 ibid.
70 Katherine Skye, *Unrest Among the Natives, The Indonesian Revolution 1945-1949 as reported by the Adelaide Advertiser and the Melbourne Age,* BA (Hons) Thesis, Flinders University, South Australia, 1986, p. 2.
71 Mohamad Bondan. pp. 2-3.
72 ibid.

Chapter 6

1 Lockwood, p. 86 .
2 *Daily Telegraph* 22.9.1945.
3 *ibid.* 25.9.1945.
4 *Daily Telegraph,* 25.9.1945.
5 Lockwood, p. 84.
6 NAA (ACT) Series A 431/1 Box 155/3.
7 CENKIM Bulletin, Brisban, 16.10.1945.

8   NAA (ACT) Series A 1838/278 Item 401/3/6/4 Pt.1.
9   Des Darragh. Correspondence, 1998.
10 *Sun*, 23.9.1945.
11 See *Melbourne Herald* 9.10.1945, *Northern Star* (Lismore) 22.10.1945, *Tribune* 6.1.1946. Many years after these events, in 1993 the *Richmond River Express Examiner* ran an article about 'The Black Hole of Casino' reiterating all the claims of Dutch ill-treatment of the Indonesians. The article attracted a furious response from a Dutchman who had been stationed in Victory Camp and now lived in the town. He dismissed the accusations as 'rot', 'half truths', 'untrue' or 'distortions,' and declared that the information on which the article was based was 'inflammatory'. See *Richmond River Express Examiner* 4 December 1993, and reply by John Ivits entitled, 'Black Hole of Casino – What Rot" held by Clarence River Historical Society, Grafton. NSW.
12 *Melbourne Herald*, 9.10.1945.
13 *Northern Star*, 22.10.1945.
14 *Melbourne Herald*, 22.10.1945.
15 NAA (Vic) Series MP 742/1 Item 115/1/291.
16 *Sun* , 22.10.1945.
17 *Sun*, 8.11.1945.
18 NAA (ACT) Series A 1838/278 Item 401/3/6/1/4/Part 1.
19 ibid.
20 NAA (ACT) Series 1838 Item 401/3/6/1/4 Part 1.
21 ibid.
22 In a scathing attack on the 'Nazi hell camp' *Tribune* reported on 8 January that local citizens had become so indignant at this (poor) treatment of the Indonesians that they had formed a Citizen's Indonesian Defence Committee.
23 NAA (ACT) Series A 461/9 Item M350/1/9 Part 1.
24 NAA (ACT) Series A 1838/278 Item 401/3/6/1/4 Part 1.
25 ibid.
26 NAA (ACT) Series A 472/1 Item W29545.
27 NAA (ACT) Series A 461/1/9 Item M350/1/9 Part 1.
28 NAA (ACT) Series A 1838/278 Item 401/3/6/1/4 Part 1.
29 NAA (ACT) Series A 461/9 Item M350/1/9 Part 1.
30 NAA (Vic) Series MP 742/1/0 Item 115/1/378.
31 NAA (ACT) Series A 461/9 Item M350/1/9/Part 1.
32 *Richmond River Express*, 22.4.1946.
33 ibid.
34 *Richmond River Express*, 22.4.1946.
35 *Tribune*, 24.4.1946.
36 NAA (ACT) Series A 9108/3 Roll 6 AG15.
37 NAA (ACT) Series A6126 XMO Item 6.
38 ibid.
39 NAA (ACT) Series 433/1 Item 49/2/518.
40 NAA (ACT) Series A 1838/278 Item 401/3/6/1/4 Part 1.
41 NAA (ACT) Series A 433/1 Item 47/2/1949.
42 NAA (ACT) Series A 1833/278 Item 401/3/1/4 Part 1.
43 ibid.
44 NAA (ACT) Series A 1833/278 Item 401/3/1/4 Part 1.
45 ibid.
46 NAA (ACT) Series A 433/1 Item 49/2/518.
47 NAA (ACT) series A 9108/3 Roll 6 A615.
48 *Tribune*, 20.9.1946.
49 *Richmond River Express* and *Northern Star*, 12.9.1946.
50 NAA (Vic) Series MP 729/8/0 Item 44/431/76.
51 ibid.
52 NAA (Vic) Series MP 742/1 Item 118/1/378.
53 NAA (ACT) Series A 433/1 Item 47/2/518.
54 NAA (ACT) Series 1838/278 Item 401/3/6/1/4 Part 2.

Endnotes

55 NAA (ACT) Series A 433/1 Item 49/2/518.
56 NAA (ACT) Series A 1838/278 Item 401/3/6/1 Part 2.
57 ibid.
58 *The Richmond River Express*, 24.9.1946.
59 ibid.
60 ibid.
61 NAA (ACT) Series A 4331 Item 49/2/5/8.
62 ibid.
63 ibid.
64 NAA (Vic) Series MP 729/8 Item 44/431/77.
65 NAA (ACT) Series 433/1 Item 49/2/8186.
66 NAA (ACT) Series A 1838/278 Item 401/3/6/1/4 Part 2.
67 ibid.
68 ibid.
69 NAA (ACT) Series 433/1 Item 49/2/8186.
70 ibid.
71 NAA (ACT) Series A 1838/278 Item 401/3/6/1/4 Part 2.
72 NAA (ACT) Series A 433/1 Item 49/2/8186.
73 ibid.

Chapter 7

1 In modern times this emotive word is sometimes still used to rekindle the spirit of the revolution for political effect, such as when former President Megawati Soekarnoputri, daughter of Soekarno, used it at her own party's political rallies.
2 N 114/190 Queensland TLC Files Noel Butlin Archives.
3 E 183/26/39 Seamens Union Files Noel Butlin Archives.
4 Robin Gollan *Revolutionaries and Reformists: Communism and the Australian Labour Movement 1920-1955*, George Allen & Unwin, NSW, 1975, p. 183.
5 N 114/190 WWF Indonesia Files Noel Butlin Archives.
6 ibid. Queensland TLC Files.
7 N 114/190 WWF Indonesia Files.
8 ibid.
9 CPD Vol 185 25. 9. 1945 p. 5811.
10 ibid. p. 5833.
11 N 114/190 WWF Indonesia Files.
12 CPD Vol 185 26.9.1945 p. 5865.
13 CPD Vol 185 28.9.1945, p. 6129.
14 ibid. 2.10.1945, p. 6197.
15 ibid.
16 Lockwood, p. 104.
17 ibid.
18 *Daily Telegraph*, 27.9.1945.
19 Lockwood, p. 108.
20 ibid. p. 319. According to Lockwood, 31 Australian unions were eventually involved in the boycott.
21 *Tribune*, 2.10.1945.
22 *New York Times*, 29.9.1945.
23 *Daily Telegraph*, 1.10.1945.
24 *Daily Mirror*, 2.10.1945.
25 NAA (ACT) Series A472/1 Item W29545.
26 Ralph Gibson, *My Years in the Communist Party*, International Bookshop, Melbourne, 1966, p. 110-111.
27 *Advertiser*, 2.10.1945.
28 *Civil Liberty*, Vol 8 No.2 October 1945, p. 3.
29 *The West Australian*, 8.10. 1945.
30 *Warta Indonesia*, 3.10.1945.

31 NAA (ACT) Series A 1838 Item 401/3/6/1/3 Part 1.
32 ibid.
33 ibid.
34 NAA (ACT) Series A 1838/2 Item 401/3/6/1/3.
35 ibid.
36 NAA (Vic) Series B 741/3 Item V/9607.
37 *Herald Sun*, 2.10.1945.
38 *The Age*, 3.10.1945.
39 *Civil Liberty*, October 1945, p. 3.
40 NAA (Vic) series MP 742/1 Item 115/1/301.
41 *Civil Liberty*, October 1945, p. 3.
42 *Sun*, 4.10.1945.
43 *The Age*, 4.10.1945.
44 *Argus*, 8.10.1945.
45 ibid. 10.10.1945.
46 *Daily Telegraph*, 4.10.1945.
47 Moh Hodrie, was among these, striking for the second time since he walked off *Oranje* in 1942.
48 NAA (ACT) Series A 433/1 Item 49/2/8187.
49 Qld TLC Files N 114/190.
50 *Courier Mail*, 9.10.1945.
51 ibid, 12.10.1945.

Chapter 8

1 Frank Bennett, *The Return of the Exiles: Australia's repatriation of the Indonesians, 1945-47*, Monash Asia Institute, Clayton, Victoria, 2003, p. 82.
2 NAA (ACT) Series A 1838/2 Item 401/3/6/1/3/Part 1.
3 ibid.
4 Bennett, p. 84.
5 NAA (ACT) Series A 5954 Item 2273/2.
6 ibid.
7 NAA (ACT) Series A 1838 Item 401/3/6/1/3.
8 NAA (ACT) Series A 433/1 Item 49/2/8187. The actual number who embarked in Sydney is open to conjecture. Marks mentioned 568, but newspaper reports of the departure mentioned between 650 and 670.
9 Hardjono and Warner (eds), p. 5.
10 *Sydney Morning Herald*, 13.10.1945.
11 *Sunday Telegraph*, 14.10.1945.
12 NAA (ACT) Series A 1838/278 Item 401/3/6/1/3/Part 2.
13 Thomas Stapleton, Unpublished manuscript presented to Archives of Department of Foreign affairs, 1981, (copy in National Library of Australia), p. 4.
14 *Sunday Telegraph*, 14.10.1945.
15 Hardjono and Warner, pp. 44-45.
16 *Sunday Telegraph*, 14.10.1945.
17 NAA (ACT) Series 5954/1 Item 2273/2.
18 NAA (ACT) Series A 1838/2 Item 401/3/6/1/3 Part 1.
19 NAA (ACT) Series A 1838/2 Item 401/3/6/1/3 Part 1.
20 ibid.
21 ibid.
22 NAA (ACT) Series A 4271/1 Item W 29545.
23 ibid.
24 NAA (Vic) Series MP 1587/0 Item 305J.
25 NAA (ACT) Series A 4271 Item W 29545.
26 NAA (ACT) Series 5945/1 Item 2273/2.
27 ibid.
28 ibid.
29 ibid.

Endnotes

30 ibid.
31 NAA (Vic) Series MP 742/1 Item 115/1/301.
32 NAA (Vic) Series MP 742/1 Item 115/1/301.
33 ibid.
34 NAA (ACT) Series A 816/1 Item 102/301/13 Part 3.
35 ibid.
36 NAA (ACT) Series A 1838/2 Item 401/3/1/3 Part 1.
37 ibid.
38 NAA (Vic) Series MP 742/1 Item 115/1/301.
39 NAA (Vic) Series MP 1049/5 Item 2026/16/9691.
40 NAA (ACT) Series A 1838/278 Item 401/3/6/1/3/Part 2.
41 Vic Paath, a petty officer and member of the Indonesia Club in Sydney was a staunch nationalist. Many years after these events he renewed his links with his wartime home when he sent his two daughters to Australia for their education. Both eventually settled in Sydney, and one of them, Marina Paath, became a lecturer in Indonesian first at the University of NSW and then in the University of Sydney.
42 NAA (Vic) Series MP 742/1 Item 115/1/301.
43 Noel Butlin Archives, E 183/26/39 and Jim Lumanauw Report, *Esperance Bay.* p. 1.
44 NAA (ACT) Series A 1838/278 Item 401/3/1/3 Part 2.
45 Lumanauw, p. 1. Plumb's own version of this meeting was that Lumanauw had 'harangued' the Indonesians and incited them to resist the disembarkation.
46 NAA (ACT) Series A 1838/278 Item 401/3/1/3 Part 2.
47 NAA (Vic) Series MP 742/1 Item 115/1/301.
48 NAA (Vic) Series MP 742/1 Item 115/1/301.
49 ibid.
50 NAA (ACT) Series A 1838/278 Item 401/3/6/1/3 Part 2.
51 ibid.
52 Lumanauw, p. 2.
53 Lumanauw, p. 3.
54 Stapleton, p. 1.
55 Stapleton, p. 8.
56 NAA (Vic) Series MP 742/1 Item 115/1/301.
57 NAA (ACT) Series A 1838/2 item 401/1/2/1.
58 ibid. Item 401/3/1/1/ Part 1.
59 Cited in Bennett, p. 191.
60 ibid. pp. 190-192.

Chapter 9

1 See for example, *Sun* and *Daily Telegraph*, 27.10.1945.
2 *Daily Telegraph*, 28.10.1945.
3 *Bundaberg News Mail*, 29.10.1945.
4 *Bundaberg News Mail*, 30.10.1945.
5 Lockwood, p. 152.
6 ibid. pp. 152-163.
7 This was the same Clarrie Campbell who was the first treasurer of SARPE-LINDO and enthusiastic member of the AIA.
8 Phyllis and John Johnson, interview, Padstow, Sydney, August 1998.
9 *Daily Telegraph*, 28.10.1945.
10 Lockwood, pp. 130-131.
11 *Daily Mirror*, 7.11.1945.
12 *Sydney Morning Herald*, 21.11.1945.
13 NAA (ACT) Series A 1838/278 Item 401/3/9/1/1 Part 1.
14 NAA (ACT) Series 5954/1 Item 2273/2.
15 NAA (ACT) Series A 1838/278 Item 401/3/6/1/ Part 2.

295

16 ibid. Part 1.
17 *Sydney Morning Herald,* 5.11.1945. Clearly the *Herald* was harking back to the earlier (June 1945) decision of the Commonwealth not to approve the training of 30,000 of their troops, which had so embittered the Dutch.
18 *Daily Telegraph,* 6.11.1945.
19 Ibid.
20 NAA (ACT) Series A 472/1 Item W29545.
21 NAA (ACT) Series A 1838/278 Item 401/3/9/1/1/ Part 1.
22 Information in this and the following paragraph is taken from Erroll Hodge, *Radio Wars: Truth, Propaganda and the Struggle for Radio Australia,* Cambridge University Press, UK, 1976, pp. 158-164.
23 *Sydney Morning Herald,* 16.11.1945.
24 ibid.
25 *Daily Telegraph,* 22.11.1945.
26 Hodge, p. 165.
27 NAA (ACT) series A 1838/278 Item 401/3/9/1/1/ Part 1.
28 Ibid.
29 NAA (ACT) series 1838/278 Item 401/3/6/1/5.
30 ibid.
31 NAA (ACT) Series A 6122/40 Item 139.
32 ibid.
33 NAA (ACT) Series A 9108/3 Roll 21 N39088/Z.
34 Laurens van der Post, *The Admiral's Baby.* John Murray, London, 1996, pp. 13-14.
35 NAA (ACT) Series A 1838/2 Item 401/4/4/1 Part 1.
36 George, p. 44.
37 Australian Public Opinion Polls Nos. 314-316, Melbourne, December 1945 – January 1946.
38 One of the final media reports for the year came from the popular magazine *Pix* (22.12.1945) which sent a cameraman to Java at a time of heavy fighting, to try to help its readers understand and assess the conflicting sides of the argument. Although ostensibly presenting the opposing views in an even-handed way, with photos to match, the pro-Dutch bias was evident in for example an account of '... cries of *Merdeka* and Nazi-style salutes,' and the astonishing logic in the caption under a photo of traditionally attired Javanese palace guards which read, 'Self-government seems an odd aspiration for a people steeped in old traditions'.

Chapter 10

1 NAA (ACT) Series A 1838/278 Item 401/3/9/1/1/ Part 1.
2 ibid.
3 ibid.
4 NAA (ACT) Series A 1838/278 Item 401/3/9/1/1/ Part 1.
5 NAA (ACT) Series A 433/1 Item 49/2/67.
6 Mohamad Bondan, p. 14.
7 NAA (ACT) Series A 5954/1 Item 2273/2.
8 WWF Files E 211/154 Noel Butlin Archives.
9 NAA (ACT) Series A 1838/2 Item 401/4/3/1.
10 NAA (ACT) Series 1838/278 Item 401/3/6/1/2 Part 2.
11 Bennett, pp. 193-194.
12 *Sydney Morning Herald,* 16.2.1946.
13 NAA (ACT) Series A 5954/1 Item 2273/2.
14 NAA (ACT) Series A 5954/1 Item 2273/2.
15 ibid.
16 ibid.
17 ibid.
18 ibid.

Endnotes

19 Bennett, p. 195.
20 Noel Butlin Archives, WWF Files E 183/26/39.
21 ibid.
22 NAA (ACT) Series A 472/1 Item W29545.
23 ibid.
24 Noel Butlin Archives, WWF Files N 114/90.
25 *Sydney Morning Herald*, 28.2.1946.
26 Lockwood, p. 194.
27 *Sydney Morning Herald*, 13.3.1946.
28 Noel Butlin Archives, WWF Files, E 211/155.
29 ibid. E 211/190.
30 ibid.
31 Lockwood, p. 199.
32 Lockwood, p. 204. At the time, Ted Roach wrote in the WWF organ, the *Maritime Worker* (20th April 1946), that 'Mountbatten flitted onto the scene, gave certain assurances to the carrying out of which we agreed. We left the matter momentarily with him'.
33 ibid. p. 207.
34 CPD Vol 186 6.3.1946 pp. 7-10.
35 ibid.
36 CPD Vol 187 20.6.1946, pp. 1647-1649.
37 *Sydney Morning Herald*, 17.7.1946.
38 *Courier Mail*, 17.7.1946.
39 ibid.
40 *Maritime Worker*, 20.7.1946.
41 NAA (ACT) Series A 6122/40 Item 40.
42 ibid. Item 138. The Digulists were Zakaria, Kandoer, Pade Sjahboeddin, Soeka, Bambang Sindoe and Aboe Kasim. The KPM men were Amir, Djadi and Rompas.
43 NAA (ACT) Series A 6122/40 Item 40.
44 ARA Ministerie van Buitenlandsche Zaken, inventaris van het Consulaat general te Sydney, Australia, 1930-1954. Inventaris No: 56/70. The members of the alleged communist group were J Walandouw F Lessiputty, Machmoed, H Mailangkay, A Sorongan and Isa Saidi.
45 NAA (ACT) Series A 6122/40 Item 138. The 3 ex-Digulists were identified as Slamet, a former schoolteacher who was 'highly intelligent,' Mas Bondan, the very active and efficient secretary, former clerk in a trading company, and Soeratmadjie, a former laborer, 'not particularly bright but very intense.' How the inquiry officer decided who was bright and who was not is not mentioned.
46 ARA Ministerie van Buitenlandsche Zaken, inventaris van het Consulaat General te Sydney, Australia, 1930-1954, inventaris No. 56/70. At this time a number of KIM leaders had managed to evade or refuse repatriation on the *Manoora*, probably because quite a few of them had Australian wives.
47 *Maritime Worker*, 20.4.1946.
48 *Sydney Morning Herald*, 22.4.1946.
49 Noel Butlin Archives, Seamen's Union Files, E 211/155.
50 ibid.
51 ibid.
52 ibid. The number of these rebels varies from 19-25 in different accounts of this incident.
53 NAA (ACT) Series A 1838/278 Item 410/3/6/1/2 Part 2.
54 NAA (ACT) Series A 433/1 Item 49/2/67.
55 NAA (ACT) Series A 571/150 Item 45/4075.
56 ibid.
57 Noel Butlin Archives. Seamen's Union Files E 183/26/39.
58 NAA (ACT) Series A 1838/391 Item 410/3/6/1/6 Part 1.
59 NAA (ACT) Series A 1838 /391 Item 410/3/6/1/6 Part 1.
60 NAA (ACT) Series A 6122/40 Item 138.

61 ibid.
62 ibid. All information in this paragraph comes from Sleeth's report in this file.
63 ibid.

Chapter 11

1 Paul Rothe and Richard Griffith, *The Film Till Now: A Survey of World Cinema*, Spring Books, London, 1967, p. 62.
2 Erik Barnouw, *Documentary: a history of the non-fiction film*, Oxford University press, London, 1993, p. 170.
3 Cited by Graeme Cutts, 'Indonesia Calling' in Jane Drakeford & John Legge, (eds), *Indonesian Independence 50 years on*, Monash Asia Institute, Victoria, 1996, p. 38.
4 NAA (NSW) Series SP 11/2 Item Joris Ivens Box 18.
5 *Daily Telegraph*, 22.11.1945.
6 Cited by Cutts, p. 39.
7 NAA (ACT Series A 472/1 Item W29545.
8 NAA (ACT) Series 1838/283 Item 401/3/9/1/4.
9 Noel Butlin Archives, Seamen's Union Files E183/26/39.
10 NAA (ACT) Series A 461/2 Item A350/1/9.
11 ibid.
12 NAA (ACT) A 1838/283 item 401/3/9/1/4.
13 CPD Vol 189 14.11.1946, p. 237.
14 Lockwood, p. 288.
15 ibid.
16 Mohamad Bondan, p. 117.
17 Information in this and the following paragraph from Philip Dorling (ed), *Australia and Indonesia's Independence. Documents 1947*, Australian Government Publishing Service, Canberra, 1994, pp. xv-xxii.
18 Evatt Papers, Flinders University, South Australia.
19 NAA (ACT) Series A 433/1 Item 49/2/518.
20 NAA (ACT) Series A 433/1 Item 49/2/67.
21 NAA (ACT) Series A 4331 Item 49/2/8186.
22 ibid.
23 Noel Butlin Archives, Seamen's Union Files P81/17.
24 *Courier Mail*, 14.11.1946.
25 NAA (ACT) Series A 433/1 Item 49/2/8186.
26 NAA (ACT) Series A 1838/278 Item 401/3/6/1/9.
27 ibid. Mungoven Report, 30.12.1946, the basis for information in this and the following paragraph.
28 NAA (ACT) Series A 433/1 Item 49/2/8186.
29 ibid.
30 NAA (ACT) Series A 1838/391 Item 401/3/6/1/6 Part 1.
31 Ibid.
32 ibid.
33 ibid.
34 Noel Butlin Archives. P81/23.
35 NAA (ACT) Series A 373/1 Item 10521.
36 Bennett, pp. 234-236.
37 NAA (ACT) Series A 433/1 Item 49/2/4823.
38 ibid.
39 CPD Vol 191, 18.4.1947, pp. 1411-1422.
40 NAA (ACT) Series A 1839/391 Item 401/3/6/6/1/6 Part 1.
41 NAA (ACT) Series 433/1 Item 49/2/4823.
42 CPD Vol 191, 30.4.1946, pp. 1701-1702.
43 NAA (ACT) Series A 433/1 Item 49/2/4823.
44 ibid.

Endnotes

45 ARA. Ministerie van Buitenlandsche Zaken, Inventaris van het Consulaat General te Sydney, Australia 1930-1954 Inventaris No. 56/70.
46 NAA (ACT) Series A 6122/40 Item 138.
47 See *Femina* magazine, Jakarta, August 1995.
48 NAA (ACT) Series A 433/1 Item 49/2/4823.
49 Ibid.
50 NAA (ACT) Series A 884/9 Item A787.
51 NAA (ACT) Series A 433/1 Item 49/2/4823.
52 ibid.
53 NAA (ACT) Series A 1068/7 item IC47/20/1/15/3.
54 Ibid.
55 *Sun*, 18.6.1949.
56 Enid Achmad, interview. Jakarta April, 2000. For the story of Mrs Jean Tahija who lived in Indonesia from 1947, when she joined her army officer husband Julius, until she died in 2000, see her memoir, *An Unconventional Woman*.
57 Jean Wachjo, interview, Wyong, NSW, September, 1997.
58 Sheila Tattersall, interview, Harbord NSW, May 1998.
59 Noel Butlin Archives, P81/1.
60 Ibid. P81/2.
61 ibid.

Chapter 12

1 Throughout 1949 there were prolonged and numerous conferences, all leading to the inevitable outcome – the transfer of complete sovereignty from the Dutch to the new nation. George, p. 66.
2 Noel Butlin Archives, N 114/190.
3 Evatt Papers, Cablegram 31.3.1947.
4 George, p. 66.
5 Noel Butlin Archives, The Campbell Collection, P81/1.
6 ibid. P 81/10
7 ibid.
8 ibid.
9 ibid.
10 ibid.
11 ibid. P 81/1
12 Molly Bondan, p. 232.
13 CPD, Vol. 192, 20.5.1947, pp. 2552-2553.
14 Bondan, p. 232
15 See NAA (ACT) Series A 461/2 Item A 350/1/9 (letter to Chifley) and Evatt Papers, Flinders University (letter to Evatt).
16 *Adelaide Advertiser*, 24.7.1947.
17 Noel Butlin Archives, WWF Indonesia Files E 211/154. Ted Roach claimed that at this time, for the first time in its history, Holland conscripted Dutch youth for war service in Indonesia.
18 Dorling, p. ix.
19 NAA (ACT) Series A 1838/278 Item 401/3/1/1 Part 3.
20 See Timothy Lindsay, *The Romance of K'tut Tantri*, Oxford University Press, Kuala, Lumpur, 1997 and K'tut Tantri, *Revolt in Paradise*, William Heinemann, London, 1960.
21 Lindsay, p. 207.
22 *Honi Soit*, 25.7.1947.
23 *Honi Soit* 31.7.1947.
24 *Honi Soit*, 31.7.1947.
25 *Maritime Worker*, 26.7.1947.
26 Noel Butlin Archives, WWF Indonesia Files E 212/675.
27 Ibid. E 211/154.

28 NAA (ACT) Series A 4355/1 item 8/3/1.
29 ibid.
30 Radio Yogyakarta, 10.8.1947.
31 Australian Public Opinion Polls, No.448-458 September 1947.
32 All information on the Medical Aid for Indonesia association comes from NAA (ACT) Series A 6122/40 Item 141.
33 Hardjono & Warner, p. 58
34 NAA (ACT) Series A 4355/3 Item 7/3/1.
35 ibid.
36 Hardjono & Warner, p. 59.
37 All information taken from Molly's letter comes from NAA (ACT) Series A 1838/391 Item 401/3/6/1/6 Part 1.
38 NAA (ACT) Series A 4355/3 Item 7/3/1.
39 ibid.
40 NAA (ACT) Series A 1838/391 Item 401/3/6/1/6 Part 1.
41 Hardjono & Warner, pp. 171-172.
42 NAA (ACT) Series A 1838/391 Item 410/3/6/1/6 Part 1.
43 NAA (ACT) Series A 1838/391 Item 410/3/6/1/6 Part 1.
44 B.D.Beddie, 'Australian Policy Towards Indonesia' in David Pettit (ed), *Selected Readings in Australian Foreign Policy*, Sorrett Publishing, Victoria, 1973, p. 124.
45 Cited in L.F.Crisp, *Ben Chifley*, Longmans, Victoria, 1961, p. 293.
46 Dorling, p. xiii.
47 Warner Levi, *Australia's Outlook on Asia*, Angus & Robertson, Sydney, 1958, p. 184.
48 *Sydney Morning Herald*, 29.1.1949.
49 CPD. Vol 201 9.1.1949. All information on this debate refers to this date.
50 NAA (ACT) Series A 1838/1 Item 1477/2/11.
51 ibid.
52 ibid.
53 NAA (Vic) Series MP 401/1 Item CL 31130.
54 *Sydney Morning Herald*, 2.3.1949.
55 Australian Public Opinion Polls No.569-578. February-March 1949.
56 Dorling, p. xxi.
57 Noel Butlin Archives,.WWF Indonesia Files, N 21/421.
58 *Sydney Morning Herald*, 2.12.1949.
59 NAA (ACT) Series A 1838 Item 403/3/1/1/ Part 17.
60 *Sydney Morning Herald*, 29.12.1949.
61 NAA (ACT) Series A 1838 Item 401/3/10/1 Part 3.
62 NAA (ACT) Series A 4357/2 Item 3517 Part 1.

References

Primary Sources
Newspapers
Argus (Melbourne)
Bintang Hindia (Jakarta)
Bulletin
Bundaberg News Mail
Daily Mercury Mackay
Daily Mirror (Sydney)
Daily Telegraph (Sydney)
Femina (Jakarta)
Honi Soit (University of Sydney)
Maritime Worker
Merdeka (Jakarta)
Minggoe Merdeka
New York Times
Pandji Poestaka (Jakarta)
Pantja Raja (Jakarta)
Penjoeloeh (Melbourne)
Persatoean Indonesia (Jakarta)
Pix
Queensland Times
Soeara Merdeka (Jakarta)
Soeleoh Merdeka (Jakarta)
Southern Cross (Adelaide)
Sun (Sydney)
Sunday Mirror (Sydney)
Sydney Morning Herald
The Adelaide Advertiser
The Age (Melbourne)
The Southern Cross (Adelaide)
The Canberra Times
The Courier Mail (Brisbane)
The Hobart Mercury
The Melbourne Herald
The Mercury (Mackay)
The Northern Star – Lismore
The Richmond River Express (Casino)
The West Australian
Tribune

Unpublished Manuscripts

Baillie, James *You Can't Help Bad Luck* (n.d.).
Freeman, Wilfred D'Estena 1995. *The First Boat People*, Archives of the Uniting Church Melbourne .
Pronk, Lieuwe 1*KPM. A most Remarkable Shipping Company 1888-1967*, Mitchell wing, State Library of NSW, Sydney.
Stapleton, Thomas 1991 Untitled Statement, Australian National Library, Canberra 1981.

Unpublished Theses

Jamal, Anhar 1990. *Di Bawah Bintang Salib Selatan: Gerakan dan Usaha Mempertahankan Kemerdekaan Indonesia di Australia (1942-1947)* Skripsi Sarjana FSUI Jakarta.
George, Margaret 1973. *Australian attitudes and Policies Towards the Netherlands East Indies and Indonesian Independence 1942-1949* PhD Thesis Australian National University Canberra.
Hogan, Terry 1972. *The Labour Movement and the Indonesian Republicans in Australia, August 1945-March 1946* BA(Hons) Thesis. University of New England Armidale.
Kattenburg, P.M. 1949. *The Indonesian Question in World Politics* PhD Dissertation Yale University.
Schneider, R.M. 1955. *Australia and Indonesia's Independence* BA Hons Thesis University of Adelaide.
Skye, Katherine 1986. *"Unrest Among the Natives" The Indonesian revolution 1945-1949 as Reported by the Adelaide Advertiser and the Melbourne Age"*. BA Honours Thesis Flinders University of South Australia.

Archives

National Archives of Australia (NAA)
NSW State Archives
Queensland State Archives
Private Collections held at The Noel Butlin Archives Centre,
The ANU Archives of Business and Labor, Canberra ACT
Waterside Workers' Federation
Seamen's Union
Trades and Labor Council Queensland
Campbell Collection
The Evatt Collection held at Flinders University, South Australia
Commonwealth Parliamentary Debates (CPD)

Audio/Visual Sources

Indonesia Calling – Joris Ivens (Documentary Film 1946).
The Dutch Connection ABC Radio National, 1999.
Hindsight – ABC Radio National, 10 November 2002.

References

Secondary Sources

Abeyasekere, Susan, 1976. *One Hand Clapping: Indonesian Nationalists and the Dutch, 1939-1942*, Monash Papers on Southeast Asia, no 5. Centre of Southeast Asian Studies, Clayton, Vic.

Adil, Hilman. 1993, *Hubungan Australia dengan Indonesia 1945-1962*, Penerbit Djambatan, Jakarta.

Album Perjuangan Kemerdekaan 1945-1950, 1975. Badan Pimpinan Harian Pusat Korps Cacad Veteran Republik Indonesia dan Badan Penerbit Alda c.v.Jakarta. Jakarta.

Anderson, B. 1972. *Java in a Time of Revolution Occupation And Resistance 1944-1946*, Cornell University Press Ithaca New York.

Anderson, David. (ed) 1991. *Australia and Indonesia, A Partnership in the Making*, Pacific Security Research Institute, Sydney.

Australian Constitutional League 1947. *Red, White-and Indonesia* (pamphlet). Melbourne.

Ball, Desmond. & Wilson, Helen. (eds) 1991.*Strange Neighbours. The Australian Indonesian Relationship*, Allen & Unwin Sydney.

Barnow, Erik. 1993. *Documentary: A History of the Non-fiction Film*, Oxford University Press London.

Bartlett, Norman 1954. *The Pearl Seekers*, Andrew Melrose London.

Beddie, D.1973. "Australian Policy Towards Indonesia" in Pettit, David (ed) *Selected Readings in Australian Foreign Policy*, Sorret Publishing Vic.

Bell, Reg A 1996. *Torres Strait Force. Cape York, Thursday Island, Merauke 1942-1945*, Australian Military History Publications. Australia .

Benda, Harry J. and McVey, Ruth. T.(eds) 1969. *The Communist Uprisings of 1926-1927 in Indonesia: Key Documents*, Southeast Asia Program, Cornell University Ithica N.Y. second printing.

Bennett, Frank C. 2003. *The Return of the Exiles: Australia's Repatriation of the Indonesians, 1945-47*, Monash Asia Institute Clayton Victoria .

Bevege, Margaret 1993. *Behind Barbed Wire*, University of Queensland Press Brisbane.

Blackmur, D. 1974. *Issues in Indonesian Nationalism 1910-1945*, Qld Institute of Technology.

Bondan, Mohamad 1971. *Genderang Proklamasi Di Luar Negeri*, Pertjetakan 'Kawal' Djakarta.

Bondan, Molly 1992. *Spanning a Revolutiong*, Pustaka Sinar Harapan. Jakarta 1992.

Bradley, Vera 1995. *I Didn't Know That*, Boolarong Press Brisbane 1995.

Campbell, Bruce.C. 1995. " The Last Colonial Act. The Expulsion of Indonesian Fishermen from the North West Coast." In *Studies in Western Australian History*, No 16.

Campbell, Rosemary 1989. *Heroes and Lovers: The Americans in Brisbane*, Allen and Unwin, Sydney.

Carey, P.B.R., 1979 'Aspects of Javanese history in the nineteenth century' in Aveling, Harry (ed), *The Development of Indonesian Society*, Queensland University Press, St. Lucia Queensland.

Chauvel, Richard 1990. *Nationalists, Soldiers and Separatists:the Ambonese Islands from Colonialism to Revolt*, KITLV Press, Leiden.

Choo, Christine 1995. 'Asian Men on the West Kimberley Coast', in *Studies in Western Australian History*, No 16.

Citra dan Perjuangan Perintis Kemerdekaan: Seri Perjuangan Ex Digul 1977, Direktorat Jendral Bantuan Sosial, Departemen Sosial Jakarta.

Connell, Daniel. 1988. *The War at Home*, Australian Broadcasting Commission Sydney.

Cowie, H.R. 1987. *Asia and Australia in World Affairs*, Thomas Nelson, Australia.

Crawford, Ian 2001. *We won the victory: Aborigines and Outsiders on the North-West Coast of the Kimberley*, Fremantle Arts Centre Press, North Fremantle.

Crisp,L.L 1961. *Ben Chifley*, Longmans Victoria.

Cutts, Graeme 1996 "Indonesia Calling" in Drakeford, Jane and Legge, John (eds), *Indonesian Independence Fifty Years On*, Monash Asia Institute Vic.

d'Alpuget, Blanche 1977. *Mediator. A Biography of Sir Richard Kirby*, Melbourne University Press Melbourne.

De Jong, Dr J. 1986. *Het Koninkrijk der Nederlanden in der Tweede Wereldoorlog*, Rijksinstituut voor Oorlogsdocumentatie Netherlands.

Dennis, Peter 1990. "Evatt and the Indonesian Revolution: the early phase" in *The Life and Work of DR H.V.Evatt* papers from a weekend conference at Bond University July14-15.

Dixon, R 1945. *Immigration and the White Australia Policy*, Current Book Distributors, Sydney.

Dorling, Philip (ed) 1994. *Diplomasi: Australia and Indonesia's Independence. Documents 1947*, Australian Government Publishing Service Canberra.

Dutch Imperialism Exposed – The Green Hell of Tanah Merah 1946, Indonesian Independence Committee Melbourne.

Duyker, Edward 1987. *The Dutch in Australia*, AE Press Melbourne.

Edgar, D.E. 1963. *Australia and her Northern Neighbours*, Halls Book Store Ltd. Melbourne.

Edwards, Hugh 1983. *Port of Pearls: A History of Broome*, Rigby Publishers Australia.

Emerson, Rupert 1960. *From Empire to Nation: The Rise to Self Assertion of Asian and African Peoples*, Harvard University Press Cambridge, Massachusetts.

Encel, S. 1971. *A Changing Australia*, Australian Broadcasting Commission Sydney.

Evans, Gareth 1991. "Australia and Indonesia" in Anderson, David *Australia and Indonesia: A Partnership in the Making*, Pacific Security Research Institute of the Institute of Public Affairs, Sydney.

Evatt, H.V. 1945. *Foreign Policy of Australia* Angus & Robertson Sydney

—— 1949. *The Task of Nations* Greenwood Press Conneticut.

Fitzgerald, Ross 1984. *From 1915 to the Early 1980's – A History of Queensland*, University of Queensland Press, Brisbane.

Fitzpatrick, Brian & Cahill, Rowan J. 1981. *Seamen's Union of Australia 1872-1972*, S.U.A. Sydney.

Ford, Jack M. 1996. *Allies in a Bind. Australia and the Netherlands East Indies in the Second World War*, Australia Netherlands Ex Servicemen & Women's Association Qld Branch .

Frederick, William H. 1989. *Visions and Heat: the making of the Indonesian Revolution*, Ohio University Press, Athens

Gelman Taylor, Jean, 2003. *Indonesia: Peoples and Histories*, Yale University Press, New Haven.

References

Gibson, Ralph, 1966. *My Years in the Communist Party*, International Bookshop, Melbourne.

George, Margaret 1980. *Australia and the Indonesian Revolution*, Melbourne University Press, Melbourne.

Gollan, Robin 1975. *Revolutionaries and Reformists. Communism and the Australian Labour Movement 1920-1955*, George Allen & Unwin NSW.

Goodman, Rupert 1992. *Hospital Ships*, Boolarong Publications Brisbane 1992.

Gouda, Frances 1995. *Dutch Culture Overseas. Colonial Practice in the Netherlands Indies 1900-1942*, Amsterdam University Press The Netherlands.

Graves, Adrian 1993. *Cane and Labour. The Political Economy of the Queensland Sugar Industry 1862-1906*, Edinburgh University Press Edinburgh.

Graham, Shirley and Adams, Brian 1983. *Australian Cinema, the First Eighty Years*, Angus &Robertson Currency Press Australia.

Greenwood, G. and Harper, N 1963. *Australia in World Affairs 1956-1960*, Cheshire for the Australian Institute of International Affairs, Melbourne.

Hamilton, Robert James "Psychopaths, communists and criminals: Brigadier Simpson and the internees of Tanah Merah" in *Journal of the Australian War Memorial* No 24 April 1994.

Hanan, David 1998. "Representations pf Indonesia in Australian Documentary films in the Late 1930s and Early 1940s" in Mobini-Kesheh, Natalie (ed) *Representations of Indonesia in Australia*, Monash Asia Institute, Centre of Southeast Asian Studies Clayton Vic.

Hardjono, Joan, Warner, Charles, (eds), *In Love With A Nation: Molly Bondan and Indonesia*, published by Charles, Warner, Picton, 1995.

Hatta, Mohammad 1972. *Portrait of a Patriot*, Mouton The Netherlands 1972.

Hills,Ernie and McIvor, Trevor.2003 'The Kite Flying Jarvos' in Talbot, Don and Larkin, John. *Toowoomba-Strange and Unusual Tales*, Toowoomba Queensland.

Hodge, Erroll 1995. *Radio Wars: truth, Propaganda and the Struggle for Radio Australia*, Cambridge University Press, UK.

Hornadge, Bill 1976. *Yellow Peril. A Squint at some Australian Attitudes to Orientals*, Review Publications Pty Ltd. Dubbo NSW.

Ind, Allison 1958. *Spy Ring Pacific*, Weidenfield & Nicolson London 1958.

Ingleson, John 1979. *.Road to Exile. The Indonesian Nationalist Movement 1927-1934*, Published for Asian Studies Association of Australia by Heinemann Educational books, Kuala Lumpur .

Jamal, Anhar 1991. "Gerakan Nasionalis Indonesia di Australia" paper given at Seminar Hubungan Indonesia-Australia: Masalah Budaya, Sosial dan Politik. Fakultas Sastra Universitas Indonesia Depok 23-26 Sept.

Jeffrey, Robin.(ed) 1981. *Asia, the Winning of Independence*, Macmillan, London.

Joint Standing Committee on Foreign Affairs, Defence and Trade 1993. *Australia's Relations With Indonesia*, Australian Government Publishing Service Canberra.

Jones, Kevin 1995. "Merdeka" in *Signals* No. 32 National Maritime Museum of Australia Sydney Sept-November.

Jong, J de 1986. *Het Koninkrijk der Nederlanden in der Tweede Wereldoorlog* Rijksinstituut voor Oorlogsdocumentatie Netherlands.

Jupp, James. (ed) 1988. *Australian People, an Encylcopaedia of the Nation, Its People and their Origins*, Angus & Robertson Australia.

Kahin, George Mc Turnan 1963. *Nationalism and Revolution in Indonesia,* Cornell University Press Ithaca New York 6th printing.

Kartomi, Margaret 1981. "The First A.I.A: the Australia-Indonesia Association" in *A.I.A. Journal* August.

—— 2002. *The Gamelan Digul and the Prison Camp Musician Who Built It An Australian Link with the Indonesian Revolution,* University of Rochester Press NY.

Kirby, Richard 1958. "A Time of Good Offices" in *Nation* 26th September 1958.

Lansell, Ross and Beilby, Peter. (eds) 1982. *The Documentary Film in Australia,* Film Victoria Melbourne.

Lea-Scarlett, Errol 1968. *Queanbeyan. District and People,* Queanbeyan Municipal Council.

Legge, J.D. 1973. *Soekarno: A Political Biography,* Penguin Books. Middlesex, UK.

—— 1988. *Intellectuals and Nationalism in Indonesia. A Study of the Following Recruited by Sutan Sjahrir in Occupation, Jakarta* Cornell Modern Indonesia Project.

Levi, Werner 1958. *Australia's Outlook on Asia,* Angus & Robertson, Sydney.

Lindsey, Timothy 1997. *The Romance of K'tut Tantri and Indonesia,* Oxford University Press Kuala Lumpur.

Lockwood, Rupert 1975. *Black Armada. Australia and the struggle for Indonesian independence, 1942-1949,* Australian Book Society Sydney.

Lowe, David. (ed) 1996. *Australia and the End of Empires. The Impact of Decolonisation in Australia's Near North 1945-1965,* Deakin University Press, Melbourne.

Lowenstein,W. & Hills,Tom 1982. *Under the Hook,* Melbourne Bookworkers Vic.

Lucas, Anton 1985. "The Tiga Daerah Affair:Social Revolution or Rebellion," in Kahin, Audrey R (ed) *Regional Dynamics of the Indonesian Revolution,* University of Hawaii Press, Honolulu.

MacKnight, C.C. 1976. *Voyage to Marege. Macassan Trepangers in Northern Australia,* Melbourne University Press. Melbourne.

McKernan, Michael 1983. *All In! Fighting the War at Home,* Allen & Unwin, Sydney.

McKie, Ronald 1960. *The Heroes,* Angus & Robertson, Sydney.

McVey, Ruth 1954. *The Development of the Indonesian Communist Party and its Relations with the Soviet Union and the Chinese Peoples Republic,* Centre for International Studies, M.I.T. Cambridge.

Markus, A. 1994. *Australian Race Relations 1788-1993,* Allen & Unwin, Sydney.

Marshall, Eric 1973. *It Pays To Be White,* Alpha Books Sydney.

Moedjanto, Drs. G. 1988. *Indonesia Abad ke-20. Dari Kebangkitan Nasional sampai Linggajati.* Penerbit Kanisius Yoyakarta.

Moenandar, R. 1969. "Pre-War Nationalist Movements and Life in Digul" in *Indonesian Nationalism and Revolution 6 first hand accounts* Monash University, Clayton, Vic.

Mook, H.J. van 1945. "Past and Future in the Netherlands Indies" Address to Institute of Pacific Relations May 1945. The Netherlands Information Bureau N.Y.

Moorhead, Richard J. (undated) *The Cruise of the Goodwill Ship,* Ruskin Press Melbourne.

Moran, Albert. 1991. *Projecting Australia. Government Film since 1945,* Currency Press Sydney.

References

Mortimer, R. 1976. "Australian Support for Indonesian Independence. A Review: in *Indonesia* No. 22, Cornell Southeast Asia Program Ithaca NY.

Mrazek, Rudolf 1994. *Sjahrir, Politics and Exile in Indonesia,* Cornell University, Ithaca NY.

Murwoto, Raden Mas 1984. *Autobiografi Selaku Perintis Kemerdekaan,* Departemen Sosial R.I. Jakarta.

Nasution, Dr. A. 1977. *Sekitar Perang Kemerdekaan Indonesia* Jilid 3, Angkasa Bandung.

Noonan, Pat 1995. "Merdeka in Mackay. The Indonesian Evacuees and Internees in Mackay, June 1943-February 1946" in Hering, Bob (ed) *Pramoedya Ananta Toer 70 Tahun.* Edisi Sastra Kabar Seberang Sulating Maphilindo 24/25.

Oey, Hong Lee 1981. *War and Diplomacy in Indonesia, 1945-199,* James Cook University, Townsville.

O'Hare, Martin & Reid, Anthony 1995. *Australia dan Perjuangan Kemerdekaan Indonesia, Australia and Indonesia's Struggle for Independence.* PT Gramedia Pustaka Utama, Jakarta.

Palmer, A.W. *A Dictionary of Modern History 1789-1945,* Penguin UK 1963.

Peel, G 1945. *What you want to know about the Dutch East Indies?* (pamphlet) Sydney.

—— 1945. *Hands Off Indonesia* (pamphlet).

—— undated *Indonesian Introduction* Current Book Distributors.

Pluvier,J.M 1965. '*Dutch-Indonesian Relations 1940-1942* ' in Journal of Southeast Asian History Vol 6 No 1 University of Singapore.

Powell, A. 1996. *War by Stealth,* Melbourne University Press, Melbourne.

Pronke, Liewe, 1998, *KPM A Most Remarkable Shipping Company 1888-1967* North Turramurra.

Central Committe of Indonesian Independence, 1946. *Republic of Indonesia* Brisbane.

Ray, J.K. 1967. *Transfer of Power in Indonesia 1942-49,* Manaktalans, Bombay.

Reid, Anthony. 1974. *Indonesian National Revolution 1945-1950,* Longman Victoria.

Rix, A. (ed) 1988. *Intermittent Diplomat. The Japan and Batavia Diaries of W Macmahon Ball,* Melbourne University Press.

Rothe, Paul and Griffith, Richard 1967. *The Film Till Now. A Survey of World Cinema,* Spring Books London.

Salim, I.F.M. Chalid 1977. *15 Tahun Digul,* Penerbit Bulan Bintang Jakarta 1977.

Saunders, Kay 1993. *War on the Homefront,* University of Queensland Press, Brisbane.

Schaper, Michael 1995. 'The Broome Race Riots of 1920' in *Studies In Western Australian History* 16.

Sharp, Nonie 2002. *Saltwater People: The Waves of Memory,* Allen & Unwin NSW.

Sheppard, W.B. 1946. *Indonesia: Asia's Stepping Stones to Australia* (pamphlet), Melbourne.

Shiraishi, Takashi, 1996. 'The Phantom World of Digoel' in *Indonesia* no. 6, Cornell University.

Sjahrir, Soetan 1969. *Out of Exile,* Greenwood Press New York.

—— 1990. *Renungan dan Perjuangan,* Penerbit Djambatan Jakarta.

Smith, Kate D. 1990. *On the Homefront: Melbourne in Wartime 1939-1945,* Oxford University Press, South Melbourne.

Snyder, L.L. 1955. *Fifty Major Documents of the Twentieth Century*, Anvil, Princeton.
Soe Hok Gie 1997. *Orang-orang di Persimpangan Kiri Jalan*, Bentang Yoyakarta.
Sparrow, Jeff and Jill 2001. *Radical Melbourne: a secret history*, The Vulgar Press, Victoria.
Tahija, Jean 1998. *An Unconventional Woman*,Viking Victoria.
Tahija, Julius 1997. *Melintas Cakrawala*, PT Gramedia Pustaka Utama Jakarta.
Taylor, Alastair 1960. *Indonesian Independence and the United Nations* Stevens, London.
Thomas, David 1971. *The Battle of the Java Sea*, Pan Books, London.
Thompson, John 1946. *Hubbub in Java*, Currawong Publishing Company, Sydney.
Turnbull, Clive, 1948. "White Australia: Policy and Passion" in Gilmore, Robert and Warner, Denis (eds), *Near North: Australia and a Thousand Million Neighbours*, Angus & Robertson, Sydney.
Van der Post, Laurens 1996. *The Admiral's Baby*, John Murray, London.
Walker, D. and Ingleson, J. 1989. "The Impact of Asia" in Meaney, Neville (ed) *Under New Heavens*, Heinemann Educational Australia.
Wallace, Gordon 1996. *Up in Darwin with the Dutch*, Surrey Hills Victoria.
Waters, Christopher 1995. *The Empire Fractures. Anglo-Australian Conflict in the 1940s*, Australian Scholarly Publishing Melbourne.
Wehl, David 1948. *The Birth of Indonesia*. Allen & Unwin London.
White, Richard 1985. *Inventing Australia: Images and Identity 1688-1980*, George Allen & Unwin Sydney Fourth Impression.
Whitlam, E.G. 1975. "Australian Indonesian Relations" in *The Indonesian Review of International Affairs*, Jakarta VI No 5.
Why Australia Should Support Indonesian Independence, Labour Council of NSW (pamphlet) undated.
Willard, Myra 1967. *History of the White Australia Policy to 1920*, Frank Cass & Co Ltd Melbourne.
Williams, Victor 1975. *The Years of Big Jim*, Lone Hand Press W.A.
Yong, Mun Cheong 1982. *H.J. van Mook and Indonesian Independence: a Study of his Role in Dutch-Indonesian Relations 1945-1948*, Martinus Nijhoff The Hague.
York, Barry 1996. *Admissions and Exclusions: "Asiatics" and "Other Coloured Races" in Australia: 1901 to 1946* Studies in Ethnic History No.9, Centre for Immigration & Multicultural Studies, Research School of Social Sciences, Australian National University, Canberra.

Index

36th Australian Employment Company (36AEC) 26, 35, 36, 40, 41, 43, 44, 55, 58, 91, 92, 93, 94, 121, 125, 240, 281

A

Aborigines 2, 3, 51, 52, 153, 278
Achmad, E. 144, 243
Aliens Security Files 13
Atlantic Charter 70, 71, 114, 148, 153, 229
Attlee, C. 171, 172
Australia-Indonesia Association (AIA) 111, 112, 113, 114, 115, 116, 128, 129, 131, 134, 163, 164, 165, 168, 169, 218, 220, 221, 233, 239, 240, 246, 251
Australian Civil Rights League 90
Australian Council of Trade Unions (ACTU) 144, 210, 211, 212, 249, 253, 257, 273
Australian-Dutch relations 59, 190, 192, 195
Australian Trade and Goodwill Delegation 5

B

Beazley, K. 238, 239
Blackbutt Camp, NSW 26, 35, 44
Bondan, Molly (nee Warner) 111, 112, 113, 114, 115, 128, 163, 165, 166, 168, 169, 174, 196, 223, 236, 241, 246, 247, 248, 261, 262, 264
Bondan, Mohamad 84, 94, 111, 121, 138, 139, 195, 196, 204, 218, 223, 229, 232, 234, 236, 239, 241, 246, 247, 248, 254, 261, 262, 264
Both (Dutch ship) 77, 79, 217
Bundaberg 183, 184
Burton, J. 154, 155, 262, 264

C

Calwell, A. 131, 132, 136, 137, 138, 140, 145, 155, 157, 158, 161, 179, 181, 193, 194, 203, 204, 205, 232, 233, 234, 236, 238, 239, 243, 265, 268, 269, 270, 271, 272
Campbell, C.H. 13, 109, 113, 115, 163, 164, 165, 186, 233, 236, 247, 250, 251, 252, 253
Casino 44, 48, 49, 50, 51, 52, 55, 91, 93, 94, 95, 100, 103, 104, 108, 123, 124, 125, 126, 127, 128, 129, 130, 131, 132, 133, 134, 135, 136, 137, 138, 139, 140, 141, 143, 156, 167, 170, 171, 184, 203, 207, 218, 219, 235, 236, 242, 281. *See also* Victory Camp
Chifley, J.B. 118, 119, 137, 145, 146, 147, 155, 161, 162, 166,

309

167, 170, 171, 172, 176, 193, 194, 202, 205, 206, 212, 215, 229, 241, 254, 259, 266, 268, 270, 282
Clark-Kerr, Sir A. 204, 205, 206, 207, 210, 213, 215, 230
Columbia Camp, Brisbane 189, 244
Commonwealth Investigation Service 240, 256, 260
Commonwealth Security Service 41, 105, 111
Communist Party of Australia (CPA) 89, 90, 104, 105, 106, 107, 151, 184, 185, 211, 260
Cowra Camp, NSW 23, 24, 25, 26, 35, 36, 37, 61, 64, 69, 73, 74, 76, 77, 78, 79, 80, 81, 82, 83, 84, 85, 88, 89, 90, 91, 92, 93, 94, 95, 96, 97, 98, 99, 103, 104, 108, 113, 116, 121, 125, 170, 281
Curtin, J. 12, 22, 56, 57, 58, 118

D
Department of External Affairs 10, 56, 72, 92, 95, 117, 120, 131, 132, 134, 138, 139, 140, 154, 162, 166, 169, 177, 178, 190, 193, 222, 231, 261, 262, 263, 265, 267, 275
de Ranitz, J.A. 132, 139
Dutch colonial rule 61, 112

E
Elliott, E.V. 110, 144, 165, 212
Evatt, Dr. H.V. 56, 57, 58, 90, 92, 100, 105, 155, 161, 193, 194, 211, 229, 231, 252, 253, 254

F
Fitzpatrick, B. 92, 127, 158
Forde, F. 13, 37, 93, 129, 132, 202
Fraser, A. 110
Freeman, Rev J. 27, 28, 30, 31, 32, 53, 54

G
gamelan 46, 47, 50, 75, 189
Gapp, L. 90, 112, 113, 188, 220, 233
Gaythorne Camp, Qld 42, 43, 159, 167, 207
Gibson, J. 19, 21
Guthrie, J. 30, 31

H
Hatta, Dr M. 66, 69, 99, 100, 120, 198, 199, 222, 261, 267, 274, 275
Healy, J. 144, 146, 222, 249, 253
Hilversum broadcast 195
HMAS *Katoomba* 75, 77, 78, 92
HMAS *Manoora* 203, 204, 205, 206, 207, 208, 209, 210, 213, 215, 230, 232, 233, 234, 235, 236, 237, 238, 239, 240, 247
HMS *Esperance Bay* 161, 162, 163, 164, 165, 166, 167, 168, 169, 170, 171, 173, 175, 176, 179, 180, 183, 194, 195, 196, 204, 205, 206, 209, 239, 241, 247
Hodgson, Col W.R. 72
Hodrie, M. 20, 22, 36, 37

I

'Indonesia Calling' 186, 225, 228, 229, 230, 248. *See also* Ivens, J.
Indonesia, medical aid for 256, 260, 261
Indonesian Communist Party (PKI) 62, 63, 64, 69, 94, 104, 106, 108, 207
Indonesian Independence Committee, Brisbane Branch (CENKIM) 110, 111, 121, 125, 129, 131, 134, 138, 144, 195, 204, 218, 223, 232, 233, 234, 237, 239, 240, 241, 246, 247, 248, 250, 251, 252, 254, 255, 261, 262, 264, 279, 281
Indonesian Independence Committee (KIM) 110, 111, 121, 157, 236
Indonesian Independence Party (PARKI) 106, 107
Indonesian nationalism 62
Indonesian Nationalist Party (PNI) 63
Indonesian Seamen's Union (SARPELINDO) 108, 109, 110, 113, 143, 144, 145, 209, 218, 219, 221, 222, 281
Indonesia Raya 53, 54, 151, 166
Ivens, J. 226, 227, 228. *See also* 'Indonesia Calling'

J

Javanese labourers 2
'Javos' (Indonesians) 38, 39, 44
Johnson, Phyllis and 'Johnno' 185, 188, 192, 225

K

Kupang, West Timor 3, 173, 174, 175, 176, 177, 178, 180, 196, 233, 236

L

Langford, Col H.R. 71, 74, 87, 89
Linggadjati Agreement 231, 249, 250, 254, 256
Lockwood, R. 10, 185, 212, 229
Long Bay Gaol 22, 110, 235
Ludruk 45, 47
Lumanauw, J. 150, 164, 174, 176, 177

M

MacArthur, Gen D. 18, 33, 72, 101, 193
Mackay, Qld 74, 77, 92, 95, 97, 98, 103, 104, 106, 107, 110, 121, 184, 203, 205, 207, 208, 209, 218
Makassar 2
Menzies, R.G. 5, 118, 119, 146, 147, 213, 214, 215, 223, 226, 269, 275, 276, 282
Merauke 43, 64, 71, 72, 73, 74, 92, 95, 97, 101, 233
Merdeka 63, 66, 143, 150, 186, 273, 275
Monk, A. 210, 211, 212
Mountbatten, Lord L. 161, 162, 167, 169, 170, 171, 172, 174, 177, 178, 179, 180, 194, 205, 206, 211, 212, 213, 217
Mungoven, T. 205, 209, 232, 233, 234, 236

N

Netherlands East Indies Forces Intelligence Service (NEFIS) 17, 75, 105, 116, 162

Netherlands East Indies (NEI) 4, 5, 6, 7, 9, 10, 12, 13, 15, 17, 18, 19, 20, 21, 22, 23, 26, 30, 32, 33, 35, 37, 52, 53, 54, 56, 57, 58, 61, 62, 64, 66, 70, 72, 76, 86, 87, 88, 91, 92, 93, 94, 95, 97, 99, 100, 101, 103, 104, 105, 106, 107, 108, 109, 110, 111, 112, 115, 116, 117, 118, 120, 121, 126, 127, 129, 130, 132, 133, 136, 138, 139, 140, 143, 146, 151, 154, 155, 157, 162, 164, 166, 170, 171, 172, 178, 183, 189, 193, 199, 200, 202, 203, 205, 210, 212, 213, 215, 218, 219, 220, 221, 226, 230, 231, 232, 235, 237, 240, 243, 244, 250, 254, 255, 262, 263, 265, 268, 271, 277, 279, 280, 281

Netherlands Government Information Service (NIGIS) 12, 33, 86, 94, 104, 121, 146, 151, 156, 193, 240, 281

Netherlands Indies Civil Administration (NICA) 242, 244

Netherlands Indies Civil Administration (NICA) 10

New Indonesia Association (SIBAR) 104, 105, 106, 108, 156

No. 18 (NEI) Squadron 18

O

O'Keefe, A. 268, 269, 270, 271, 272

P

pearling industry 3

Peel, G. 113

Penjoeloeh 11, 29, 33, 35, 45, 46, 47, 54, 104, 108, 226

Plumb, K. 105, 162, 167, 169, 170, 173, 174, 175, 176, 177, 180

Port Melbourne 27, 30, 31, 155

R

Renville Agreement 267

Roach, T. 205, 211, 212, 253, 258

Roemah Indonesia 31, 33, 43, 45, 46, 54, 55, 151, 155, 158, 240

Roeslan, R.M. 31, 52, 53, 54

Royal Netherlands Indies Army (KNIL) 9, 10, 15, 23, 26, 43, 45, 47, 48, 50, 53, 104, 106, 246

Royal Netherlands Packet Line (KPM) 4, 10, 15, 22, 23, 32, 43, 44, 46, 53, 55, 56, 75, 104, 108, 109, 112, 125, 143, 148, 150, 163, 164, 165, 187, 189, 197, 198, 202, 203, 216, 218, 219, 221

S

Sardjono 69, 87, 94, 104, 105, 207

Sastroamidjojo, Dr O. 253, 261

Seamen's Union of Australia 26, 108, 109, 110, 221

Simpson, Brig W. 41, 42, 43, 84, 86, 88, 89, 90, 91, 92, 93, 94, 95, 99, 100, 101, 105, 117, 158
Sjahrir 69, 120, 199, 204, 206, 210, 212, 213, 214, 230, 241, 250, 251, 254, 259
Soegito, S. (nee Tattersall) 244, 245, 246, 275, 276
Soekarno 63, 64, 69, 119, 120, 143, 146, 148, 153, 154, 162, 165, 197, 198, 199, 213, 227, 255, 259, 264, 267, 273, 275, 276
Stapleton, T. 165, 177, 178, 302
Stirling Castle incident 191, 192, 195
sugar cane industry 2, 3

T

Tahija, J. 15, 17
Tanah Merah 64, 65, 67, 68, 69, 70, 71, 72, 74, 75, 86, 101, 103, 105, 107, 110, 150, 203, 219, 223, 281
Tanah Tinggi 67, 68, 70, 72, 74, 75, 77, 79, 83, 88, 99, 100, 103
Technical Battalion, Casino 48, 104, 108, 123, 124, 125, 281
Toowoomba Camp, Qld 26, 35, 39, 44, 91, 93, 95, 103, 104, 121
trepang fishing 2, 3

V

van Aerssen Beyeren, Baron F.C. 12, 53, 56, 57, 58, 117, 119, 164, 189, 195, 202, 211, 213, 229

van der Plas, Dr C.O. 6, 7, 10, 22, 37, 40, 42, 43, 53, 71, 72, 73, 74, 78, 81, 83, 84, 86, 88, 91, 92, 95, 99, 100, 101, 105, 116, 198, 199, 281
van Echoud, J.P.K. 26, 36
van Holst Pellekaan, J. 91, 93, 203
van Mook, Dr H.J. 10, 12, 57, 58, 116, 170, 171, 204, 205, 206, 210, 212, 214, 215, 230, 250
van Oyen, Lt-Gen H. 57, 117
Victory Camp 48, 123, 125, 126, 127, 136, 140, 184

W

Wallangarra, NSW 26, 35, 36, 37, 38, 39, 40, 41, 42, 43, 44, 55, 59, 93, 108
'war brides' 225, 237

www.ingramcontent.com/pod-product-compliance
Lightning Source LLC
Chambersburg PA
CBHW020315010526
44107CB00054B/1853